INTEGRATED CIRCUITS
AND
COMPUTER CONCEPTS

Books by Sy Levine

A LIBRARY ON BASIC ELECTRONICS
    Volume One - Basic Concepts and Passive Components
    Volume Two - Discrete Semiconductors and Optoelectronics
    Volume Three - Integrated Circuits and Computer Concepts

A LIBRARY ON BASIC ELECTRONICS

VOLUME THREE

INTEGRATED CIRCUITS AND COMPUTER CONCEPTS

SY LEVINE

Printed in the United States of America

Published by ELECTRO-HORIZONS PUBLICATIONS

114 Lincoln Road East
Plainview, New York 11803

ACKNOWLEDGEMENT

The completion of any single book is rarely, if ever, based on the exclusive efforts of the nominal author. With this third, and last volume in this series, this truth is infinitely more apparent than was evident when the first book was begun.

To my devoted wife, Esther, and my good friend, Jerry Worthing, the two people who have provided me with their consistent and skillful support, I would like to extend all my thanks, love and grateful appreciation for their time, creative efforts, and constructive suggestions in helping to bring this series to its successful conclusion.

S.L.

PREFACE

This third book in the 3-volume series, A LIBRARY ON BASIC ELECTRONICS, is written for those men and women whose need for a conceptual comprehension of electronics has become increasingly urgent. This series of books is dedicated to those people who feel the impact of the technology and are motivated to explore its complexities, to obtain a working knowledge of electronics, and to improve their technical communication skills. The books are intended for people in purchasing, sales, marketing, production, advertising, management, and electronics schools who may find this information beneficial in their daily work.

BASIC CONCEPTS AND PASSIVE COMPONENTS, the first volume of the series, examined basic electronic concepts, their rules, contents and terminology, while providing extensive insight into electronic technology. Passive components were studied with regard to how they are made, how they work, how they are specified on a data sheet and how they relate to each other in electronic circuitry and systems.

VOLUME TWO, DISCRETE SEMICONDUCTORS AND OPTOELECTRONICS, continued the study by examining the active components of circuitry. More of the totality of electronic circuitry was developed to provide a comprehensive picture of this technology and state-of-the-art developments.

PART ONE of this third, and last volume, INTEGRATED CIRCUITS AND COMPUTER CONCEPTS, examines the technologies of both hybrid and monolithic integrated circuits, how they are made, how they are packaged, and where they are used. PART TWO deals with the world of digital circuit techniques and basic computer concepts. It includes a discussion of binary arithmetic (the language of the computer), logic circuits, memories and other elements of the computer. As with the previous volumes, the information in this volume incorporates a presentation of future trends in integrated circuit and computer technology. Specific reinforcement exercises (and answers), glossaries and a definitive index for easy reference are included.

It is the author's hope that this series of books will provide the reader with a meaningful grasp of electronics technology and will lead to opportunities for greater personal productivity and gratification.

TABLE OF CONTENTS

PART II - COMPUTER CONCEPTS

PART ONE
INTEGRATED CIRCUITS

INTRODUCTION TO
INTEGRATED CIRCUITS

The challenge inherent in the study of basic electronics begins with basic concepts, continues through the exploration of passive components and then, goes on to examine the subject of discrete semiconductors and optoelectronics. Eventually, this investigation leads to the study of the integrated circuit (IC) and to the technology that opened the path to the creation of the microcomputer - the newest, most promising electronic giant of the Twentieth Century.

An enormous leap forward in electronic circuit technology and packaging miniaturization was made possible when discrete components in a circuit were replaced with monolithic and hybrid ICs. This scientific phenomenon was comparable to the revolutionary advance in electronic circuit design that occurred when vacuum tubes were replaced with discrete semiconductors.

IC technology has made it possible to produce electronic systems that are significantly more versatile, more durable, smaller, less expensive and require much lower electrical power to operate compared with electronic equipment that had been manufactured prior to 1962. The unique characteristics of IC technology have inspired the design of many significant and innovative products, including: electronic medical implants and prostheses, satellite communications equipment, video games, very small, light-weight television receivers, digital watches and hand-held calculators.

Because of its many singular features, IC technology has opened the way to the creation of the personal computer (PC) with its unlimited applications for business, home and schools. This extraordinary machine vastly exceeds the capabilities of the room-size, power-hungry, heat-generating, slow, multi-million dollar computers of the 1950s.

Before integrated circuits were available, it was necessary to provide data sheet information on the maximum ratings, characteristics and physical dimensions of every discrete passive component and semiconductor in the design of a circuit or system. With the IC as the basic element in an electronic system, specifications of the multitude of individual components have been replaced with design information for only *one* component - the integrated circuit.

The IC is regarded as a *single component*, complete in itself, with the capability of performing the function(s) of an entire electronic circuit or system. Individual discrete components are no longer interconnected to form circuits that are joined to create a system; **the IC itself is the circuit or system**.

ICs are made in either **hybrid** or **monolithic** form and are discussed in detail in CHAPTER ONE - HYBRID INTEGRATED CIRCUITS, CHAPTER TWO - SILICON-BASED MONOLITHIC INTEGRATED CIRCUITS and CHAPTER THREE - GALLIUM ARSENIDE-BASED MONOLITHIC ICs.

The integrated circuit is a unique and remarkable scientific development. It has changed the nature of electronic circuitry and packaging, significantly affecting the structure of our daily activities. This new technology has dramatically impacted on medical services, transportation, educational methods, communications and media techniques, banking services, and almost every aspect of our working and leisure lives.

To become familiar with the complexity of the integrated circuit and its many applications, continuing research and study is essential. By accepting these exciting technological and educational challenges, informed men and women will be at the forefront of the dynamic world of electronics and its infinite potential for the future.

A BRIEF HISTORY
OF INTEGRATED CIRCUITS

During the early part of the 20th Century, some research had begun on crystalline-structured solids for use in electronic circuitry. During this period, however, the scientific community expressed little interest in this investigation and minimal funding was available. In 1936, Bell Laboratories in New Jersey, the research arm of American Telephone and Telegraph, instituted a well-funded program to improve the sound quality of the telephone. The study centered around a variety of materials, such as: selenium (Se), germanium (Ge) and silicon (Si). It was discovered that when modifying a solid crystalline mass by using a combination of chemical and metallurgical techniques, the electrical characteristics of the material would change. When connected in a circuit having a D.C. supply voltage, the modified material (originally nonconductive) now allowed electrical current to flow in the circuit. Based on these findings, in 1948, three Bell Laboratories physicists, **John Bardeen, Walter Brattain** and **William Shockley**, invented the tiny germanium transistor and, in 1956, they were awarded the Nobel Prize in Physics for their efforts.

Until then, the vacuum tube was the only component in an electronic circuit which made electronic amplification and switching possible. The mighty vacuum tube, however, was destined to be replaced by the remarkable transistor, the device with essentially similar functions but having many more features and advantages. A transistor was made from a **solid** crystalline mass, rather than being made like a vacuum tube (several individual metal parts connected within an evacuated glass envelope). The term, "solid-state" came into popular use to describe the solid structure of the transistor. This device was one of a diverse group of solid-state components, called *semiconductors*, and it provided the impetus to launch the Semiconductor Industry in 1954, inaugurating the technical and social phenomenon universally referred to as the "Semiconductor Revolution."

By the late 1950s, semiconductor technology had undergone major changes. Although germanium devices were still being used in isolated applications, silicon was replacing germanium as the preferred semiconductor material, offering electrical, thermal and manufacturing advantages. Silicon semiconductors were more stable, operated over a wider temperature range, and were more reliable than equivalent devices made of germanium.

To reduce transistor production costs, improved mass production techniques (*batch processing*) were used. To further reduce costs, one of the fabrication steps was modified to create a simpler transistor structure. Because of its plateau-shaped geometry, the device was referred to as a *mesa transistor*. Despite its low processing costs, the mesa transistor had a major drawback: its exposed elements could be damaged by the etching acids used in the fabrication process and by the possibility of environmental contamination. In 1959, **Jean Hoerni** and **Robert Noyce**, two of the co-founders of Fairchild Semiconductor Company located in California, modified the existing semiconductor production process to overcome the problems inherent in the mesa transistor structure. They developed a new transistor shape, called *planar*, and added a series of processing steps, called *passivation layers*. Passivation consisted of growing a protective, insulating layer of silicon dioxide on the surface of a chip before and after each fabrication step.

By the end of the 1950s and into the 1960s, semiconductors, such as: diodes, SCRs, TRIACs and bipolar transistors (initially, just called "transistors"), were rapidly replacing vacuum tubes in existing circuits and in the initial design of equipment. Innovative electronic products appeared on the scene which combined discrete semiconductors with discrete passive components (resistors, capacitors and inductors) in use for many years. New and unique packaging techniques were now used to help enhance circuit performance and circuit/system reliability. Component miniaturization resulted in reduced system size and weight. The need for fewer components decreased the need for electrical power. In many cases, auxiliary cooling systems were eliminated by using semiconductor devices instead of vacuum tubes, further reducing system size, weight and cost.

In the late 1950s, a new production and packaging concept was conceived to assemble discrete components on an easily replaceable, prewired, insulated material called a *printed circuit (PC) board*. The components were mounted on the board by inserting their leads through selectively drilled holes. On the opposite side of the board, the leads were soldered in place, their excess lengths were trimmed and the board was cleaned and tested in preparation to being connected to other sections of a system. This packaging method was called *modularization* and provided an inexpensive, easy way to assemble, handle, and duplicate a section of an electronic circuit or system while enabling the quick removal and replacement of a PC board containing a defective component.

In 1957, new packages, called *micromodules*, were developed by the U.S. Air Force to improve circuit and system performance characteristics and further reduce weight and space inherent in conventional PC boards. The components used in a micromodule were closely stacked on top of one another and interconnected to form a required circuit. This assembly became the forerunner of a production and packaging technique that eventually led to *hybrid integrated circuit* technology.

The first hybrid integrated circuits (ICs) consisted of interconnected, discrete components with their leads inserted and soldered to the bottom of a single PC board to produce an array, circuit, or subsystem. The hybrid IC was protected in a conformally-coated epoxy, or in a package having external terminals, and specified as a **single, replaceable component.** Inherent in this type of packaging technique were the costs of double-packaging: the initial individual component packaging cost and the added cost of packaging the completed hybrid IC.

With the need to eliminate the extra handling and added costs of double-packaging while further reducing the weight and space of a hybrid IC, newer component manufacturing techniques were developed. Passive component chips were made that were electrical equivalents of their discrete counterparts; semiconductor chips were already available for this purpose. Other production methods (and equipment) were developed to permanently attach these chips to the surface of ceramic or glass substrates, selectively printed with interconnecting conductors. The entire assembly was enclosed in an appropriate package or conformally-coated with protective epoxy.

This new type of hybrid IC was still specified as a single, replaceable component that used less space, weighed less, offered superior performance characteristics and was more reliable than a completed PC board assembly with equivalent functions.

In 1958, in an attempt to further simplify the modularized concept of production and packaging, **Jack Kilby**, an engineer working for Texas Instruments, conceived the idea of manufacturing all components of a circuit on a thin wafer of germanium. The circuit consisted of the equivalent of five discrete components (1 capacitor, 3 resistors and 1 transistor) interconnected with four gold wires, four metal lugs serving as, the input and output terminals, and a small metal bar used as the ground (circuit reference). The entire assembly was 0.040 inches by 0.062 inches and was held together with wax.

Although well received by the scientific world as a major technological breakthrough, Kilby's device experienced processing problems, wiring difficulties, circuit instabilities and, as a result, was not commercially successful.

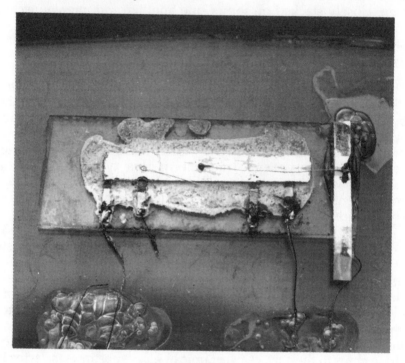

First Monolithic IC

Despite technical and commercial setbacks, the circuit concept Jack Kilby established introduced the electronics world to the *monolithic integrated circuit* - a single semiconductor chip into which chemical elements are diffused to produce a complete circuit and specified as a **single, replaceable component**.

In March 1961, Fairchild Semiconductor's Jean Hoerni and Robert Noyce, the inventors of the planar and passivation techniques, developed the first silicon-based monolithic IC - a "flip-flop" circuit commonly used in computers as counters. The initial production units were purchased by the National Aeronautics and Space Administration (NASA), the agency that funded research and development costs; this first practical monolithic IC was then made available to commercial equipment manufacturers. In a very short time, the use of monolithic IC devices received overwhelming industry acceptance, revolutionizing all forms of electronic design, packaging and circuit applications.

The first monolithic IC chip (0.06" in diameter) contained the equivalent of four bipolar transistors and five resistors, all metallurgically interconnected to form a circuit.

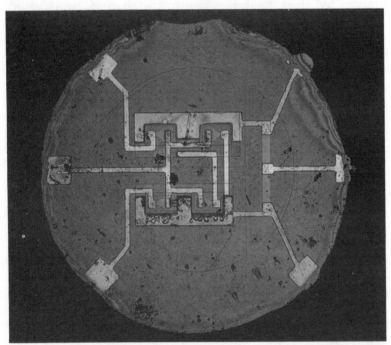

The First Successful Silicon-based Bipolar Monolithic IC Chip

This first monolithic IC was followed by far more complex ICs that were manufactured by the major semiconductor companies throughout the United States and other industrialized areas of the world. Since the first monolithic ICs included bipolar transistors as part of their structure, they were referred to as "bipolar monolithic ICs".

In 1961, Texas Instruments introduced the first discrete *field-effect transistors* (FETs), specifically, junction FETs (JFETs). Even though their circuit functions were essentially the same, they were operated by a different mechanism than the one used in bipolar transistors and had improved characteristics compared with the older devices. To differentiate between bipolar transistors and field-effect transistors, FETs were initially called "unipolar" transistors, but the term, "JFETs" eventually was commonly used. In 1962, Siliconix Inc., a California-based semiconductor manufacturer, introduced the discrete metal-oxide semiconductor FET (MOS FET). This device technology eventually led to the development of the MOS monolithic IC chip.

In 1969, Intel Corporation, a newly-founded monolithic IC manufacturer, based in Northern California, produced the first semiconductor memory, using MOS IC technology. In 1971, Intel engineers **Ted Hoff, Frederico Faggin** and **Stan Mazor** developed the first MOS monolithic IC microprocessor on a single silicon chip for use in the first hand-held calculator. The success of this chip paved the way for the concept, design and production of microcomputers, the implementation of computer technology in monolithic IC form.

Developments in semiconductor processing methods brought about many improvements in MOS monolithic IC technology, especially in the area of photolithography. More efficient variations of MOS monolithic ICs were created, such as: CMOS (Complementary MOSFET), BiMOS (a combination of bipolar and MOS technology on the same chip). These different silicon-based monolithic ICs afforded greater performance capability, higher chip densities, less power dissipation, and lower processing costs.

In 1974, Texas Instruments introduced the first monolithic IC microcomputer (also called a microcontroller), containing all the elements of a complete computer. This bipolar monolithic IC chip was designed specifically for consumer electronics to be used in desk-top and hand-held calculators, digital watches, copying machines, toys, games, tape recorders, fire and burglar alarm systems, and a variety of home appliance controls. The concept of implementing computer circuitry in monolithic IC form was very rapidly developed and eventually, the huge, multi-billion dollar, personal computer (PC) industry was spawned. From the first commercially-feasible monolithic IC, with the equivalent of nine components interconnected in a circuit, to the present stage of development, a monolithic IC chip can contain more than one million component functions in its complex, single-chip structure, no larger than ¼ " x ¼ ".

Despite the tremendous strides that have taken place in a relatively short time, even more impressive monolithic IC applications can be anticipated. The dedication, energy and imagination of creative minds have brought an extraordinary technology to fruition. Without doubt, the dynamic growth of IC technology will continue to produce electronic wonders into the next century and far into the future.

 CHAPTER
ONE

HYBRID INTEGRATED CIRCUITS

DEFINITIONS

HYBRID IC COMPONENTS

HYBRID IC ASSEMBLY

GENERAL COMMENTS ON
HYBRID ICs

REINFORCEMENT EXERCISES

HYBRID INTEGRATED CIRCUITS

DEFINITIONS

A hybrid integrated circuit (IC) consists of many individual passive and/or semiconductor components, in chip or packaged form, interconnected and soldered onto a pre-wired, ceramic substrate. The hybrid IC can be an array, circuit, several circuits or a complete system either enclosed in a package, or encapsulated in a protective coating that conforms to the shape of the complete IC. A hybrid IC is considered to be a single component.

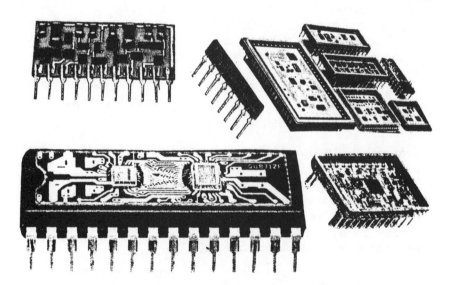

Examples of Hybrid Integrated Circuits
Figure 1

THE SUBSTRATE — THE HYBRID IC SUPPORT STRUCTURE
A **substrate** is the mechanical support structure for the components and conductors of a hybrid IC and is made of a ceramic material, such as: alumina (aluminum oxide) or beryllia. The material must withstand temperatures above the melting point of solder, resist any chemical reactions resulting from contact with other elements and solvents, provide electrical isolation, and have the capability of conducting heat efficiently.

HYBRID IC COMPONENTS

Passive components (resistors, capacitors, inductors, etc.) and semiconductors (diodes, transistors, etc.) are made in pellet or chip form for use in hybrid ICs. The component pellets and chips function in a manner similar to that of their larger, packaged, discrete counterparts and are selected for their specific characteristics and performance capabilities.

RESISTOR CHIPS - MATERIALS AND STRUCTURE

Resistor chips for hybrid ICs are manufactured in **thick film, thin film,** and **bulk metal foil** format, each with its own resistance, tolerance, power range, and dimensions. The following types are the most commonly used:

THICK FILM RESISTORS

Thick film resistor chips are usually thicker than 0.001 inch and are used for general-purpose commercial, industrial, and consumer applications where the value of the temperature coefficient (TC) of the device is not critical. The resistive element is made of **cermet,** a combination of ceramic and metal; palladium-silver and ruthenium dioxide are the most commonly used. The resistor chip is constructed as follows:

- Two nickel-plated, solder-coated, silver electrodes are attached to the ends of a ceramic substrate.
- The resistive element is deposited and fused under high temperature to the substrate. If necessary, it can be laser-trimmed to an accuracy of 0.01%.
- Finally, glass and epoxy resin coats are applied to cover the chip to form a protective layer. See Figure 2.

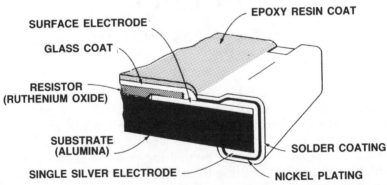

Cross-section of a Typical Thick Film Resistor Chip
Figure 2

THIN FILM RESISTORS+

Thin film resistor chips are used in military and space applications where tight tolerance, low temperature coefficient, and high reliability are required. Nichrome (an alloy of nickel and chromium) and chromium-cobalt are commonly used as the resistive elements.

- When applying an extremely thin resistive film (less than 0.000001" thick) to a ceramic or glass substrate, the resistive film is vaporized under heat when subjected to ion bombardment. This process is called **sputtering**.

- Two electrode areas are then attached to the ends of the resistor chip. The electrodes are coated with a thin film of gold for effective soldering and resistance to corrosion.

Available resistive values of thin film chips are very limited, ranging from 10 to about 1000. Typical resistive tolerance is 0.1%; typical TC is from 10 ppm/°C to 50 ppm/°C.

BULK METAL FOIL RESISTORS

Bulk metal foil resistors generally exhibit a typical TC of 0.5 ppm/°C. Standard tolerances for these chips are 0.01% and they can be trimmed to any value within 0.005%. Made of a uniformly alloyed, metal foil resistive material, bulk metal foil resistors offer considerable improvement in performance characteristics compared with other chip resistors.

CAPACITOR CHIPS — MATERIALS AND STRUCTURE

MULTI-LAYER CERAMIC (MLC) CAPACITORS

Ceramic capacitor chips, made in a multi-layered, single-structured (monolithic) form, are manufactured as follows:

- Ceramic powder is suspended in water to form a mixture that is then cast into layers 0.001" to 0.003" thick. One surface of each ceramic layer is metallized with aluminum to create the conductive areas for each capacitor chip.

- The aluminum electrodes and ceramic layers are stacked to form a laminated (interdigitated) block in which the electrode and ceramic layers alternate.

- Additional silver or palladium-silver alloy electrodes are attached to the interdigitated block and covered with a barrier layer of nickel to prevent loss of silver.

- A coat of solder is deposited on the silver electrodes to enhance bonding to the substrate contact areas. See Figure 3.

- The capacitor is formed into a monolithic block by cold-pressing ceramic powders into a predetermined shape and bonding them under high temperature to create a cohesive, strong structure. This entire process is called **sintering**.

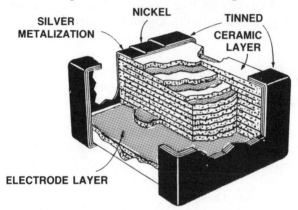

Cross-section of a Multi-layer Ceramic (MLC) Capacitor Chip
Figure 3

Special MLC chips are manufactured for high voltage use, however, applied voltages of about 10% above its rated value can cause a decrease in capacitance. Capacitance values range from 1.0 pF (picofarads) to 10 uF (microfarads) at tolerances of 0.01%. Laser trimming produces tighter tolerance chips at relatively low cost. Maximum voltage ratings range between 500 and 5000 volts. The multi-layered structure provides high values of capacitance in relatively small physical sizes.

TANTALUM OXIDE CAPACITORS
Tantalum oxide is used to create chips with capacitance levels ranging from 0.1 uF to 150 uF at working voltages from 4 volts to 50 volts D.C. These levels are higher than the capacitance levels of ceramic. As with discrete capacitors, higher voltage ratings are associated with lower capacitance values.

These chips are constructed in molded form and have the highest capacitance per unit volume of any dielectric (the nonconducting material of a capacitor which is sandwiched between the two conducting areas).

Since an unprotected tantalum chip will degrade in the presence of moisture, an epoxy-resin coating is used to protect the chip prior to final testing and shipping.

SILICON CAPACITORS

A capacitor is defined as a component that has two conducting areas with a dielectric (nonconductive material) sandwiched between them. A silicon-based semiconductor diode (P/N junction) can be made to serve as a fixed or variable silicon capacitor by applying an appropriate D.C. voltage across its terminals.

• When a reverse D.C. voltage, (plus to the N-region, or cathode), is applied across the diode terminals, an extremely high resistance area (depletion region) is formed between the P and N-regions (conducting regions), causing the diode to serve as a capacitor. See Figure 4a.

• The diode can also act as a *variable* capacitor (**varactor**); as the applied voltage varies, the capacitance value will vary *inversely*. The capacitance variation ranges between 1 pf and several hundred pF (see Figure 4b), depending on the value of applied voltage and chip size.

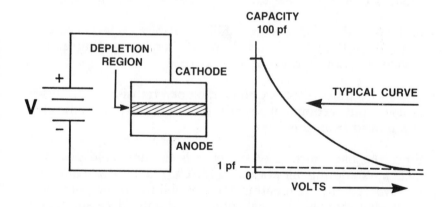

Diode Cross-section   Characteristics
Figure 4a   **Figure 4b**
Silicon Diode Serving As a Silicon Capacitor

SEMICONDUCTOR CHIPS
For use in hybrid ICs, semiconductor chips can be supplied as:
• Unpackaged back-bonded chips
• Unpackaged face-bonded chips
• Discrete semiconductors sealed in suitable packages

During fabrication, processing is done on the "top" surface, or "face" of the chip; the opposite side is normally called the "back" surface. The surface of a chip that is permanently attached to a hybrid IC substrate is called the "bonded" surface.

UNPACKAGED BACK-BONDED CHIPS
Unpackaged back-bonded chips are attached to the metallized areas on the surface of a hybrid IC substrate. Wires are connected between the bonding pads on the top surface of the chip and the metallic pads on the substrate, where required. The actual assembly process is described later in this chapter.

ADVANTAGES
• Since lead lengths from unpackaged back-bonded chips are wire-bonded to the metallized pads on the hybrid substrate and are shorter than those of packaged devices, the chance of stray capacitive effects created by long leads are minimized.

• Back-bonded chips are more readily available and less expensive to produce than face-bonded chips, thereby creating greater device selection options at a lower cost.

• The back surface of a back-bonded bipolar transistor chip serves as its output section (collector) and most of the heat in the chip is removed from this large area.

• Since the back surface of the chip is flat and gold-plated to facilitate soldering, air pockets at the chip-to-substrate interface are avoided. By eliminating the possiblility of air pockets, a necessary, intimate thermal contact at the interface surfaces is provided, allowing the metallized section of the ceramic substrate to act as an efficient heat sink.

DISADVANTAGES
• The exposed wires connecting the bonding pads on the back-bonded chip and the metallized areas on the hybrid IC substrate make the completed hybrid circuit assembly vulnerable to the stress of a harsh environmental and to physical damage when improperly handled.

UNPACKAGED FACE-BONDED CHIPS
Face-bonded chips are shipped in special containers (carriers) that provide access to the bonding pads on the face of a chip. Chips in this form are often referred to as:

- Beam-lead chips
- Flip chips
- Leadless-inverted devices (LIDs)
- Beam-tape devices

These chips are inverted, or flipped, face down, and then permanently attached to the metallized areas of the hybrid IC substrate by aligning and soldering the chip's bonding pads to appropriate metal contacts on the substrate.

ADVANTAGES
- Only one step is needed to attach the chip and electrically connect a chip's bonding pads to a hybrid IC substrate, resulting in some reduction of hybrid IC assembly costs.

DISADVANTAGES
- Since the thermal path to the substrate is only through the bonding pad surfaces, heat generated in the chip is not transferred efficiently from the chip to the substrate.

- Selection of face-bonded chips is limited because relatively few semiconductor chips of this type are manufactured.

- Face-bonded chips require more processing and are more costly than back-bonded chips.

PACKAGED SEMICONDUCTOR CHIPS (DISCRETE SEMICONDUCTORS)
From an assembly aspect, it may be more desirable to mount packaged chips having 3 or more terminals onto a hybrid IC substrate. These components include: SCRs, TRIACs, bipolar transistors, FETs, and monolithic ICs.

ADVANTAGES
- Packaged components are less prone to damage that may be caused by improper handling during hybrid IC assembly.

- Packaged components can be subjected to stabilization bake, thermal shock, and power burn-in prior to hybrid IC assembly.

- A greater selection of semiconductor components in packaged form is available and in some cases a specific component is only available in packaged form.

DISADVANTAGES
• Packaged components have a higher profile and take more room on a hybrid IC substrate than components in chip form.

• Generally, packaged semiconductor components cost more than the same component in chip form. These chips must be assembled in packages that have terminals suitable for mounting onto the surface of a hybrid IC substrate.

Some presently available packages used to mount semiconductors onto a hybrid IC substrate are shown in Figure 5. They include: Small Outline Transistor (SOT), SOIC, Leadless Chip Carrier (LCC), Flat Pack, and Leaded Chip Carrier packages.

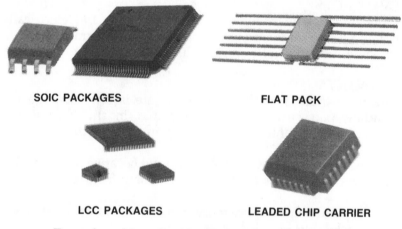

SOIC PACKAGES   **FLAT PACK**

LCC PACKAGES   **LEADED CHIP CARRIER**

Examples of Low-Profile, Multi-terminal Packages
Figure 5

When electrical and/or size requirements dictate the use of specific component types, either unpackaged back-bonded chips, face-bonded chips, or packaged semiconductors can be assembled onto a substrate to create a desired hybrid IC.

HYBRID INTEGRATED CIRCUIT ASSEMBLY

Hybrid IC assembly (see Figure 6) begins with screen-printing a pattern of conductive ink on a ceramic substrate surface. The ink is used to interconnect components mounted onto the substrate to form an array, circuit, or sub-system. The air around the substrate is then heated to activate the ink's adhesive properties to permanently attach the conductive interconnect pattern to the surface of the substrate. Either an epoxy bonding or reflow solder method continues the assembly process.

TYPICAL HYBRID IC ASSEMBLY PROCESS

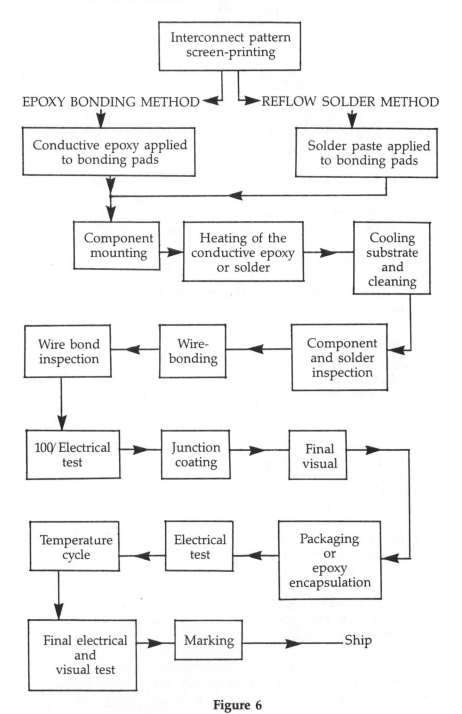

Figure 6

EPOXY BONDING METHOD
During screen-printing, an epoxy resin containing metal particles (usually silver or gold) is simultaneously applied to the designated bonding pads on the substrate to facilitate electrical conductivity and heat transfer.

REFLOW SOLDER METHOD
The screen-printed substrate is immersed in a pot of molten solder to plate (tin) its metallized surfaces. The substrate is allowed to cool and solder paste is forced through a coarse screen onto the substrate's metallized bonding pads.

• The desired components are then mounted on designated bonding pads and the hybrid IC assembly placed into a heated chamber where the temperature must be high enough to either cure the epoxy resin or to melt the solder paste.

• After the resin is cooled, or the solder paste cooled and solidified, the components become permanently attached to the the hybrid IC substrate bonding pads. The components of the hybrid IC are now ready to be interconnected.

WIRE-BONDING TECHNIQUES
Very thin gold or aluminum wire, 0.0007" to 0.001" in diameter, is used as the connecting material in hybrid ICs. For chips having higher current-carrying capability, larger wire, 0.002" in diameter and greater is used.

The proper sized wire must be used to connect the metallized bonding pads on the surface of the component chips to the bonding pads inside the hybrid package. The external terminals of the package connect to the bonding pads inside the package. Three optional wire-bonding methods are:

• **Thermo-compression bonding** - By compressing one end of a connecting wire placed on a metallized bonding pad at 270° C, the wire is permanently bonded to the pad.

• **Ultrasonic bonding** - Mechanical ultrasonic vibration at the wire-to-bonding pad interface produces the required energy to attach the wire to the bonding pad.

• **Thermosonic bonding** - After the substrate is heated to 150° C, an ultrasonic wave is applied to supply the energy needed for proper wire-bonding at the bonding pad-to-wire interface.

INSPECTION AND PACKAGING
- Before packaging, the hybrid IC assembly is cleaned and visually inspected with a high-power binocular microscope to locate scratches, solder splashes, improper wire-bonds, or any contaminants on the substrate surface. Unacceptable units are repaired, if possible, or rejected.

- After 100% electrical testing to the required specifications, acceptable hybrids IC assemblies are then enclosed in plastic or hermetically-sealed packages. Examples of hybrid IC lead-frames and packages are shown in Figure 7.

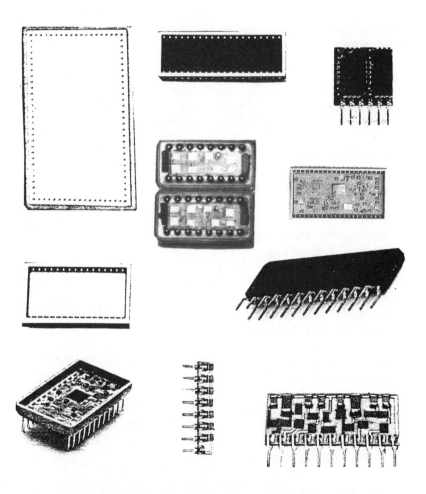

Examples of Hybrid IC Lead-Frames and Packages
Figure 7

HERMETICALLY-SEALED PACKAGES

To prevent any detrimental external gasses, water vapor or any other impurities from penetrating a package to contaminate the circuit inside, hermetically-sealed packages are used. A solder joint provides an airtight and waterproof seal between the open case and its cover. This hermetic seal is required for all packaged components intended for military and aerospace use. To maintain a true hermetic seal over a wide operating temperature range, the package case, cover, leads, and lead insulation (if required) are made of materials with similar thermal expansion characteristics, such as: Kovar (an iron-nickel-cobalt alloy), glass, silica (silicon dioxide), and alumina (aluminum oxide).

Hermetically-sealed packages are also used for commercial, industrial and consumer applications, if the equipment operates in environments that might damage components of the hybrid IC.

NONHERMETICALLY-SEALED PACKAGES

Molded plastic and conformally-coated epoxy packages are not hermetically-sealed; they only provide a means of carrying, mounting and protecting the circuit from physical damage.

MOLDED PLASTIC PACKAGE

• An unpackaged hybrid IC assembly is mounted and soldered on a selected lead-frame.

• Gold or aluminum wires are connected between the appropriate bonding pads on the hybrid IC substrate and bonding pads on a molded lead-frame.

• The molded lead-frame is filled with epoxy. Any air bubbles formed in the epoxy are removed by a partial vacuum method. The epoxy is cured by heating the area around the package and is then allowed to cool.

• The external metal terminals of the molded package are trimmed and properly bent for insertion into a PC board.

CONFORMALLY-COATED EPOXY PACKAGE

• Instead of being placed in a lead-frame mold and processed, epoxy is coated around a completed component-mounted, wire-bonded substrate assembly.

• The epoxy is cured by heating the area around the package and is allowed to cool, and then, the external metal terminals are trimmed and bent, if necessary.

The completed hybrid ICs are tested to determine conformance to the electrical and mechanical specifications listed on the data sheets. Any additional special tests and/or pre-conditioning that may be required are also performed. Approved parts are then marked, inventoried, and/or shipped, as required.

For hybrid ICs intended for high-reliability, military and aerospace applications, all pre-conditioning procedures and tests required by military specifications are performed. For details on hybrid ICs intended for military and aerospace use, refer to CHAPTER FIVE - IC HIGH-RELIABILITY CONSIDERATIONS.

GENERAL COMMENTS ON HYBRID INTEGRATED CIRCUITS

When compared with a system built with discrete components, the overall size and weight of a system is considerably reduced when using hybrid ICs as individual multi-function components. These devices contain interconnected chip components instead of the larger, packaged discrete components normally mounted on a PC board. In addition, a proper layout of a PC board using hybrid ICs can improve circuit and system performance (faster switching speed and/or higher frequency response) by decreasing the distance between components. To a great extent, other component characteristics, such as: tolerances and thermal properties in a hybrid IC are similar, and sometimes superior, to the characteristics of their discrete counterparts. Some chip components, such as thick film resistor chips, can be laser-trimmed to 0.01% tolerances.

A first generation hybrid IC consisted of large, packaged passive and semiconductor components mounted on a substrate by inserting the component leads through holes in the substrate. They were then soldered to appropriate soldering pads on an interconnect pattern on the bottom surface of the substrate to create an array, circuit, etc. Although it appeared to be similar to a conventional PC board, the hybrid IC was encapsulated to form a single, replaceable part of a larger system.

Second generation hybrid ICs, consisting of smaller, but functionally-equivalent component chips, used more advanced assembly methods instead of those methods used with the larger, discrete components. This new approach reduced costs by the elimination of expensive and time-consuming "double-packaging" (discrete component package plus the final hybrid IC package) inherent in the production of earlier hybrid ICs.

State-of-the-art (third generation) hybrid ICs consist of circuit components made to be mounted and attached to the surface of a substrate. These new hybrid ICs consist of passive components and semiconductors in chip and packaged form that are connected to create arrays, circuits, and systems functionally similar to the second generation hybrids. The main difference between the two is that the components used in the third generation hybrid IC are specifically made with physical configurations compatible with an assembly method that allows components to be mounted onto the surface(s) of a substrate. This assembly technique is called Surface Mounted Device (SMD) technology.

SMD technology offers a means of further reducing the weight, size, and cost of an electronics system, while improving its performance characteristics and reliability. Like any new technology, there are other factors associated with it.

- SMD technology requires the use of new assembly equipment for the automatic placement, soldering, cleaning, and testing of the finished SMD assembly. The cost of all this new equipment is quite high, requiring large production quantities to justify the initial expense. For companies involved with only small quantity production of hybrid ICs, SMD technology may not be a cost-effective approach.

  There are, however, several new companies that are providing SMD "foundry" services for small quantity production runs. Foundry companies purchase the required production equipment and SMD components and accept production orders from those equipment manufacturers who require this technology to offer a more competitive marketing position for their products.

- SMD component availability is improving even though, at the present time, only about 40% of all available electronic components are in SMD form.

It is assumed that with increased industry acceptance, the availability of SMD components will continue to increase and the costs of SMD assembly, testing, and other related production equipment will decrease.

Because hybrid IC technology has provided improved circuit and system performance, reduced production costs, and offered improved reliability, it has evolved into a viable choice for many circuits and systems.

REINFORCEMENT EXERCISES

Answer TRUE or FALSE to each of the following statements:

1. A hybrid IC consists of a group of passive and semiconductor components, in chip or packaged form, permanently attached to the surface of a pre-wired substrate to create an array (a group of similar devices), a circuit, a sub-system, several sub-systems or an entire system.

2. A completed hybrid IC is specified as a single component and not as a group of separate, interconnected discrete passive and semiconductor components.

3. The hybrid IC's substrate provides mechanical support for components and interconnecting conductors, electrical isolation of the circuit elements and heat transfer capability.

4. Since ceramic does not resist chemical reactions to other elements and solvents and cannot withstand temperatures as high as the melting point of solder, silicon is used as the substrate material in making a hybrid IC.

5. Thick film resistor chips are mainly used for general-purpose commercial, industrial and consumer applications where a chip's temperature coefficient is not critical.

6. Multi-layer ceramic (MLC) capacitor chips cannot be laser trimmed to produce tight tolerance chips. Furthermore, these capacitor chips will not withstand the slightest overvoltage across their terminals, even for a short time.

7. Solid tantalum oxide capacitor chips are constructed in molded form for use in hybrid ICs. Since these chips have the lowest capacitance per unit volume of any dielectric, they are not used where high capacitance value devices are needed; they are used only for protection against high humidity environments.

8. Since unprotected tantalum will not degrade in the presence of moisture, there is no necessity to protect the chip prior to final testing and shipment.

9. A silicon diode chip can act as a variable capacitor by varying the forward voltage across its terminals. As voltage increases, the capacitance of the chip increases.

10. Only components in chip form are mounted on a hybrid IC substrate, regardless of the number of terminals on the chip. Packaged components are never inside a hybrid IC.

11. One of the major advantages in using face-bonded semiconductor chips is that nearly every semiconductor available in discrete form, or as a packaged monolithic IC, is also available as an unpackaged face-bonded chip. This feature provides greater device selection options.

12. Both back-bonded and face-bonded semiconductor chips are used, where indicated, enhancing the advantages of a hybrid IC. The face-bonded type, however, is more commonly used.

13. Thermo-compression, ultrasonic and thermosonic bonding are used to wire-bond thin gold or aluminum leads between the bonding pads on component chips and appropriate metallized contact areas on a hybrid IC substrate.

14. Hermetically-sealed or plastic packages are used to enclose hybrid ICs, depending on the application. In some cases, an unpackaged hybrid IC assembly is conformally-coated with an epoxy material.

15. Hermetically-sealed packages (made of ceramic and Kovar), with expansion and thermal characteristics similar to glass, silica and alumina, do not permit gas or water vapor penetration. They are mainly used for military and aerospace applications.

16. Modern hybrid IC packaging methods do not use surface mounted device (SMD) components.

17. Hybrid ICs are only applicable for custom circuit design when design time is limited and if the quantities required are very low.

Answers to these reinforcement exercises are on page 187.

CHAPTER
TWO

SILICON-BASED MONOLITHIC INTEGRATED CIRCUITS

INTRODUCTION AND
DEFINITIONS

SILICON-BASED MONOLITHIC IC
PRODUCTION PROCESS

HOW ELEMENTS OF A MONO-
LITHIC IC CHIP ARE FORMED

SELECTION OF IC PACKAGES

MONOLITHIC IC SELECTION
CRITERIA

GENERAL COMMENTS ON ICs

REINFORCEMENT EXERCISES

SILICON-BASED MONOLITHIC ICs

INTRODUCTION AND DEFINITIONS

A silicon-based **monolithic** IC is a *single* chip with specific chemicals (dopants) diffused into its silicon material to produce the *functions* of circuit components. The number of component functions in a single monolithic IC chip is called **chip density**. The sections of the IC that perform the component functions are interconnected by metallic depositions and/or diffusions to create an array, a completed circuit, several circuits, a sub-system, several sub-systems, one or many completed electronic systems on a single IC chip.

The term "monolithic" is derived from the Greek words "mono" (one) and "lithos" (stone). It denotes a single chip structure.

Compared with a hybrid IC that has more than one component mounted on a ceramic substrate, a monolithic IC consists of only one chip that is also the substrate. Since all component functions are contained *within* this structure, it is called an **active substrate**. The substrate consists of many interconnected layers of various elements that comprise the total chip. An unpackaged silicon-based monolithic IC chip is usually no more than ¼" x ¼", depending on circuit complexity and the level of monolithic technology, while hybrid IC dimensions are not limited to any particular size. See Figure 8.

Typical Hybrid IC   Large Monolithic IC Chip

Figure 8

Silicon is the preferred material to be used as the active substrate for all semiconductors. It has maintained this special status in the production of monolithic ICs because:

- Compared with other materials suitable for semiconductor use, silicon is relatively low in cost and is easily processed.

- After preconditioning, silicon-based semiconductors exhibit extremely stable electrical characteristics.

- The nominal operating and storage temperature capability of silicon-based semiconductors (from -55° C to +150° C) is wider than germanium-based semiconductors that range from -55° C to +100° C. The change in characteristic per ° C change in temperature (temperature coefficient, or TC) of silicon is lower than germanium. As temperature changes occur in a circuit, the characteristics of a silicon semiconductor will not change as much as a germanium semiconductor.

In those applications where the specific characteristics of silicon are not suitable, gallium arsenide (GaAs), a compound of gallium and arsenic, has become an alternate monolithic IC substrate material. Despite higher production costs, GaAs-based monolithic ICs offer several performance characteristics that are superior to equivalent silicon-based devices. See CHAPTER THREE - GALLIUM ARSENIDE-BASED MONOLITHIC ICs.

A silicon or GaAs monolithic IC is a single component in either chip form or enclosed in an appropriate package with its external terminals internally connected to metallized bonding pads on the surface of the chip. A packaged monolithic IC can be connected to its system by inserting it into an appropriate socket on a PC board containing the system's other components, or, the package leads can be soldered to the PC board.

An unpackaged monolithic IC chip can be connected to a PC board by wiring its bonding pads to the metallic bonding pads on the PC board surface. In spite of the apparent contradiction in the terminology, a monolithic IC, packaged or unpackaged, is often called a "chip", or "microchip"; these "chips", in either form, are often used as component elements of a hybrid IC.

Monolithic ICs are products of the combined technologies of photolithography (a photo-printing method for reproducing circuit patterns on wafers), chemistry, and metallurgy. Improved photolithographic methods are producing higher chip densities, which, in turn, increase switching speed characteristics of silicon. Increased switching speed is one of the main reasons the performance gap between silicon and GaAs-based monolithic IC technology is closing.

The techniques of producing and processing blank silicon wafers into finished chips for use as discrete semiconductors was investigated in VOLUME TWO - DISCRETE SEMICONDUCTORS. There are some basic differences in the production of discrete semiconductor chips and monolithic IC chips. To achieve a clearer understanding of this important procedure, a detailed review of the entire wafer fabrication process is relevant.

SILICON-BASED MONOLITHIC IC PRODUCTION PROCESS

Ordinary beach sand is the basic raw material required to produce silicon-based monolithic IC chips. Silicon dioxide (SiO_2), the main constituent of beach sand, must be refined to initiate the process of semiconductor production. See Figure 9.

Silicon Rod
(Ingot)

Wafer

Monolithic
IC Chips

Beach Sand

From Beach Sand to a Completed Monolithic IC Chip
Figure 9

SILICON INGOT AND BLANK WAFER PRODUCTION

To refine silicon dioxide, the raw material must be heated to a temperature of 1420° C (the melting point of silicon) to produce pure silicon in the form of high-purity **polycrystalline** bars. The term "polycrystalline" describes the *nonuniform* lattice structure of a silicon rod (or ingot). In its polycrystalline state, however, silicon is not suitable for use in the processing of semiconductor devices.

To provide workable semiconductor material, polycrystalline silicon bars must be further refined to create a silicon ingot that exhibits an identically-oriented formation (uniformly-latticed), **single-crystalline** structure that is maintained throughout the crystalline ingot. To produce single-crystalline ingots, either of two methods are used - the **Czochralski** or **float-zone** techniques.

CZOCHRALSKI METHOD

• A bar of polycrystalline silicon is melted in an oxygen-free high-temperature oven.

• A single-crystalline silicon seed is introduced into the melt causing a portion of the melt to freeze onto the seed. The liquid silicon in the melt is then formed into a cylindrical ingot of pure single-crystalline silicon.

FLOAT-ZONE METHOD

• A polycrystalline silicon bar is placed in an oven having an oxygen-free atmosphere. The heat radiating from a radio frequency (RF) induction coil melts the bottom of the bar causing a drop of silicon to suspend from the bar.

• A single-crystalline silicon seed is then introduced into the silicon drop. With careful temperature control of the melted section, silicon is chemically grown on the seed in the form of a single-crystalline structure. The RF induction coil is slowly raised along the length of the bar and causes the molten region of silicon to move along its length. The bar begins to dissolve and grow onto the seed to form a silicon ingot having a single-crystalline lattice structure.

The ingot is machined to form a rod of uniform diameter. A "flat" is ground along the length of the ingot so that each wafer sliced from the rod will have a reference edge parallel to its natural crystal plane. A diamond saw is used to cut the ingot into wafers about 0.02 inches thick.

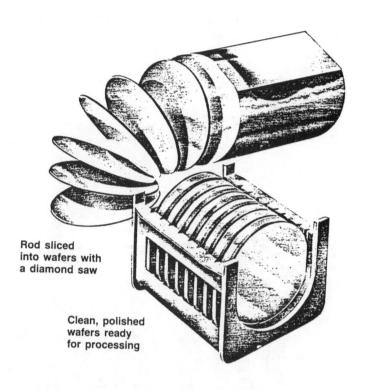

**Rod sliced
into wafers with
a diamond saw**

**Clean, polished
wafers ready
for processing**

From Silicon Ingot to Wafers Ready for Processing
Figure 10

The wafers are etched, lapped and one side polished to a mirror finish to remove any damage caused by the sawing. The blank wafers are now ready for further processing. See Figure 10.

Monolithic IC processing begins by the penetration of specific chemicals, in vapor form, into selected areas of an active substrate. This process is referred to as **diffusion**. With the aid of templates, called **photomasks** (masks), a series of diffusion patterns (layouts) are created to allow successive diffusions to change the electrical properties of selected areas on the substrate. Each step of the diffusion process requires a different pattern to create the interconnected component functions on each layer of the completed monolithic IC chip.

Computer-aided design (CAD) is a modern technique used to assist in the layout of the different photomask patterns for each layer of a monolithic IC chip. CAD uses a software program that includes a library of circuit cells (layouts of parts of standard circuits) that can be displayed on the computer monitor.

The circuit layout display can be manipulated by a "light pen", and/or by computer keyboard commands. Circuit cells are moved, added and/or removed (Figure 11), to produce a graphic representation of a single layout pattern for one layer of a single monolithic IC chip (not the entire wafer). This pattern is referred to as a **reticle**.

Computer Aided Design (CAD) Used to Layout Photomask Patterns
Figure 11

OPTICAL PHOTOMASKING -
THE INITIAL STAGE OF PHOTOLITHOGRAPHY

- Before a photomask can be created, a photographic enlargement of the reticle is checked, corrected and redrawn. By a step and repeat photographic process, the reduced image of the reticle is reproduced in rows and columns on a metal master mask for as many times as space on the mask allows. The process is repeated for each reticle and a set of different master masks is produced. A single mask is made for each diffusion - the number of masks in a set depends on the number of diffusions required by the complexity of the IC chip.

- A final working mask, in the form of a glass plate, is made from each master mask in the set to serve as a template. The dimensions of each mask must be compatible with the size of the blank wafer previously prepared for further processing.

The number of individual, identical patterns on each mask depends on the diameter of the silicon wafer and the size of the IC chip. Larger, more complex circuits require larger patterns, therefore, more space on the wafer (or more silicon "real estate") is necessary for each IC chip. Only one mask is used to reproduce its unique pattern onto only one layer of the silicon substrate.

Each mask contains several accurately spaced patterns, called **registration marks**. During wafer fabrication, these patterns are used to align each mask precisely in relation to other masks in the set. A typical photomask is shown in Figure 12.

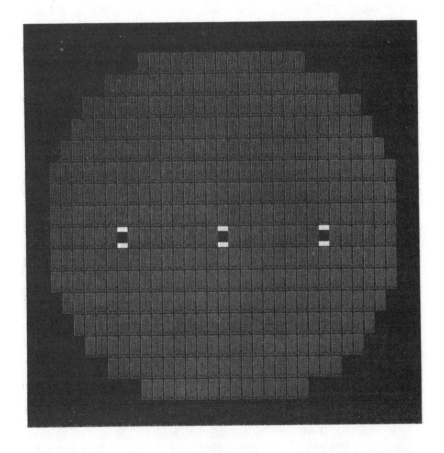

Example of a Photomask for One Layer of a Monolithic IC Wafer
Figure 12

The use of CAD has been a vital factor in improving photomask quality and reducing production time, costs of masks, and the IC chip itself. The older method of drawing circuit layouts by hand for wafer design has been replaced by CAD.

Although the optical mask-making process described above is a popular technique in the design of photomasks, the practical limit to the thinness of a line in a photomask pattern (and the pattern on an IC layer) is about 1 micron (1 micrometer). One micron is equal to 40 millionths of an inch (0.00004 inches).

Using this conventional method, productivity and reliability levels are severely reduced as the limit of the thinness of a line is exceeded. More advanced mask-making methods are being used to achieve thinner lines, resulting in much greater functional capability for newer monolithic IC chips.

SILICON WAFER FABRICATION

THE EPITAXIAL LAYER
Wafer fabrication begins by depositing a thin layer of silicon on the highly polished surface (top) of a wafer. The Si layer, called **epitaxy** or the **epitaxial layer**, must have the same crystalline structure as the original wafer and is used to prepare the wafer for passivation, the next processing step.

PASSIVATION (GLASSIVATION)
The passivation process provides an isolating film (Figure 13a) of silicon dioxide before each diffusion step to aid in selectively diffusing the required dopants into a wafer. Passivation combines silicon (Si) and water vapor (H_2O) in a high temperature chamber to grow a thin layer of silicon dioxide on the top (epitaxial surface) of the wafers in the chamber.

FINAL PHOTOLITHOGRAPHY -
TRANSFERRING MASK PATTERNS TO A WAFER
• The passivated surface is coated with **photoresist**, a light-sensitive emulsion, and the first mask aligned on the wafer. Photoresist **polymerizes** (hardens) when exposed to ultraviolet light coming through the mask. See Figure 13b. Since radiated areas of photoresist are hardened, they cannot dissolve when immersed in a developer solution and remain in those areas where ultraviolet light passed through the transparent areas of the mask. See Figures 13c and 13d. After removing the mask, unhardened areas of the silicon dioxide layer are then etched away in a hydrofluoric acid solution. See Figure 13e.

- The hardened photoresist is then etched away with a sulphuric acid solution. See Figure 13f. The exposed area of the pure silicon wafer is now ready for the first diffusion step. A separate mask is required for each diffusion step.

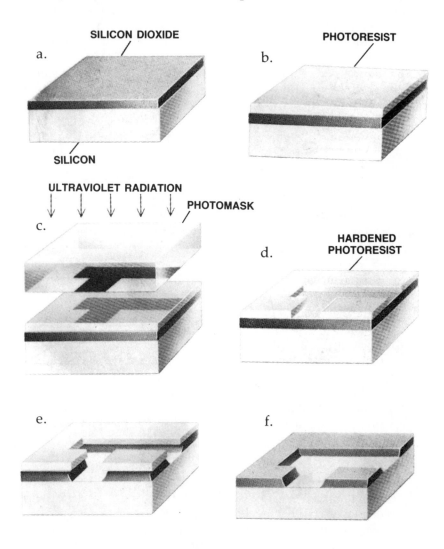

From Photomask to the Final Photolithographic Process
Figure 13

DIFFUSION AND METALLIZATION
Diffusion, or **doping**, is the process that changes the electrical characteristics of the layers of a wafer by having specific chemicals in gaseous form, called **impurities** or **dopants**, penetrate and diffuse through selected areas of the wafer. Boron and phosphorus are the chemical elements used as dopants to create the functions of components and conductors of a silicon-based monolithic IC.

For large quantity production (**batch processing**), 100 blank silicon wafers or more are put in a high-temperature diffusion chamber (all at the same time) in an atmosphere of the required dopant. The dopant is absorbed into the exposed silicon area on each wafer causing these areas to change from pure silicon (inherently infinite resistance) to a material that is highly conductive (essentially zero resistance).

• A new layer of silicon dioxide (passivation layer) is grown over the first diffusion layer. The process is repeated with each succeeding mask precisely aligned on the wafer. Using boron and phosphorus respectively, a P-type or an N-type region is created, depending on the specific dopant used in each diffusion step. Properly patterned and placed in the correct relationship to each other, P-type and N-type layers become the various component elements of the IC.

• Although not used for diffusion, **metallization masks** are included in a photomask set to provide a means of creating interconnect patterns between selected layers of the substrate. A thin film of gold or aluminum is deposited on the patterned surface of the substrate layer. The selection of gold or aluminum depends on the particular technology used to produce a specific monolithic IC chip.

FINAL METALLIZATION AND PASSIVATION
• To facilitate attachment of leads from the surface of an IC chip to external circuit(s) and/or system(s), a film of gold (or aluminum), about one micron thick, is deposited on the substrate's final metallization pattern to form bonding pads.

The bonding pads are conductive areas that provide a connecting point from the IC chip to the inside terminals of an IC package or to the appropriate bonding pads on a PC board.

• A final passivation layer is grown on the wafer surface, excluding the bonding pads, to complete the wafer fabrication.

BLANK SILICON WAFER TO MONOLITHIC IC CHIP

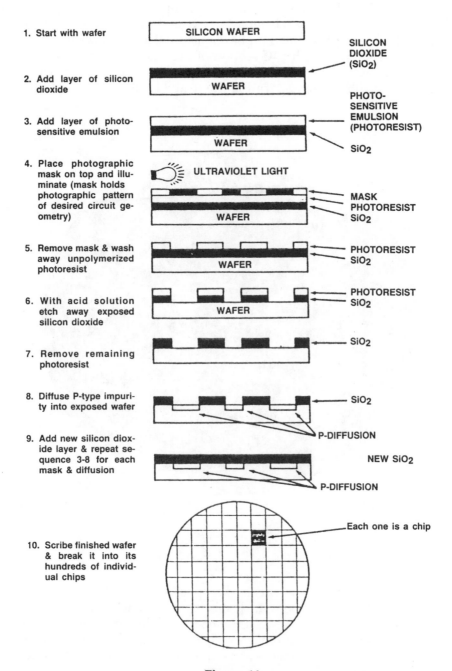

1. Start with wafer

2. Add layer of silicon dioxide

3. Add layer of photo-sensitive emulsion

4. Place photographic mask on top and illuminate (mask holds photographic pattern of desired circuit geometry)

5. Remove mask & wash away unpolymerized photoresist

6. With acid solution etch away exposed silicon dioxide

7. Remove remaining photoresist

8. Diffuse P-type impurity into exposed wafer

9. Add new silicon dioxide layer & repeat sequence 3-8 for each mask & diffusion

10. Scribe finished wafer & break it into its hundreds of individual chips

Figure 14

WAFER PROBING

The uncut, finished wafer (shown in Figure 15) contains a large number of identical sections that must be separated into individual chips. Before the wafer is scribed and separated, it is subjected to wafer probe testing. Using a test fixture that resembles a "bed of nails", the multi-pointed probe contacts the appropriate bonding pads of each monolithic IC section of the wafer in a step-by-step sequence. One by one, each section of the wafer is electrically examined to roughly determine the usability of each monolithic IC chip.

A Completed Monolithic IC Wafer

Figure 15

If the tested chip is electrically acceptable, the probe is stepped to the next chip and the same test is repeated. Each defective chip is marked with an ink spot; if the results of the wafer probe tests indicate the existence of too many defective chips, the entire wafer is discarded. Acceptable wafers now need to be scribed and separated into individual IC chips.

Because of its many multi-layered pattern, each IC chip is an intricate, three-dimensional structure that must be reproduced in exact detail (within allowable tolerances), so that all usable chips of a wafer are identical. See Figure 16.

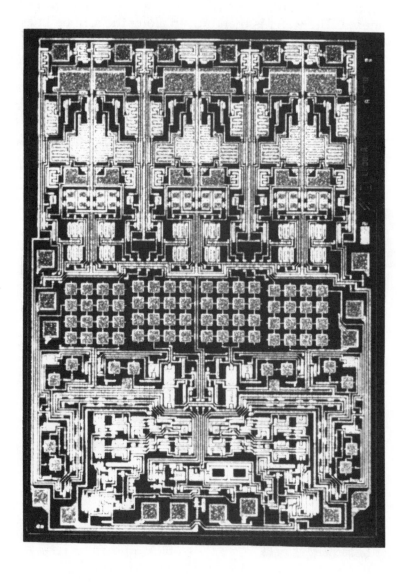

A Single Monolithic IC Chip - Enlarged 25 Times
Figure 16

COMPLETING THE MONOLITHIC IC PRODUCTION PROCESS

WAFER SCRIBING AND SEPARATION

Either a diamond-pointed scriber or a laser beam is used to scratch (scribe) the wafer surface between the rows and columns of the IC patterns. The wafer is then broken along the scribed lines to produce individual monolithic IC chips.

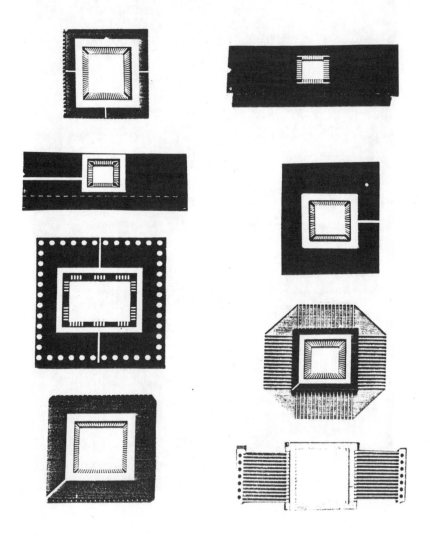

Examples of Headers and Lead-frames
Figure 17

DIE ATTACH

A thin piece of solder, (**solder form**) having the same surface area as the chip, is accurately positioned inside an open IC package (**header** or **lead-frame**). A chip (die) is placed on top of the solder form and the solder is heated to its melting point. When the solder cools and solidifies, the chip has been permanently attached. Headers and lead-frames provide a mounting and support surface as well as a heat transfer interface. See Figure 17.

LEAD BONDING (WIRE BONDING) AND PACKAGING

- Thin gold wires (about 0.001" in diameter) connect the bonding pads on the chip to the bonding pads on the header that, in turn, connect to the external package terminals. For more details about thermo-compression, ultra-sonic or thermosonic wire-bonding techniques, see CHAPTER ONE.

- Before the package is sealed, the chip and package are visually examined under a powerful binocular microscope for any defects, such as: scratches on the chip, silicon flaking from the chip, solder residue in the package, poor lead bonds or other unacceptable mechanical imperfections.

- Finally, the IC chip is sealed into a nonhermetic plastic package and the lead-frame trimmed, or, hermetically sealed in a suitable package.

OPTIONAL PRECONDITIONING PROCEDURES

When intended only for high quality commercial and industrial use, some packaged ICs require several preconditioning procedures to provide an improved level of quality. They include:

- STABILIZATION BAKE - Under a non-operating condition, the completed devices are placed in a 125° C oven for a period of one to two days. The high-temperature bake serves to stabilize their electrical characteristics, providing a high level of device reliability. This pre-conditioning procedure is required for all monolithic ICs conforming to military specifications and is sometimes performed for commercial, industrial and commercial semiconductors as a normal procedure.

- THERMAL SHOCK - A sampling of a given lot of ICs are placed in a chamber set at 100° C for about hour. They are then plunged into a chamber set at -55° C. If the leads are not bonded properly, they will detach. If the sampling lot passes this test, the entire lot is assumed to be satisfactory.

An alternate procedure for determining acceptable wire bonds is to subject a sample lot to destructive lead-pull tests before the package is closed. If the sample lot is acceptable, the entire production lot is assumed to be satisfactory.

• POWER BURN-IN - The devices are placed in an oven at 125° C for a period of 168 hours (1 week) and operated at 80% of their rated power. Although this procedure is generally not required for nonmilitary devices, some commercial and industrial applications dictate that power burn-in be performed. By applying accelerated-life conditions, ICs with fabrication defects might likely fail during burn-in.

There is, however, no obligation on the part of the manufacturer to perform these pre-conditioning tests and/or procedures for non-military devices. Historically, a stabilization bake has been performed on all semiconductors since the industry began, regardless of the intended applications.

When specifically processed for military or aerospace use, all monolithic ICs undergo additional pre-conditioning and screening, with appropriate documentation supplied as required by the monolithic IC specification, MIL-M-38510. Upon approval, the part is designated as a high reliability device and assigned a part number according to the military specification for that particular part or the series of similar parts.

FINAL TESTING
To verify compliance with data sheet specifications, IC lots are subjected to electrical tests using automatic test equipment (ATE) before being sorted. The packages are branded with part numbers and date-codes (week and year of production), packaged in IC carriers, placed in inventory and/or shipped to their assigned destination.

All military and aerospace specifications for monolithic IC devices are written by DESC (Defense Electronics Supply Center), the agency responsible for the procurement of military electronic components and for establishing and maintaining a qualified parts list (QPL) for monolithic ICs. The list identifies those ICs approved for military and aerospace applications. In addition, DESC is responsible for the periodic inspection and for monitoring the "approved" status of the production facilities used by the semiconductor companies producing these parts. For more details on military specifications, refer to CHAPTER FIVE - IC HIGH-RELIABILITY CONSIDERATIONS.

HOW ELEMENTS OF A SILICON-BASED MONOLITHIC IC CHIP ARE FORMED

The transistor elements of a monolithic IC determine the particular technology used to create a monolithic IC. These technologies are identified as:

• Bipolar - using diodes, bipolar transistors, capacitors and resistors.

• MOS (NMOS, PMOS CMOS) - using resistors, NMOS and PMOS FETS.

• BIMOS - using all component equivalents of bipolar and MOS technologies.

COMPONENT EQUIVALENTS FOR BIPOLAR TECHNOLOGY

Diode - A 2-terminal (anode and cathode) device that functions as a conductor or a nonconductor, depending on the polarity of the applied voltage. It can be described as an electronic switch controlled by a polarity-sensitive voltage. A diode is formed by first diffusing boron, and then, phosphorus, into a silicon substrate to create adjacent P-type and N-type layers to produce a P-N junction.

Bipolar transistor - A 3-terminal (collector, base and emitter) component that functions as an amplifier or as a digital switch with gain when properly connected as part of a circuit. It is formed by diffusing an additional region of N or P-type material adjacent to a P-N junction to form either an NPN or a PNP bipolar transistor.

Capacitor - A 2-terminal voltage storage component formed by sandwiching a dielectric (nonconducting material) between two conducting areas. P-type or N-type materials (highly conductive regions) can serve as conductive areas. Pure silicon or silicon dioxide (essentially infinite resistance) can serve as the dielectric to complete the capacitor.

Resistor - A 2-terminal device with a finite (between zero and infinity) ohmic value. It is formed by using a proper dopant concentration for boron-doped or phosphorus-doped regions to create a desired resistance value on selected areas of the diffusion layers of a monolithic IC wafer. For example, for lower resistance, a more concentrated dopant is used.

COMPONENT EQUIVALENTS FOR MOS TECHNOLOGY

N-channel MOS (NMOS) FET - A 3-terminal (drain, source, gate) device that can serve as an amplifier or switch when properly connected as part of a circuit. It is formed by the diffusion of boron into a substrate to create a P-type region. Diffusing phosphorus into the next layer creates N-type regions in selected substrate areas. A thin layer (about 50 microns) of silicon dioxide (SiO_2) is grown on the surface of the substrate and etched, in selected areas, to permit electrical contact to the N-type regions. A layer of aluminum is then deposited on part of the SiO_2 to create the gate area. See Figure 18. To form a P-channel MOS (PMOS) FET, the sequence of diffusing boron and phosphorus dopants are interchanged.

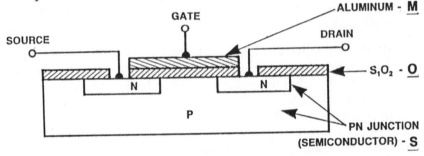

Construction of an Element of an NMOS Monolithic IC
Figure 18

CMOS FET - Elements of NMOS and PMOS FETs are interconnected on the substrate to create a 4-terminal Complementary MOS (CMOS) device to serve as a digital switch. See Figure 19.

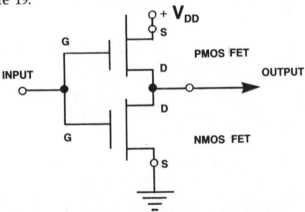

Schematic Diagram of a CMOS Switching Circuit
Figure 19

The CMOS switching circuit in Figure 19 operates as follows:
- When a positive digital (step-function) voltage is applied between the input terminals (gate to ground) of the normally- OFF NMOS FET, the positive voltage between gate and source of the NMOS section causes its channel (drain-gate) to be at its lowest value of resistance. The NMOS FET acts as a turned ON digital switch. At the same time, since the voltage between the gate to source of the PMOS FET is now zero, its channel resistance is essentially infinite, acting an extremely high resistance load for the turned ON NMOS section.

- When the input signal reverts to zero voltage, the opposite action occurs - the PMOS FET turns ON and the NMOS FET turns OFF, becoming the high resistance load for the turned ON PMOS FET switch. The high resistance of the turned OFF NMOS channel allows very little current to flow and the ON resistance of the turned ON PMOS switch is very low. As before, there is practically no power being dissipated in the CMOS switch.

COMPONENT EQUIVALENTS
FOR BIMOS (BIFET) TECHNOLOGY
BIMOS ICs are a combination of bipolar and MOS technologies; their component equivalents are formed in the same way as described for the separate technologies. The common component equivalents for BIMOS include the following: bipolar transistors, MOS FETs, diodes, resistors, and capacitors.

SELECTION OF IC PACKAGES

While there is relatively little "high-technology" involved with IC packaging in the manufacture of sophisticated ICs, only the chip requires more attention than the package. The success or failure of a particular device can often hinge on the use of a proper package. As IC chips are becoming larger, more complex and provide greater capability, more terminals are needed on the IC package to carry information signals to and from the chip. Package configuration, heat transfer capability, lead spacing, package size, ease in placement, insertion and removal from a PC board, as well as the techniques of soldering are major considerations in the selection process.

The need to optimize chip performance by further package miniaturization, to reduce space between components, has stimulated the creation of newer packages and improved packaging techniques for high-density, high-performance IC chips.

JEDEC PACKAGE (8-PIN TO-5)
The first monolithic IC chips were used in military/aerospace applications and required a package that was capable of being hermetically-sealed. Originally used as a transistor package, the 3-pin TO-5 was modified by the addition of 5 more terminals to accommodate newer monolithic IC chips. It was referred to as an 8-pin TO-5 (Figure 20a). Eventually, 8-pin, 10-pin, and 12-pin TO-5 packages were made available in low cost, plastic versions as well as in the hermetically-sealed types. Since the leads in the 12-pin TO-5 packages were spaced very closely together, they were difficult to insert in PC boards. Newer packages with different configurations were developed to be used with the larger, more complex monolithic IC chips.

FLATPACK
This package (Figure 20b) is made of ceramic and Kovar for use in military equipment. Its lead spacing (0.05" centers), package length (0.250"), optional width varying from 0.125" to 0.250", and thickness varying from 0.35" to 0.60" became the industry's standard. Terminals extend horizontally from its body for soldering or welding to the designated contact areas on a PC board and are easily accessible for visual examination, repair, or electrical probing.

The first Flatpacks were 12, 14, and 16 pin types and were soon made available in 18, 22 and 24 pin versions. Plastic Flatpacks were also made available for non-military applications. This small, low-profile, IC package was the first that was made to mount on the surface of a PC board rather than through it.

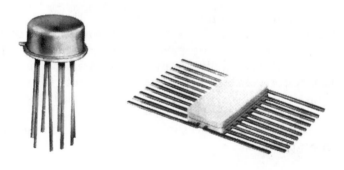

(a)   (b)
8-pin TO-5   22-pin Flat Pack
Early Monolithic IC Packages - TO-5 and Flatpack
Figure 20

DUAL IN-LINE PACKAGE (DIP)

Because of the requirements for a lower-cost package with a greater number of pins, a 14-lead variation of the Flatpack with 0.10" spacing between terminals (Figure 21) was made to be plugged into a PC board socket and was called a Dual In-Line Package (DIP). It followed the manufacture of the Flatpack by about two years. Compared with the cost of 8 to 30 cents per terminal for an equivalent ceramic and Kovar Flatpack, the plastic, nonhermetic DIP costs about 1 to 3 cents per terminal.

The DIP was eventually made available in a variety of sizes (4 to 64-pin configurations), in both plastic and ceramic/Kovar versions and accommodates larger, more complex IC chips. Its leads can be soldered to a PC board for low-profile assembly or, can simply be inserted and removed from a PC board socket, providing a convenient means of component testing and handling.

The long internal leads of a DIP, however, may increase circuit resistance, capacitance, and inductance and adversely influence circuit operation by producing signal delays that result in circuit instability. The plug-in features of a DIP are being superseded by the space-saving benefits of the surface mounting assembly techniques being achieved with newer IC packages having the same pin count.

Dual In-Line Packages (DIP)
Figure 21

Despite the favorable features and popularity of the DIP, it is being replaced by Small-Outline IC (SOIC), Leadless Chip Carrier (LCC) and Leaded Chip Carrier packages. These new IC packages are overcoming the former space inefficiency and electrical compromises of the DIP while satisfying the need for more circuit functions on a high-density monolithic IC chip.

SMALL-OUTLINE IC (SOIC) PACKAGE

The SOIC is a plastic, extremely small, low-cost IC package (Figure 22a) that uses a minimum of PC board space and is intended for use in SMD packaging. Its external "gull-winged" leads are mounted and soldered to either surface of a PC board or to a hybrid IC substrate. See Figure 22b. Short external terminals and short internal leads make the SOIC a rugged package with a minimum of undesirable capacitance and inductance.

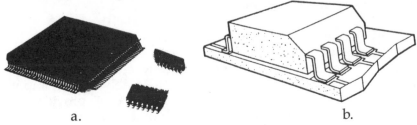

a.   b.

Small-Outline IC (SOIC) Packages
Figure 22

LEADLESS CHIP CARRIER (LCC) PACKAGE

The ceramic Leadless Chip Carrier (CLCC), a low-profile package (Figure 23a) is used for hermetically-packaged, high-density, monolithic IC chips. This package can be mounted to the surface of a PC board. Leads from bonding pads on the IC chip are soldered to metallized contacts located at the periphery of the chip cavity. Conductors from these contacts are connected internally to contacts on the bottom edges of the package.

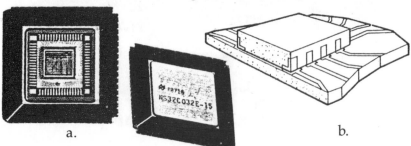

a.   b.

Ceramic Leadless Chip Carrier (CLCC) Package
Figure 23

The **Plastic Leadless Chip Carrier** (PLCC), a plastic version of the LCC, is intended for commercial, industrial and consumer use and is about one-eighth the cost of the CLCC. Both types of packages are available in a variety of sizes to accommodate all monolithic IC chips up to a pin count of 84. Its terminals, on 0.05" centers, are located on the edges of the package.

Packaging of a monolithic IC chip in a CLCC (or PLCC) and then mounting on a PC board is accomplished as follows:

• Either solder paste is applied or a solder form is placed on the gold-plated surface of the LCC cavity. A chip is placed in the cavity and the air around it is heated to melt the solder. When the solder cools and solidifies, the chip is permanently attached to the inside of the LCC cavity.

• Gold leads (0.001″ in diameter) are wire-bonded between the bonding pads at the edge of the chip and the appropriate contact areas (bonding pads) at the perimeter of the LCC cavity. Short leads reduce stray capacitances and inductances within the Leadless Chip Carrier, minimizing its adverse affects.

• The package is sealed by soldering an appropriate lid to the gold-plated top surface of the carrier.

• The external terminals on the bottom-side edges of the sealed package are then accurately positioned and soldered to matching bonding pads on a PC board. CLCCs and PLCCs are suitable for surface mounting assembly of monolithic IC chips.

Because the external terminals of the package are firmly soldered to the PC board (see Figure 23b), problems may arise because of the resulting rigidity. As the ambient temperature changes, the soldered terminals can separate from the PC board if the temperature coefficients of expansion of the LCC terminals and PC board are not compatible. PC board materials are being changed to overcome this incompatibility.

LEADED CHIP CARRIER

These packages, both hermetic and nonhermetic types, are made to accommodate monolithic IC chips with pin counts up to 84. Leaded Chip Carriers (Figure 24a), have J-shaped terminals that tuck under the package body which can be inserted into an appropriate socket in a conventional, through-hole PC board or soldered to metallic pads on a PC board. See Figure 24b.

Compared with the leads of a gull-winged type package, J-shaped terminals of a Leaded Chip Carrier provide much more compliance (flexibility), thereby avoiding problems of incompatible coefficients of expansion between the package terminals and the PC board bonding pads. Since J-shaped leads flex as PC board bonding pads expand and contract, they can be more readily used with ceramic, glass or low-cost epoxy PC boards.

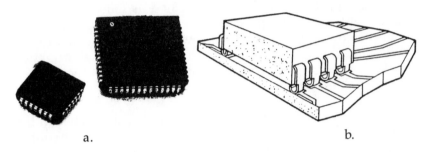

a.   b.

Leaded Chip Carriers
Figure 24

PIN GRID ARRAY (PGA)
When a monolithic IC chip requires a package with a pin count
of more than 84, a *pin grid array* (PGA) is used. It is made in both
ceramic (CPGA) and plastic (PPGA) for hermetic or nonhermetic
sealing, with its pins arranged in a rectangular array (0.1" spacing
between rows and columns). See Figure 25a. Some PGA packages
can have as many as 320 pins with lead spacing as close as 0.0125".

a.   b.

Pin Grid Array (PGA) Packages
Figure 25

The alternate "cavity-up" version (Figure 25b) has no pins at the
center of the package, making room for the chip cavity. Although
this orientation reduces the number of available pins, the chip is
placed in close proximity to the upper surface of the package where
a heat sink may be attached.

The "cavity-up" version of a PGA package can dissipate up to 12 watts of power. The techniques of IC chip assembly and package closure are the same as those of an LCC. The pin terminals on the bottom of a PGA, however, are easily inserted or removed from a PC board socket, thereby providing the advantage of the plug-in feature of a DIP.

With almost unlimited ability to accommodate any required number of pins, a PGA package is more area-efficient than most other package types. Because of the densely-arrayed (more than 84 pins) configuration, a PC board layout, using PGA packages, may require very careful, and somewhat difficult, manipulation.

MONOLITHIC IC SELECTION CRITERIA

Technology, chip density, and application (other than price and availability) are the major considerations in selecting a specific monolithic IC chip for use in a system. This can be restated as follows: The characteristics inherent in a specific technology, the number of component functions per chip and its intended application will determine its selection.

Monolithic IC technology is initially classified by the type of transistor the IC uses to produce either amplification or switching in a circuit. These transistor types are referred to as bipolar, MOS (NMOS and PMOS), a combination of both bipolar and MOS technology (BIMOS) and CMOS (NMOS and PMOS FETs). Each technology has its own unique performance characteristics.

BIPOLAR MONOLITHIC IC TECHNOLOGY
Bipolar transistor designations, NPN or PNP, identify direction of current flow and supply voltage polarity.

ADVANTAGES:
- The output sections (collectors) of amplifiers and switches in a bipolar IC have the power capability to drive more loads than those in a functionally-equivalent MOSFET monolithic IC.

- Switching speed and frequency response is about 10 times faster (higher) than that of a functionally-equivalent MOS monolithic IC. Normally, operating an amplifier or switch at higher power improves speed and/or frequency response, while operating at lower power reduces switching speed and/or frequency response.

DISADVANTAGES:
- Several hundred to about 1000 times more power is consumed than equivalent MOS IC devices providing the same function. As a result, larger power supplies, auxiliary cooling devices (fans, blowers, etc.) and other cooling techniques are needed to remove the heat generated by the increased power.

- Separate coupling capacitors and load resistors are required in a circuit, therefore, more diffusion steps are needed than for an equivalent MOS IC function.

- Amplifier and switching circuits have a low input resistance characteristic, therefore, the output resistance of the previous circuit is more heavily loaded, reducing its gain. To increase resistance of an input section of a circuit to a high enough value to avoid an excessive load on the previous circuit, more components are needed. Adding more components increases the number of diffusion steps needed for the same function while circuit complexity and production costs rise.

MOS MONOLITHIC IC TECHNOLOGY
MOS FET designations, N-channel (NMOS) or P-channel (PMOS), identify direction of current flow and supply voltage polarity.

ADVANTAGES:
- Power consumption is several hundred times to about a thousand times less than with equivalent bipolar technology ICs.

- The input resistance of a MOS amplifier and/or switch is very high (essentially infinity) and will not significantly load the output of a previous circuit, resulting in no adverse effect on its gain.

- MOS technology is essentially immune to electrical noise. In addition, critical regulation of a voltage supply is not required. In most automobiles, a noisy electrical environment and a poorly regulated power supply (storage battery) are very common conditions, making MOS technology most suitable for automotive electronics applications.

- Unlike bipolar transistors, MOS FETs have interstage coupling capacitors built into their structure; the need for separate coupling capacitor diffusion layers are eliminated, production costs are reduced and chip density is increased by a factor of approximately 5.

CMOS MONOLITHIC IC TECHNOLOGY

Complementary MOS FETs (NMOS and PMOS) are connected as shown in the circuit configuration of Figure 19. This CMOS FET digital switching circuit is the major element of CMOS monolithic IC technology.

ADVANTAGES:

• In a CMOS FET switching circuit, no **external** load is required; the NMOS and PMOS alternately serve as the load. The output section of a bipolar transistor or an NMOS (or PMOS) FET switch (or amplifier), however, requires a separate component as the circuit load (usually a fixed resistor). The complementary configuration of a CMOS FET switching circuit eliminates the need to diffuse the required load resistors, simplifying IC layout and reducing production costs.

• With very little current through the PMOS channel and very little resistance in the NMOS channel (and vice versa), practically no power is being dissipated in the CMOS FET switch.

• CMOS monolithic ICs use the least power of all silicon-based monolithic IC technologies and are most applicable for use in battery-powered, portable equipment.

• A major consideration in the use of monolithic ICs with very high chip densities has been the removal of heat generated in the IC transistor and resistor components. Because of lower heat generation, as well as efficient use of wafer real estate, CMOS monolithic technology has made the presently available, extremely high-density IC chips possible.

DISADVANTAGE:

• Compared with equivalent bipolar monolithic IC chips, CMOS monolithic IC chips have lower switching speed and frequency response, by a factor of approximately 10.

Similar factors influence the switching speeds of both bipolar and CMOS monolithic IC technology. With higher operating power, faster switching speed can be achieved. Conversely, if the operating power is reduced, switching speed is reduced. Selection of a specific monolithic IC technology often depends on this major trade-off - power versus speed.

Improved photolithographic techniques have made possible the production of CMOS monolithic IC chips with switching speeds that are approaching, and in some cases, overtaking the switching speeds of bipolar monolithic ICs. This comparison, however, is generally made between new CMOS monolithic ICs and older bipolar monolithic ICs. The same improved photolithographic techniques that result in faster CMOS monolithic ICs are also increasing the switching speed of bipolar monolithic IC chips. The switching speed differential that exists between the newer bipolar and the newer CMOS monolithic IC devices is still about the same - a factor of approximately 10.

BIMOS (BIFET) MONOLITHIC IC TECHNOLOGY

By combining both bipolar and MOS FET functions on a single IC chip, where required, BIMOS (BIFET) monolithic ICs offer the advantages and minimizes the disadvantages of each technology.

For example, bipolar elements are used in that part of an IC where the relatively high-speed characteristic of bipolar technology is needed. The low power, high input resistance, and high density circuit characteristics of CMOS technology are used in appropriate sections of the IC. Using this "optimizing" technique, BIMOS technology affords improved performance characteristics with less operating power (and less generation of heat).

CHIP DENSITY

Chip density is defined as the number of circuit component functions per monolithic IC chip and is classified as follows:

- SSI - Small-Scale Integration - maximum chip density of 30
          - used only for bipolar technology
- MSI - Medium-Scale Integration - chip density from 30 to 100
          - the first MOS monolithic IC chip was in this range
- LSI - Large-Scale Integration - chip density from 100 to 1000
          - used for both bipolar and MOS monolithic IC technology
- VLSI - Very large-scale integration - chip density from 1000 to over 1 million - mostly used for CMOS technology

The chip density designations for different levels of integration (as shown above) have been the industry de facto standard used by monolithic IC manufacturers as approximate, or "ball park", values. Without established standards, the specified chip density of a monolithic IC may vary among different manufacturers, particularly, for LSI and VLSI classifications. As with any non-standard parameter, variations will depend on the manufacturers' marketing approach and will continue to vary until proper standards are accepted by the industry.

GENERAL COMMENTS ON MONOLITHIC ICs

STANDARD NUMBERING SYSTEMS FOR MONOLITHIC ICs
The industry-sponsored agency responsible for establishing standard numbering systems for electronic parts and packages used in commercial, industrial and consumer applications is the Joint Electron Device Engineering Council (JEDEC), an arm of the Electronic Industry Association. Although JEDEC has been successful in establishing standard IC package dimensions including terminal spacing and configurations, for many available IC packages, they have had very little success in standardizing a numbering system for the device itself. Chip manufacturers either use their own in-house numbering system for these parts, or, they use the popular (industry-accepted) IC part numbers originated by other chip manufacturers. Monolithic ICs that are approved for use in military and aerospace equipment by the Defense Electronics Supply Center (DESC), an agency of the Dept.of Defense, are assigned part numbers that reflect the required level of reliability. See CHAPTER FIVE for more details.

PRODUCTION YIELD AND PRICE OF A MONOLITHIC IC CHIP
A group of ICs being processed at the same time is called a **production lot** or **batch**. The **yield** from any given production lot of monolithic ICs is defined as the ratio (expressed as a percentage) of the completed, usable chips, to the total number of chips (usable or defective) in a group of wafers from a single production lot. To a great extent, yield is dependent on process control and quality of the IC production process, including labor, material, and equipment.

Ideally, all completed wafers of a production lot will have a 100% yield and chips from each wafer will exhibit identical characteristics (within specified tolerances). All usable chips, even from the same wafer, generally do not have identical performance characteristics; new families of ICs are often generated to accommodate variations in performance.

Although 100% yield from any given IC lot is rarely, if ever, achieved in IC monolithic manufacturing, acceptable yields can be obtained by controlling processing procedures and proper handling of wafers, chips, and other materials by:
• Precise alignment of masks on wafers
• Uniform temperature throughout the diffusion chambers
• Efficient photographic, diffusion and assembly facilities
• Periodic calibration of test equipment
• Keeping human error to a minimum.

Yields vary from wafer-to-wafer and from lot-to-lot; the cost of a completed chip is only partially influenced by yield. Because chips are processed in wafer form, compared with a small diameter wafer, more available chips per wafer, for the same processing costs, will be produced on a larger diameter wafer. Blank silicon wafers, 3" to 5" in diameter, were commonly used for many years; at the present time, larger wafers (6" to 8" in diameter) are generally being used.

Included in the eventual pricing of any IC, the following costs must be considered: packaging (including sealing), maintenance and calibration of processing and test equipment, material, labor, sales, and marketing, and all capital investments. Perhaps, the dominant consideration in the final price of any component is the competitor's price for an equivalent device.

Large, successful semiconductor companies are moving in the direction of using automated production equipment (robotics) in all stages of the manufacturing process. Although the initial outlay for this capital equipment is extremely high, the use of robotics can be very effective in reducing manufacturing costs while producing a high yield that is consistent with the manufacture of good quality, low-priced ICs. Automated equipment costs can be readily amortized over the huge production quantities that are normally basic to successful semiconductor manufacturing.

A monolithic IC that is intended for military and/or aerospace applications must conform to its applicable military specifications (including preconditioning, packaging, test procedures, and documentation). The final price of the IC chip can be as much as 100 times more than an equivalent device made for commercial, industrial, and consumer use. Similar monolithic ICs intended for use in either commercial, industrial and consumer equipment, or "high-reliablity" components used in military and aerospace equipment are manufactured by the same personnel, using the same production equipment and, except for the package, the same materials. It is for this reason that monolithic IC chips have proven to be very reliable in non-military as well as military applications.

See CHAPTER FIVE - IC HIGH-RELIABILITY CONSIDER-ATIONS for more detailed information.

REINFORCEMENT EXERCISES

Answer TRUE or FALSE to each of the following statements:

1. If an array, electronic circuit, subsystem or complete electronic system is structured on a single chip (active substrate), the end product is called a monolithic integrated circuit.

2. A monolithic IC is generally referred to as a "chip" in unpackaged form, but not as a "chip" when the monolithic IC is assembled in an appropriate package.

3. Monolithic ICs are manufactured through the combined technologies of chemistry, metallurgy and photolithography.

4. Although a hybrid IC is not limited to any particular size package, a monolithic IC in chip form is generally limited to an area no larger than ¼″ by ¼″.

5. Switching circuits in silicon-based monolithic ICs are much faster than those produced by GaAs-based monolithic ICs, despite improvements in semiconductor technology.

6. Silicon ingots are manufactured by similar techniques for both discrete semiconductor chips and monolithic IC chips. Although the chip manufacturing process is essentially the same for both discrete semiconductors, the monolithic IC proces has many more steps and uses computer-aided design (CAD) to produce and verify the IC photomasks.

7. Wire-bonding is the process whereby thin gold wires are connected to the bonding pads on a chip and the bonding pads on a header. The bonding pads on the header are internally connected to external terminals on a package.

8. Bipolar, MOS, CMOS, and BIMOS are the names of the different technologies used in the production of monolithic ICs, each having advantages and disadvantages when compared with each other. The selection of the preferred technology to be used in any system design is dictated by the end application.

9. A bipolar monolithic IC has a much lower switching speed and higher chip density than a CMOS monolithic IC. A bipolar IC uses less substrate space than an equivalent CMOS IC performing similar circuit functions.

performing similar circuit functions.

10. CMOS monolithic ICs use relatively little power and are applicable for use in battery-powered, portable equipment.

11. Increasing the power dissipation of a CMOS monolithic IC will decrease its switching speed and frequency response.

12. A Leaded Chip Carrier package is used for enclosing a high density monolithic IC chip having up to 84 external connections. This package type uses only J-shaped terminals and, therefore, is not suitable for mounting to the surface of a PC board.

13. Packages with J-shaped terminals, require less board space than gull-winged leaded packages. In many cases, however, packages with gull-winged terminals are preferred since the soldered connections between a PC board and the J-shaped terminals cannot be as easily examined.

14. A Leadless Chip Carrier (LCC), made in a low-cost plastic body for commercial, industrial or consumer applications, has gull-winged terminals that are applicable for mounting to the surface of a substrate or PC board.

15. Industry-standard chip density values have been established for monolithic IC chips eliminating some of the confusion that existed when different component functions per chip were being used for the different designated levels of integration, specifically: SSI, MSI, LSI and VLSI.

16. The cost of producing ICs with the use of automatic production equipment is prohibitive and, to a great extent, not recommended for profitable production of monolithic ICs.

17. The price of an integrated circuit is based mainly on the yield in any given production lot and has little to do with package type, end-application, production costs, sales and marketing costs, capital investments, and competition.

Answers to these reinforcement exercises are on page 125.

 CHAPTER THREE

Gaas-BASED MONOLITHIC INTEGRATED CIRCUITS

INTRODUCTION

COMPARISONS BETWEEN GaAs AND SILICON

GaAs MONOLITHIC PROCESS

ASSEMBLY AND OPERATIONAL CONSIDERATIONS

REINFORCEMENT EXERCISES

GALLIUM ARSENIDE MONOLITHIC ICs

INTRODUCTION

Gallium arsenide (GaAs), a compound of gallium and arsenic, has been used as a substrate material for discrete semiconductors since the early 1970s. GaAs is specifically used to produce discrete diodes and field effect transistors operating in the microwave (super high and extremely high) frequency ranges. Because of its light-generating properties, GaAs is also used to produce light emitting diodes (LEDs).

Although silicon has been the dominant semiconductor substrate material, GaAs ICs are now presenting a serious challenge to the leadership of silicon-based monolithic IC chips. Compared with silicon devices, GaAs monolithic ICs offer improved performance characteristics for the following applications:

• High speed digital logic circuits

• Telecommunications and satellite systems working at microwave frequencies and fiber optic systems operating at even higher frequencies (the infrared regions)

• Data conversion systems operating beyond the present frequency limit of silicon (about 1 Gigahertz)

• High speed test instrumentation systems

• Military and aerospace applications where semiconductor components may be adversely affected by the presence of nuclear radiation - GaAs provides excellent radiation hardness (resistance to nuclear radiation)

The recent growth in the number of new companies committed to the development and production of GaAs monolithic ICs for all available applications is reminiscent of the very early days of silicon monolithic IC production; processing costs and material were relatively high and design information was at a minimum.

As with all previously developed semiconductor technologies, major improvements in GaAs-based monolithic IC technology will depend on further advances in processing techniques, more efficient chip geometries and more skillful circuit design.

COMPARISONS BETWEEN
GALLIUM ARSENIDE AND SILICON

ADVANTAGES:
Compared with silicon-based equivalents, GaAs-based monolithic
IC technology features:

- Switching speeds and frequency responses about 6 to 10 times faster for equivalent circuits.

- The "ON" resistance of a GaAs monolithic IC switch is lower than either bipolar or CMOS, resulting in reduced power dissipation and decreased heat generated in the circuit.

- GaAs circuits are capable of operating at lower levels of supply voltages (as low as 2.5 volts) - silicon-based monolithic ICs normally operate at a supply voltage between 5.0 to 24 volts.

- GaAs circuits generate less electrical noise and are capable of amplifying weaker signals without distortion or internal circuit noise.

- GaAs offers much higher **radiation hardness** - the measure of a circuit's ability to resist destructive radiation measured in **rads**. Typically, radiation hardness values for GaAs are as high as 10^8 rads versus 10^4 rads for silicon, a decisive advantage for military and aerospace electronic systems.

DISADVANTAGES:
Despite their obvious advantages, GaAs monolithic ICs are being used mainly to complement silicon-based monolithic ICs rather than to replace them in applications where silicon ICs can not be used. The disadvantages of GaAs monolithic ICs include:

- Limited availability of gallium (extracted from bauxite and residues of zinc processing). In comparison, silicon, the second most abundant element, is an ingredient of silicon dioxide (sand), the third most abundant compound available.

- Single-crystalline GaAs ingots, from which blank wafers are sliced, are more expensive and more difficult to process because arsenic is toxic and volatile at the high temperatures used to produce these ingots. To avoid unpredictable device behavior, additional and costly processing steps are needed to manufacture GaAs ingots and do not encourage the production of low-cost, high-volume monolithic IC chips.

The cost of a 3" diameter GaAs wafer is about $175, compared with a 6" diameter silicon wafer (4 times the area) that typically costs $30. GaAs-based monolithic ICs are presently not competitive in the high-volume commercial, industrial and consumer market areas. They could be most cost effective for those applications that require the special characteristics afforded by GaAs monolithic ICs - high speed digital switching and very high radiation hardness values.

GaAs monolithic IC technology is still relatively new. The required design skills for GaAs-based monolithic ICs and efficient production techniques have not, as yet, been sufficiently developed to reduce GaAs IC production costs and increase production yields. Despite some preferable GaAS monolithic IC characteristics, the lower-priced, readily available silicon-based monolithic ICs are being used when there is no need for improved performance at a higher price.

GALLIUM ARSENIDE MONOLITHIC IC PROCESSING

INGOT AND WAFER PRODUCTION
The processing of a GaAs monolithic IC wafer has fewer steps than an equivalent silicon wafer. Unlike silicon, GaAs ingots are made of two elements (gallium and arsenic) that must be controlled to manufacture acceptable wafers. Under a high temperature condition, arsenic is often volatile, and sometimes, toxic. It tends to bubble out of the high temperature melt from which crystals are pulled. To prevent volatility or toxicity of the GaAs, the crystal was initially grown in a sealed, silicon dioxide "boat" containing an abundance of arsene gas that contains arsenic. This process is called the **horizontal Bridgman method**.

This method produced small diameter, D-shaped ingots that were inconvenient for efficient wafer processing. In addition, the GaAs crystals were often contaminated from the silicon in the silicon dioxide boat. To neutralize the electrical properties of silicon and achieve a desired yield for stable gallium arsenide devices, the boat was doped with chromium and oxygen.

The problems created by the horizontal Bridgman method were overcome by a modification of the Czochralski method. (See CHAPTER TWO). GaAs ingots are now manufactured by a high-pressure, liquid-encapsulated Czochralski (LEC) technique using a floating layer of boric oxide to contain the arsenic.

Although Czochralski-grown GaAs ingots contain more imperfections than Bridgman-grown crystals, the cylindrical-shaped, wider-diameter Czochralski-grown ingots are more compatible with standard wafer processing equipment, reducing the cost of the blank wafer. By precisely controlling the proper temperature distribution in the GaAs melt, higher quality Czochralski-grown ingots are more readily produced, resulting in increased yields and reduced costs of the blank GaAs wafer.

PHOTOLITHOGRAPHY AND WAFER PROCESSING
Similar techniques are used to produce GaAs and silicon-based monolithic IC chips. Starting with a blank wafer, the process continues with photolithography, diffusion, metallization, wafer probe, scribing, and separation into individual chips. Standard processing equipment and manufacturing techniques are used throughout the entire process.

There are, however, some differences in the wafer fabrication process between GaAS and silicon substrates. A silicon-based VLSI MOS chip contains the functions of either PMOS, NMOS or a combination of both (CMOS) FETs. These devices require an input (gate terminal) that is insulated from the channel of the device through a nonconducting layer of silicon dioxide.

With a silicon substrate, the oxide layer is grown simply by heating the wafer in a diffusion chamber in an atmosphere of water vapor. With a GaAs substrate, it is almost impossible to create thin insulating films, since neither gallium nor arsenic oxidize easily.

To insulate the gate, a MESFET (metal-semiconductor FET), a modified MOSFET, incorporates a metal gate electrode in its structure. The metal gate electrode makes direct contact with the GaAs substrate to form a **Schottky diode**, a device used instead of the SiO_2 insulating film used in the MOSFET structure.

A MESFET is either a depletion type (D-MESFET) or an enhancement type (E-MESFET) and is the main element of most GaAs monolithic IC chips. The depletion type (normally-ON) D-MESFET and enhancement type (normally-OFF) E-MESFET refers to the device's condition when no voltage is applied to its input terminal (gate). To turn the D-MESFET OFF, a *negative* voltage is applied to its gate; the E-MESFET is turned ON by applying a *positive* voltage to its gate. In both cases, the source terminal (common to input and output) is connected to the reference with voltage polarities designated with respect to the source.

GALLIUM ARSENIDE MONOLITHIC IC CHIP PACKAGING

Packages used for GaAs monolithic IC chips are similar to those used for microwave hybrid ICs, since they are specifically made to house devices that operate at frequencies above 1 Gigahertz.

GaAs monolithic ICs use conventional thermo-compression wire-bonding techniques. Gold leads, 0.001" (1 mil) in diameter are used to connect the bonding pads on the chip to the metallic contacts inside the package.

There are two types of GaAs monolithic IC packages.

• The first, a 40-pin Leadless Chip Carrier (LCC), has a conventional LCC "footprint". Its cavity is a redesigned silicon IC package accommodating very high-frequency/super-speed GaAs ICs. The bonding pads on the surface of a GaAs chip are wire-bonded directly to 50-ohm transmission paths etched into the carrier package. The package modification serves to eliminate speed and frequency limitations caused by stray inductances that are inherent in the wiring inside the package.

• The second package type, a 32 or 36-pin Flatpack, with 0.012" (12 mil) terminals on 0.03" (30 mil) centers, has an internal bonding scheme that optimizes speed and frequency response throughout the package. A GaAs IC chip is bonded onto an intermediate substrate within the package that has transmission lines similar to those in the modified LCC. The transmission lines connect the chip to internal package contacts with extremely short 1.0 mil gold wires which, in turn, connect to the external terminals of the package.

ASSEMBLY AND
OPERATIONAL CONSIDERATIONS

COOLING

High-current GaAs monolithic ICs can get quite hot and cooling techniques must be considered in selecting a package type. If it is impossible to mount the IC to a heat-sinked surface, forced-air cooling is recommended. Regardless of the type of package used, maximum IC power capability and maximum operating temperature ratings must not be exceeded, under any condition.

RADIO FREQUENCY (RF) SHIELDING

As with any circuit operating at very high switching speeds and/or very high frequencies, proper shielding of the package and adjacent circuit components must be provided to prevent radio frequency interference (RFI). Generally, GaAs IC package shells are internally connected to the reference terminal (ground); several of the package's external terminals are usually available for connecting to ground.

Conducting paths of a PC board are referred to as "traces". Some of these conducting paths are used to shield the circuit against RF and are called "guard traces". The layout of the board must be carefully designed to minimize stray capacitances between the traces and between the traces and ground.

TESTING

GaAs monolithic ICs are now able to perform complex analog and digital functions at frequencies and switching speeds only discrete components could previously have accommodated. Because of their extremely high operating frequency and high-speed switching capabilities, GaAs monolithic ICs require special methods for testing and analyzing high-speed digital systems and complex data paths.

Initial functional tests may be performed at speeds lower than the device's full capability to allow conventional automatic test equipment (ATE) to be used. When high-speed components, such as GaAs monolithic ICs, are operated in an actual system, subtle circuit conditions come into play that may affect system operation in an unpredictable and undesirable manner. Normally, these effects can not be detected by the usual tests performed in laboratory simulation. Some of the factors causing changes that reduce performance capability include: poor system layout, improper wiring patterns and insufficient interface circuitry.

Since not all systems require the full switching speed and frequency response capability of the IC, an alternative evaluation method is to install the GaAs monolithic IC(s) into the actual circuit or system and run a series of operational tests under "worst-case" conditions. This test method may not always be the most practical or lowest-cost approach to device evaluation, however, it is probably the most reliable.

GaAs ICs are now exhibiting high-performance characteristics and are being used more and more in complex, state-of-the-art equipment and have proven their technical value. By reducing some of the high costs of material, production and testing, their reduced price will make them commercially more attractive and more competitive with silicon-based equivalents.

REINFORCEMENT EXERCISES

Answer TRUE or FALSE to each of the following statements:

1. Gallium arsenide, a compound made of two chemical elements, gallium and arsenic, is used as a substrate material in the manufacture of monolithic ICs.

2. As a monolithic IC substrate material, GaAs has been in use since the early 1970s and is presently being used as much as silicon for the production of monolithic ICs.

3. Compared with the highest performance silicon monolithic ICs, GaAs monolithic ICs typically provide higher switching speed and higher frequency response characteristics by a factor of approximately 6 to 10.

4. GaAs has been used in the manufacture of discrete diodes and transistors operating in the microwave frequency region and as light emitting diodes (LEDs) for only about 5 years.

5. The present specific uses for GaAs-based monolithic ICs include high performance (high-switching speed and high frequency response) systems, both analog and digital, and in applications where silicon-based circuits can not work as efficiently to produce the desired operation.

6. GaAs monolithic ICs are not intended for use in: telecommunications and satellite systems operating at frequencies above 1 Gigahertz, fiber optic systems working in the infrared region and high-speed test instrumentation systems.

7. Some of the preferred uses for GaAs ICs are in high speed data conversion systems and in high-speed computer-related digital logic circuits.

8. In military and/or aerospace applications, silicon-based monolithic ICs are preferred to GaAs-based ICs in areas of high radiation levels since silicon's radiation hardness is far superior to GaAs.

9. A completed GaAs monolithic wafer costs much more than an equivalent silicon-based monolithic IC wafer mainly because more processing steps are required to complete GaAs-based monolithic IC wafers; it is not due to the raw wafer cost

differential between the two materials.

10. The manufacturing techniques and equipment used to produce
    GaAs IC chips, starting from the raw wafer, through final wafer
    separation, to completed packaged GaAs IC devices, are very
    similar to the methods used in the production of packaged
    silicon-based monolithic ICs.

11. Some of the differences between silicon and GaAs are that
    GaAs generates less electrical noise and can amplify weaker
    signals without distortion or internal circuit noise. GaAS ICs
    can also operate at lower supply voltages.

12. In switching applications, the "ON" resistance of a GaAs switch
    is lower than a turned-on silicon CMOS, offering reduced
    power dissipation and less heat generation.

13. Since GaAs monolithic ICs use relatively little power, and no
    appreciable heat is generated, there is never any need for heat
    sinks or fans in systems using GaAs ICs only.

14. Since GaAs monolithic IC chips normally operate at very high
    switching speeds and/or very high frequencies, proper
    shielding must be provided against radio frequency interference
    (RFI) for both the IC package and adjacent circuit components.

15. The two packages generally used for GaAs monolithic chips
    are modified versions of the Leadless Chip Carrier and the
    Flatpack. Each package type has a redesigned cavity to
    eliminate speed and frequency limitations caused by stray
    inductances inherent in the wiring inside the package.

16. Special wire-bonding techniques are used to connect leads
    between the bonding pads on the GaAs substrate and metallic
    areas inside the package which, in turn, connect to the external
    terminals.

17. GaAs monolithic IC technology has established itself as a
    worthy technical competitor with silicon-based monolithic ICs.
    As GaAs IC technology improves and costs decrease, the
    technical and commercial dominance of silicon is expected to
    decrease.

Answers to these reinforcement exercises are on page 127.

 CHAPTER
FOUR

INTEGRATED CIRCUIT APPLICATIONS

INTEGRATED CIRCUIT APPLICATIONS

INTRODUCTION

Before the advent of ICs, discrete passive components and discrete semiconductor components were interconnected to form an electronic circuit. In many cases, this approach is still being used. Similar, and even more complex, circuits can now be produced as a single component IC, in either hybrid or monolithic form. The device (discrete circuit or IC) designed into a system will depend on the required size, weight, power, cost, reliability, and availability of the desired type of circuit.

In either hybrid or monolithic form, an integrated circuit is mainly classified by its application. IC manufacturers have provided extensive catalogs and data sheets of their "product line" in an attempt to furnish necessary technical information on their products' features (electrical, mechanical, and thermal characteristics) to users and potential users.

In an effort to provide a logical means of easily locating the various products listed in their catalogs and for purposes of reference and comparison, IC manufacturers generally organize this information in terms of the circuit's intended application(s). In many cases, different types of these ICs have been lumped into an applications category that is not valid for their intended use. Unfortunately, this practice has often tended to confuse, rather than inform.

DEFINITIONS

DIGITAL
Changes and transitions that have a distinctive step-function motion by suddenly moving from one step to another are referred to as being *digital* in nature. Although many changes in ordinary, everyday activity occur in a gradual, or non-digital manner, such as: the movement of time, or day changing into night, some conditions encountered in a gradually changing world are digital transitions. A "yes" or "no" response can illustrate a digital concept. For example, an ordinary light switch (not a light dimming control) is either in an ON or OFF position and there is a very rapid transition between the two distinctly different states.

In electronics, a circuit whose step-function input voltage causes its output to change in a step-function manner from a specific value of voltage to another is a *digital circuit*. The transition between the two voltage values is accomplished in essentially zero time. Each voltage value of this "two-state" circuit can be used to represent a particular state, such as: ON/OFF, ZERO/ONE, TRUE/FALSE, HIGH/LOW, MARK/SPACE, or any other predetermined condition. Since the term "binary" refers to a two-state condition, the circuit is more accurately called a *binary digital circuit*.

ANALOG
This term defines a general class of electronic circuits in which the output voltage varies as a **continuous** function of the input. This type of circuit is often called a "non-digital" circuit since there is no step-function (digital) activity exclusively performed within its structure.

LINEAR
The term "linear" means "straight-line", where, for example, the direction of a straight line will not deviate from its path within a specified (usually very limited) tolerance. In electronics, a "linear" circuit in one whose output voltage is **proportional** to its input voltage, generally, over a well-defined range of input voltage, output voltage, and frequency. The degree of deviation of the output voltage of a linear circuit from a proportional (straight-line) response to its input voltage is called "distortion". A well-designed linear circuit has very little, or no distortion that might degrade the quality of the output voltage.

NON-LINEAR
Although a linear circuit can be referred to as an analog circuit, an "analog" circuit is not necessarily a "linear" circuit. Some analog circuits are specifically designed to provide an output voltage that is **not proportional** to its input, even though the output will vary as a function of the changing input voltage. This is referred to as a *non-linear* circuit.

INTERFACE
An electronic interface provides the means of interconnecting or linking two types of circuits or systems. An interface circuit is neither purely analog nor purely digital; it has sections of both types within its structure. Interface techniques provide compatibility between circuits having different modes of operation.

IC APPLICATIONS CATEGORIES

It has been customary practice in the electronics industry to designate circuits that have no digital elements as part of their structure as "linear" circuits and IC manufacturers have generally listed their non-digital products in the LINEAR section of their catalog. A more appropriate (and less confusing) label for this product line group would be "ANALOG", since this general designation encompasses those circuits that are either linear or non-linear and are **not** digital in structure.

To accurately define the several types of IC applications, they are categorized as: DIGITAL, ANALOG, and INTERFACE ICs. Within the ANALOG group, the sub-categories are LINEAR and NON-LINEAR.

DIGITAL   **ANALOG**   **INTERFACE**

LINEAR   **NON-LINEAR**

Within these major applications categories (DIGITAL, ANALOG, and INTERFACE), an IC can be referred to as being either a "STANDARD CIRCUIT" or a "CUSTOM CIRCUIT". A system using many circuits to form a complete entity within itself might be constructed of either standard or custom ICs, or both.

STANDARD INTEGRATED CIRCUITS - HYBRID AND MONOLITHIC

Standard (off-the-shelf) ICs are part of a manufacturer's product line, with the component part numbers listed in a catalog, with their ratings, characteristics, and dimensions specified in the catalog and/or the component data sheet.

Standard ICs are generally made in large quantities to be sold at a comparatively low price and are available for immediate delivery from a distributor or IC manufacturer, depending on the desired amount and/or any contractual agreements between the two parties. Normally, manufacturers of standard ICs are responsible for one-time design and tooling costs of the ICs, which are readily amortized over large production quantities.

An efficient, cost-saving approach to system design is to assemble readily available standard hybrid and/or monolithic ICs that can accommodate a great variety of system needs, thereby eliminating the costs of added design, packaging inherent in the production of circuits made with discrete components. This group of ICs includes some of the more popular devices replacing existing circuits without "re-inventing the wheel".

CUSTOM INTEGRATED CIRCUITS

A custom hybrid or monolithic IC is intended to satisfy the specific electrical, mechanical, and environmental needs of any unique system(s) produced by the purchaser, usually an original equipment manufacturer (OEM).

Custom IC production time can be quite long, typically several months, or possibly several years, as in the case of an extremely complex custom monolithic IC (generally not available for purchase on the open market). A custom IC can be manufactured in very large or very small quantities, depending on OEM production requirements.

One-time costs of mask design and tooling are generally paid by the purchaser, not the custom IC manufacturer, regardless of the quantities produced, unless, other arrangements have been made between the two parties. As with a standard IC, the actual selling price of a custom IC, in either monolithic or hybrid form, will be influenced by the tooling and production costs, end-application (military or aerospace versus commercial, industrial or consumer), and the quantity required.

Although a non-standard circuit has always been identified as a "custom" IC, many custom monolithic ICs are now being referred as an ASIC or *Application-Specific Integrated Circuit*. Variations in the design approach, specifically selected to optimize function, size, cost and delivery time, are identified as "fully custom, "semicustom" (standard cell) or "gate array" ASICs.

A *fully custom* IC is designed and produced as a completely unique product, based to a great extent, on the requirements and performance specifications established by the purchaser to provide an exclusive approach to a technical problem.

A *semicustom* IC uses standard IC cells or modules and is often referred to as a "standard building block" design. Equivalent standard IC cells for the different IC process technologies are available and offer a wide selection to optimize a circuit design. Libraries of these standard-cell modules are stored in computer data banks to be accessed by the IC designer. Through appropriate computer keyboard commands, the stored modules are displayed, manipulated, interconnected, verified, and are then placed into the final IC layout. With the semicustom, or standard building block approach, some degree of circuit uniqueness is lost, since the same final device can be easily duplicated and used by competitive companies.

A *gate array* IC consists of a multitude of prefabricated individual logic gates, interconnected during the IC metallization processes to provide the logic system uniqueness dictated by the purchaser's requirements. This method is the fastest and least expensive way to design an IC chip, however, since the pre-interconnected gate array chip is intended for many uses, some logic gates in the array are frequently not needed in a particular application and are left unused. The present gate array approach often results in some unnecessary processing and is used in the design of only digital monolithic IC chips.

ASICs can be produced in the appropriate processing technology (bipolar, CMOS, etc.) with the advantages of the specific technology serving to optimize the circuit's function. They can be custom circuits designed to perform one or two simple, but special, functions. They can also be extremely complex ICs that encompass many intricate functions for a single system, or several systems. The major reasons for developing an ASIC are to reduce operating power, size, and cost of a custom circuit designed to satisfy a specific application, while creating a monolithic IC with relatively short production lead time.

Although the greater number of ASICs being manufactured at the present time are digital in nature, there are also many analog ASICs being used. In addition, monolithic IC designers are combining analog and digital circuitry on the same ASIC chip to offer improved performance characteristics for a system. This is particularly true as CMOS technology is being advanced and higher levels of chip density are being achieved.

DIGITAL CIRCUITS

A *digital* pulse is a step-function voltage that moves instantly from a predetermined voltage level to a second level that has a more positive or more negative voltage value. It stays at the second voltage level for a specific time and then instantly returns to its original level.

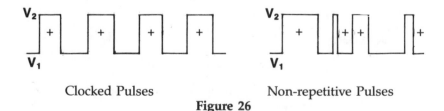

Clocked Pulses   Non-repetitive Pulses

Figure 26

Digital pulses (signals) can be generated as *clock pulses* that recur at a constant repetition rate to synchronize other circuits, or as *non-repetitive* pulses that have no fixed repetition rate or pulse width. The characteristics of these pulses are determined by other circuits or systems. See Figure 26.

In the circuit shown in Figure 27, the digital input and output pulses, as well as the polarity of the supply voltage, is positive with respect to the circuit reference. As the input digital pulse changes instantly from one state to the other, its output voltage also changes in a similar manner. Since the input pulse is only a "two-state", or binary voltage, the value of its output voltage will be either zero or its maximum value. No "in-between" voltage levels exist at either input or output.

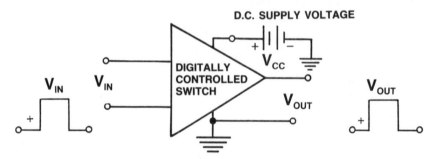

Block Diagram of a Digital Circuit
Figure 27

DIGITALLY-CONTROLLED SWITCH
- During the standby (non-operating) state of a normally-OFF, digitally-controlled switching circuit (Figure 28), zero voltage is applied to its input terminals. Since R_{CE} (the resistance of the normally-OFF switch) is essentially infinite, no current will flow through the load (R_L and no electrical power (I_2R) will be used in either load or switch.

V_{IN} = ZERO $\leftarrow R_{CE} \cong \infty$ I_L = ZERO R_L $I_L^2 R_L$ = ZERO $I_L^2 R_{CE}$ = ZERO V_{CC}

Normally-OFF, Digitally-controlled Switch
Figure 28

• When a digital pulse of the proper amplitude and polarity is applied to its input terminals (Figure 29), the resistance of the switching section (R_{CE}) suddenly changes to essentially zero. The switch turns ON and current flows in the load (R_L). Although power ($I_L^2 \times R_L$) is being consumed in the load, since R_{CE} is essentially zero, the switch consumes essentially no power even though load current (I_L) is flowing.

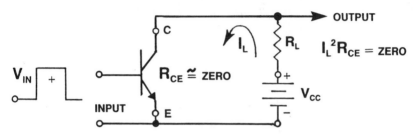

Turned-ON, Digitally-controlled Switch
Figure 29

In this application, the digitally-controlled switch is not being used in a complex manner, but merely as the electronic equivalent of a single-pole, single-throw mechanical switch. It acts in a general-purpose high-speed switch function and often operates as only part of a more sophisticated IC chip.

The major applications for digital ICs, however, are in the areas of computer systems and related circuitry. Both standard and custom hybrid and monolithic ICs used for these applications consist of digital circuits, such as: microprocessors, logic gates, flip/flops, registers, semiconductor memories, computer-support circuits, and even a complete microcomputer circuit on a single monolithic chip. Computer and computer-related circuits are examined in PART TWO - COMPUTER CONCEPTS.

ANALOG CIRCUITS

Electronic circuits are used successfully to sense, measure, monitor, modify, amplify, operate, and control changing conditions and natural phenomena. Circuits in which the output voltage varies as a **continuous** function of its input are called "analog circuits". Since they include no digital activity, they are sometimes referred to as "non-digital circuits" and encompass both linear and non-linear analog circuitry.

LINEAR AMPLIFIERS

In the linear amplifier block diagram shown in Figure 30, the sine wave output voltage (V_{OUT}) is an amplified version of its input voltage (V_{IN}). Regardless of how input and output signals are designated (current, voltage, or power), the relationship of output divided by input is called "gain" or "amplification factor". Pertinent information, such as: maximum power, current, voltage, operating temperature range, frequency capability, and distortion values under various conditions of output power and load are generally listed on the device data sheet.

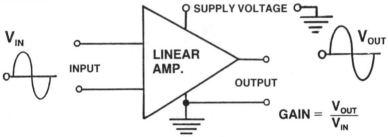

Block Diagram of a Linear Amplifier
Figure 30

OPERATIONAL AMPLIFIER
Applications of linear monolithic ICs have increased relatively slowly and steadily but not with the dramatic impact of digital monolithic ICs. An important exception is the *operational amplifier*, commonly called "op amp", the first commercially successful linear monolithic IC that provided industry with a versatile, stable linear amplifier as a single component.

The op amp was originally designed to perform mathematical operations, such as: addition, subtraction, integration, and differentiation and derives its name from these operations. The circuit is now used for a considerably broader range of applications. Its features can be readily used to greater advantage since it is inherently an extremely stable, versatile, general purpose amplifier, with low-noise and wide frequency range characteristics. Some of its parameters, such as: frequency response and gain can be changed, and precisely adjusted, by modifying the relationship of external components (either resistors and/or capacitors).

IC op amps are available in a variety of power and frequency capabilities,in both hybrid and monolithic IC form as a single, dual, triple, or quad and in different types of hermetically and nonhermetically sealed packages.

The op amp circuit shown in Figure 31 features an input section (differential amplifier) that will provide linear amplification to a desired input signal and effectively eliminate input circuit noises and other undesirable input voltages.

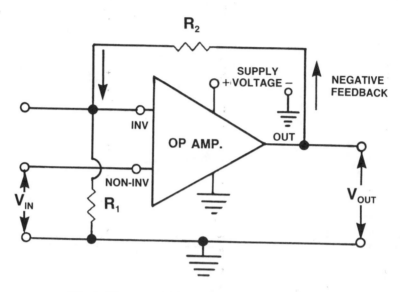

Block Diagram of an Operational Amplifier
Figure 31

The "feedback resistors" (R_1 and R_2) connect a portion of the output voltage to the input in a "closed-loop" configuration. The values of R_1 and R_2 are chosen to produce a "negative feedback" voltage that reduces the gain of an "open-loop" (no feedback) circuit to a predetermined amount, R_1 divided by (R_1 + R_2).

In addition, since the output voltage is 180° out-of-phase with the input voltage, the negative feedback circuit reduces the effects of any sudden or gradual change in circuit operation which are due to a change in supply voltage, operating temperature, loading of the op amp, or aging of its circuit elements by this same feedback ratio, R_1 divided by (R_1 + R_2). This results in improved circuit stability and performance.

By careful selection of the external resistors, R_1 and R_2, for low temperature coefficient (TC), tight tolerance, low noise, and precise circuit gain can be achieved. In a hybrid IC, either thick or thin film resistor chips can be laser-trimmed for an exact circuit gain.

DIFFERENTIAL AMPLIFIER - OP AMP INPUT SECTION

Since the op amp's input section is a differential amplifier (Figure 32), it has two separate input terminals, either of which, or both, may be connected to a prior circuit's output.

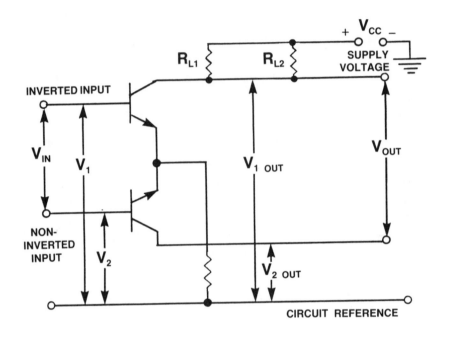

Differential Amplifier - Schematic Diagram
Figure 32

Any voltages common to both input terminals (shown in Figure 32 as V_1 and V_2) represent circuit noise or other undesirable voltages and are called *common-mode voltages* (V_{CM}). Because the output voltages V_{OUT1} and V_{OUT2} are amplified, inverted versions of V_1 and V_2, and are 180° out of phase with each other, they cancel each other. If their values are equal, the op amp output voltage is zero ($V_{OUT1} - V_{OUT2} = 0$).

If no input signal applied between the input terminals of the differential amplifier, V_{IN} is zero, output voltage (V_{OUT}) is zero and is free of any noise or other undesirable voltages.

When a desired signal (V_{IN}) is applied between the two input terminals (INVERTED and NON-INVERTED), the resultant V_{OUT} is a stable, noise-free, amplified version of input signal, V_{IN}.

AUDIO AMPLIFIERS - PREAMPLIFIER AND POWER

In a record player/audio amplifier system (Figure 33), the music (in the form of grooves on the record) is converted to voltage variations by the phonograph cartridge. These signals are then amplified by the first linear audio amplifier section (pre-amplifier). The output of the pre-amplifier, too weak to drive the loudspeaker, is coupled to a second linear audio amplifier section (power amplifier), further amplifying the signal to provide enough power to drive the loudspeaker.

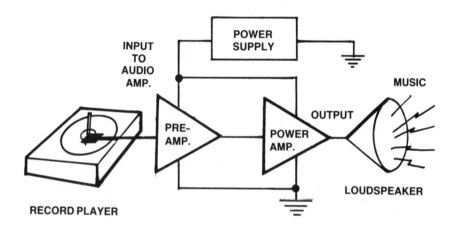

Record Player/Audio Amplifier System - Block Diagram
Figure 33

The loudspeaker converts the amplified voltage variations to mechanical vibrations to fill a room, auditorium or hall with music. With a high quality system (record player, phonograph cartridge, audio amplifier, and loudspeaker), music coming from the loudspeaker will be the amplified, distortion-free version of the music represented by the record grooves.

Low-cost, low-distortion audio amplifier monolithic ICs (both singles and duals for monaural and binaural systems) are available as separate, pre-amplifiers and power amplifiers. With the addition of a volume control, PC board, disk player, tape recorder, loudspeaker and an appropriate power supply, an entire music system can be assembled easily, quickly, and inexpensively, with practically no design time required.

NON-LINEAR CIRCUITS

D.C. VOLTAGE REGULATOR

Relatively low-cost, monolithic IC voltage regulators provide high performance capability in both hermetically-sealed and non-hermetic sealed packages. Compared to the simple resistor-zener circuit voltage regulator discussed in VOLUME TWO - PART ONE of this series (DISCRETE SEMICONDUCTORS), they provide:

• Greater output current and power capability
• Improved line voltage regulation
• Improved load regulation - 0.02% at 2 amperes load current
• Short-circuit protection and automatic re-set
• Internal thermal overload protection and automatic re-set

Individual monolithic IC regulators are produced to operate at the following fixed output voltages: 5, 6 ,8, 10, 12, 15, 18 and 24 volts. They are available as a dual (two regulators in one package) and as positive and negative voltage regulators.

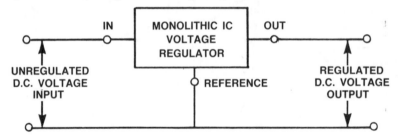

Monolithic IC D.C. Voltage Regulator
Figure 34

If the external terminals of a monolithic IC voltage regulator (Figure 34) are connected as shown in Figure 35, and a fixed resistor and potentiometer are added as shown, the circuit can now serve as a variable output D.C. voltage regulator.

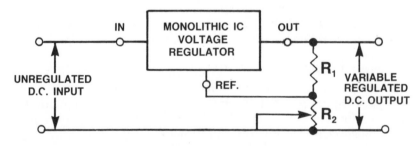

Block Diagram - Variable Output D.C. Voltage Regulator
Figure 35

COMPARISONS BETWEEN DIGITAL AND ANALOG CIRCUITS
From several aspects, the digital approach to circuitry can be preferable to circuits providing similar functions in analog form. Digital techniques may offer the following advantages:

• POWER CONSUMPTION - Depending on the specific IC technology used, the power consumed could be as little as one thousandth of that used with analog circuits being used in a similar system. Digital circuitry lends itself for use in low-power, battery-operated, portable equipment.

• ERROR-FREE TRANSMISSION AND STORAGE - Although analog circuits have the capability of achieving precise levels of accuracy, a storage and/or transmission medium may inject errors into the system. These errors can be alleviated if the analog information is converted to digital data, stored and transmitted digitally, and then reconverted into the desired analog voltages.

Once conversion into digital form is accomplished, or if the information is originally in digital form, calculations of any accuracy can easily be obtained with the use of a digital system having sufficient capability (even with component tolerances of $\pm20\%$). Typically, monolithic IC component elements have tolerances between $\pm10\%$ and $\pm20\%$.

• REAL ESTATE EFFICIENCY - More digital functions can occupy the same space on a hybrid IC board, or be diffused into a monolithic IC chip, than with similar systems using analog circuitry, while reducing material and production costs.

More and more, systems that have previously been using analog circuits exclusively are being replaced, either in whole or in part, by digital systems, such as: digital audio tape and disk recorder/player systems, industrial control systems, telephone systems, and precision automatic test equipment.

A wide variety of relatively new products are being designed with digital circuit techniques and are being manufactured at relatively low cost for consumer, industrial, commercial, medical, military and aerospace applications. Some of these products include: satellite communications equipment, electronic medical diagnostic equipment, computerized cameras, hand-held and desk-top calculators, and of course, new, remarkable digital computers that have created a technical and industrial revolution throughout the world's industrialized areas.

INTERFACE CIRCUITS

ANALOG-TO-DIGITAL (A/D) AND
DIGITAL-TO-ANALOG (D/A) CONVERTERS

As digital ICs are replacing the more traditional analog ICs, the need for electronic circuits that will be able to effectively convert from one technique to the other is rapidly intensifying. To meet this need, IC manufacturers have been producing more precise, faster, smaller, lower power-consuming, and less expensive circuits in hybrid and monolithic IC form. These circuits are referred to as analog-to-digital (A/D) and digital-to-analog (D/A) converters.

The function of an A/D converter is to sense a changing voltage of an analog circuit and convert different levels of the analog voltage into individual digital codes. An A/D converter will perform the reverse action by changing each input digital code into a corresponding analog output voltage.

A block diagram of a typical electronic thermometer and digital readout system using an A/D converter is shown in Figure 36.

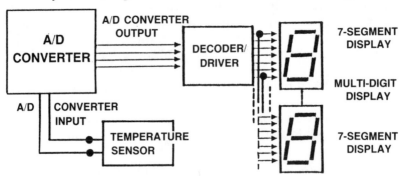

Temperature Sensor, A/D Converter, and Digital Display System
Figure 36

• The temperature sensor will generate an analog voltage at its output that is analogous to the temperature in a room. The sensor's output is connected to the A/D converter input. As the temperature changes, the analog voltage (V_{IN}) will also change proportionately.

• For each different change in value of input voltage V_{IN}, a different digital code (V_{OUT}) is generated at the output of the A/D converter. Since each value of V_{IN} is the analog voltage of a different temperature, each digital code at the A/D output represents the corresponding temperature.

- The A/D converter output is connected to the input terminals of a decoder/driver, with each of its output voltages providing the power for a display segment. Each digital code will represent the corresponding temperature of the room.

- A seven-segment, multi-digit display that is connected to a decode/driver output will display the corresponding temperature in the room for each digital code at its input.

RESOLUTION CAPABILITY OF A/D AND D/A CONVERTERS
The precision of this system is determined by the accuracy of the temperature sensor and the *resolution* of the A/D converter. Resolution in a system is defined as the smallest measurable change in the variable output of that system. The level of resolution of the system depends on the number of input voltage levels (V_{IN}) that can be accurately converted into digital codes by an analog-to-digital (A/D) converter, or converted into analog voltages by a digital-to-analog (D/A) converter.

For example, a simple (4 bit)* A/D converter in a system generates 16 (2^4) different digital codes at its output, over the entire range (zero to +10 volts) of incoming analog voltage. The 4-bit D/A converter in a system generates a different voltage level for each of the 16 digital codes at its input; system accuracy is 6.25%. Replacing the converters with more complex (higher resolution) types will greatly improve system accuracy.

With a relatively simple, low-cost digital circuit, 1 in 256 (an accuracy of less than 0.4%) can be measured. Levels of resolution and resulting accuracies are illustrated below for different A/D and D/A converter systems.

CONVERTER SIZE	RESOLUTION	ACCURACY
4 bit	1 out of 16	6.25%
8 bit	1 out of 256	0.39%
12 bit	1 out of 4096	0.024%
16 bit	1 out of 65,536	0.0015%

A/D converters and D/C converters, in a variety of sizes and in both hybrid IC and monolithic IC form, are being manufactured in a wide selection of hermetically-sealed and nonhermetically-sealed packages.

*The computer term "bit" designates the number of elements in a "digital word" and is studied in detail in PART II - COMPUTER CONCEPTS (CHAPTER SEVEN).

COMPARATOR

This circuit is basically a high gain amplifier without feedback and compares the level of the changing analog voltage at its input to a reference voltage. When the changing analog voltage has reached the reference voltage, a digital output voltage change is presented at its output.

The comparator (Figure 37) can be used as part of a system to help maintain a preset, constant level of room temperature. If the reference voltage is made variable, different levels of room temperature can be selected.

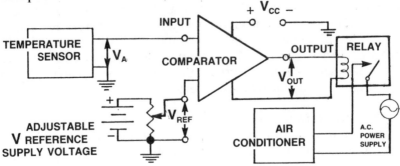

Comparator Used to Stabilize Room Temperature
Figure 37

- The temperature sensor is used to sense room temperature and generate a D.C. voltage (V_A), the electrical analog of the changing temperature. As room temperature increases, the increasing analog voltage (V_A) at the comparator's input terminals is compared to the reference voltage, V_{REF}.

- When the changing V_A, equals the preset reference voltage (V_{REF}), the comparator is activated, causing its output voltage (V_{OUT}) to suddenly change from zero volts to the level of the supply voltage (V_{CC}). This, in turn, energizes the relay coil connected to the comparator output, turning the A/C ON. As room temperature decreases, the comparator input voltage V_A decreases. When the value of V_A moves below V_{REF}, the comparator output voltage (V_{OUT}) will suddenly go OFF.

- With the comparator output voltage, V_{OUT}, at zero, the relay and air conditioner will turn OFF in a step-function manner. After several of these cycles, the system will stabilize and the temperature of the room will stay constant, within the design specifications of the system.

MULTIPLEXING WITH ANALOG SWITCHES

If a digitally-controlled switch (turned ON by a digital pulse connected to its input terminals) allows an analog (linear) signal to pass through its low-resistance switching section during its ON state, it is designated as an *analog switch*.

A single analog switch (Figure 38) operates as follows:

• When a digital pulse (V_D) is applied to its input terminals, the analog switch is energized and the resistance of its switching section (R_{A-B}) changes from essentially infinity to essentially zero.

• The A.C. signal (V_S), previously only at point A, is now connected to point B, with a minimum of distortion or attenuation. Point B can now be connected to any electrically-compatible point in a circuit or system.

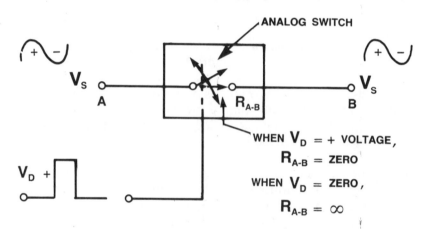

Block Diagram - Single Analog Switch
Figure 38

The analog signal (V_S), now connected to point B, can be used to control other circuits, or, can be amplified and/or processed for use in other systems.

The amount of distortion and/or attenuation will depend on the particular circuit technology used and the dynamic range of the circuit. MOS technology is generally preferred for use in analog switching circuits. A MOS FET has the unique capability of conducting equally well in either direction during its ON state, while providing a relatively high dynamic range for analog signals.

The technique used to connect several transmission lines or channels to a common transmission line in a sequenced or timed manner is called *multiplexing*. Conversely, multiplexing is also a technique of connecting a single transmission line to several channels in the same manner. Multichannel IC analog switching circuits are manufactured in hybrid and monolithic IC form for use in a variety of multiplexing techniques.

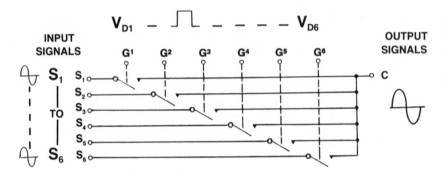

Functional Diagram - Multiplexing System
Figure 39

The system (Figure 39) operates as follows:
• When an appropriate digital switching voltage (V_{D1} through V_{D6}) is applied to a single analog switch input (G_1 through G_6), the selected switch will close.

• Any one of the six analog signal sources (S_1 through S_6) is connected individually to the common transmission line connected to point C. A human operator, or a programmed computer, can set the proper sequencing and timing of the switching action.

• The common transmission line can be connected to any desired point in another system that is electrically compatible with the multiplexing circuit.

Variations of this multiplexing technique, or similar types of multiplexing systems, are effectively used to automatically, and/or manually, switch analog signals from various sources to a common transmission line and vice versa. Multiplexing is used for audio, RF, video and cable TV (CATV) switching circuits in such diverse equipment as: entertainment systems used in airliners, high-speed computer-controlled telephone communications systems and satellite communications.

REINFORCEMENT EXERCISES

Answer TRUE or FALSE to each of the following statements:

1. An integrated circuit, either in hybrid or monolithic form, is mainly classified by its application or how the IC is used.

2. Because of the various available applications of ICs, they should be categorized into only three separate and distinct groups: digital, linear, and interface circuits.

3. A linear amplifier provides current, voltage and/or power amplification, producing a proportional (straight-line) relationship between the amplifier's input and output signals.

4. A digital pulse (signal) moves in a step-function manner, from one designated voltage level to a second designated voltage level, with the transition between the two voltage levels accomplished in essentially zero time. It stays at the second voltage level for a specified time and then instantly returns to its original voltage level.

5. In digital circuits, the two voltage levels of a digital pulse can be used to represent any specified state or condition, such as: ON/OFF, HIGH/LOW, TRUE/FALSE, ZERO/ONE, MARK/SPACE, HOT/COLD, etc.

6. The major applications for digital ICs are in the areas of computer systems and related circuitry. Digital hybrid and monolithic ICs used for these applications include: logic gates, semiconductor memories, microprocessors, and even a complete microcomputer on a single monolithic chip.

7. Because analog ICs generally use less power and provide more accuracy than digital ICs performing equivalent functions, they are preferred for use in military and aerospace applications where these requirements are critical.

8. An operational amplifier is only used for specific mathematical operations such as addition, subtraction, integration and differentiation, and not as a linear amplifier.

9. In an operational amplifier, common-mode voltages in the input section are amplified to improve the circuit's performance characteristics.

10. A differential amplifier has two separate input terminals, either of which, or both, may be connected to a prior circuit's output. It is generally used as the input section of an operational amplifier.

11. Low-distortion audio amplifier monolithic ICs (both singles and duals for monaural and binaural systems) are available as separate pre-amplifiers at relatively low cost.

12. With increased negative feedback in an op amp, voltage gain goes down; circuit stability and frequency response go up.

13. Relatively low-cost voltage regulators are available in monolithic IC form to provide desirable features, such as: re-settable short-circuit and thermal-overload protection.

14. An interface IC provides the means of interconnecting or linking two types of circuits or systems and is neither purely linear nor purely digital; it has sections of both types within its structure, providing compatibility between circuits and systems having different modes of operation.

15. When a group of digital codes are connected to the input of a 8-bit D/A converter, the resolution that is achieved at its output is 1 out of 8, for an accuracy of 12.5%

16. The one-time design and tooling charges to produce the photomasks for custom ICs are always paid for by the IC manufacturer, regardless of the quantities produced.

17. An application-specific integrated circuit (ASIC) is a custom IC in monolithic form, designed and produced as a full custom, semicustom or gate array IC.

18. With the use of computer-aided design (CAD) and similar computer-aided techniques, designers can tailor each ASIC chip in a system to the needs of that specific section of the system, optimizing performance and use of space.

19. Although most of the available ASICs are in the analog category, digital and interface techniques are presently being used for ASICs, but to a lesser extent.

Answers to these reinforcement exercises are on page 129.

CHAPTER
FIVE

IC RELIABILITY CONSIDERATIONS

INTRODUCTION

MIL-M-38510 PART NUMBER
DESIGNATIONS

MILITARY STANDARD MIL-STD-883

THE ELEMENTS OF MIL-M-38510

QUALITY CONTROL PROGRAMS

CAUSES OF IC FAILURE

HIGH COST OF OMITTING
INCOMING INSPECTION

RELIABLE ICs FOR COMMERCIAL
APPLICATIONS

IC RELIABILITY CONSIDERATIONS

INTRODUCTION

Reliability refers to the combined **quality** and **longevity** of any component, circuit or system.

QUALITY is the degree of excellence inherent in a component, circuit, or system and is determined by:

• The potential and actual limitations and failures in the composition and structure of a final product.

• The combined nature of the design, materials used, and the level of personnel competency.

• The kind of test equipment and test procedures, production equipment and techniques, plant facilities, process control and quality control used to produce a final product.

Specific pre-conditioning and testing programs are required by DESC for high-reliability, military and aerospace applications. Similar screening techniques are dictated by "company policy" of the OEM and/or component manufacturers for selected commercial, industrial, and consumer use.

LONGEVITY is the minimum period of time a component, circuit, or system will operate, as specified, under the electrical, mechanical, and/or environmental stresses and conditions that the final product has been designed to withstand. In addition, the longevity of a component, circuit, or system depends primarily on the quality that was built into the product during design and manufacturing. After manufacture, however, longevity is influenced by additional factors that include:

• Proper handling by shipping and receiving personnel

• The ability to avoid excessive voltage, current, heat or other inadvertent stresses (beyond maximum ratings) under all specified conditions of operation and environment

• Appropriate use of the final equipment by the end-user

When the term "reliability" is used, it is interchangeable with the term "high-reliability", or "hi-rel". A hi-rel IC does not mean "perfection" in performance capability, combined with infinite longevity. The work required to achieve a technically perfect final product would be prohibitive in cost and time and it would be commercially impractical. Hi-rel implies the establishment of a predetermined level of assurance that the hi-rel ICs, and the equipment in which they are assembled, will function at a specified performance level over an estimated length of time, according to their specifications.

Before a component is assembled into a circuit or system, special attention is required to eliminate or, at least, minimize the high cost of maintenance and/or prevent a complete disaster resulting from component failure in actual operation.

Military and aerospace requirements include the need for operation over temperature ranges of -55° C to +125° C or, for special applications, from -176° C to +150° C. In many cases, hi-rel ICs are subjected to stresses of mechanical shock, vibration, and acceleration. Component-deteriorating environmental stresses include fungus, salt air, chemical solvents, humidity, and similar contaminating agents.

The Defense Electronics Supply Center (DESC), an arm of the U.S. Dept. of Defense (DOD), is the sole government agency responsible for the initiation of high-reliability (hi-rel) specifications for all electronic components, including hybrid and monolithic ICs. They are used by all branches of the U.S. Armed Forces, NASA (National Aeronautical and Space Administration), FAA (Federal Aviation Agency) and the Weather Bureau. These specifications are used in manufacturing, preconditioning, packaging, branding, testing, and shipping of hi-rel ICs to provide a confidence level (expressed as a percentage) to assure the user that all approved ICs will conform to specified electrical, mechanical, and environmental requirements. The following are some of the items in the hi-rel specifications that establish this criteria:

- A predetermined level of reliability (quality and longevity)
- Specified procedures for packaging, preconditioning, testing, branding, and shipping
- Standard incoming inspection procedures and quality control methods and documentation
- A means of qualifying and enforcing periodic inspection of IC manufacturing facilities for proper processing and quality control techniques

In cooperation with DESC, and also under the jurisdiction of DOD, DCAS (Defense Contract Administration Service) has the authority to monitor the facilities and procedures of suppliers of approved hi-rel ICs; DCAS can impose its own controls to correct any non-conformity to applicable specifications.

DCAS is also responsible for the approval (certification) of the processing and quality status of standard military electronic products and for all Government Source Inspection. A resident (or visiting) Government Source Inspector establishes test conditions for incoming and outgoing inspection and has the responsibility to accept or reject any lot. Only the DOD, however, and not DCAS, has the option to impose Government Source Inspection (GSI) on any IC or IC manufacturing facility and, when necessary, can require Government Source Inspection.

Military and aerospace applications dictate the need for the most stringent hi-rel requirements and quality assurance. The extreme demands of modern military and aerospace equipment often require operation under hazardous conditions as well as in the harsh environment of space. Contamination and stress from external sources necessitates the controlled production of ICs to assure their ability to withstand these stresses while still functioning within required specifications.

The general military specification for ICs is designated as MIL-M-38510, with detailed preconditioning procedures and test methods defined by MIL-STD-883. Although there is no specific applicable military specification for hi-rel hybrid ICs, like hi-rel monolithic ICs, they are processed in accordance with the general military specification MIL-M-38510 and must conform to similar procedures, test methods, facilities qualification, and certification.

Military Standard, MIL-STD-1772, specifies the procedures for supplier certification and qualification, product qualification, environmental screening tests, rework procedure, process control, and quality control for hi-rel hybrid ICs.

Military specifications established by DESC, incorporate the latest revisions that reflect any technological improvements in preconditioning and test procedures. The performance, size, and reliability, as well as the cost of the required ICs, are influenced by the revisions that reflect the cooperative efforts among DESC, the manufacturers of the ICs and the military electronic equipment and the users of the equipment.

MIL-M-38510 PART NUMBER DESIGNATIONS

A hi-rel IC, in compliance with MIL-M-38510, consists of the JAN prefix, the general specification number, the detail specification number, and a coded part number, as follows:

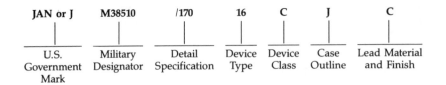

JAN or J	M38510	/170	16	C	J	C
U.S. Government Mark	Military Designator	Detail Specification	Device Type	Device Class	Case Outline	Lead Material and Finish

- JAN or J - U.S. Government (DESC) certification mark
- M38510 - Designator for military specification MIL-M-38510
- /SLASH NUMBER - MIL-M-38510 establishes the general requirements for all hi-rel ICs. The detailed characteristics of a particular IC series (or group of similar devices) are listed in an additional specification referred to as a *slash sheet* and becomes part of the specifications for that device. JM38510/170 is the designation for the detailed specifications and characteristics of the military version of the CD4000, a CMOS monolithic IC logic series.
- DEVICE TYPE - The coded designation of a specific IC in a series of similar ICs (e.g.: CD4000 series). There may be many different ICs in any series (approximately 150 in the CD4000 series of logic gates), each providing a different function. The CD4016 is a quad bilateral switch, CD4028 is a BCD-to-decimal decoder, etc.
- DEVICE CLASS - Reliability level is based on the electrical, mechanical, thermal and environmental requirements of a specific system. Screening levels are commensurate with a system's intended applications and are designated as follows:
  Class C - used for easily repairable ground systems
  Class B - used in aircraft, naval and ground systems
  Class S (most stringent) - used for space flight equipment
- PACKAGE OUTLINE - This letter is the code for a specific IC package. The letter "J" designates a 24-pin DIP.
- LEAD MATERIAL AND FINISH - This letter is the code for an IC package's specific lead material and finish. The letter "C" designates gold-plated Kovar terminals.

The JM38510/17016CJC brand on the lid of a package identifies the part as a DESC-certified CD4016, screened to the Class B reliability level of MIL-M-38510, in a 24-pin dual in-line package that has gold-plated Kovar terminals.

MILITARY STANDARD MIL-STD-883

This military standard provides the "how-to" procedures for MIL-M-38510 and establishes standard methods for testing the electrical, mechanical, and environmental characteristics of hi-rel hybrid and monolithic ICs to determine their ability to withstand the conditions surrounding military and aerospace operations. Suitable laboratory conditions are specified to simulate actual service conditions existing in the field for the rated life of the device.

MIL-STD-883 is categorized into test classes that list a group of different methods for the electrical, mechanical, and environmental tests for different types of ICs.

QUALIFICATION TO MIL-M-38510

Before any JM38510 device can be shipped, regardless of its screening level, a qualification cycle on the specific series must be performed and certification must be granted by DESC.

The required qualification program is used to provide the assurance that the design, manufacturing process, assembly, inspection, and testing of the IC complies with the MIL-M-38510 specification, its applicable slash sheet and MIL-STD 883. The appropriate revision for both specifications must be used.

PRODUCTION LINE QUALIFICATION
The fabrication, assembly and testing lines used for JM38510 devices must be officially certified by a DCAS inspector for MIL-M-38510 use, specifically including the following:

- Process control
- Facility cleanliness

- Equipment calibration
- Documentation

CERTIFICATION PROCESS
- The first step is a formal request from the IC manufacturer to DESC for a certification audit. DESC administers certification for both Class B and Class S. Class B auditing is conducted by DESC personnel. The Class S audit is conducted by representatives of DESC, the U.S. Air Force, NASA and the Space and Missiles Systems Organization (SAMSO).

- Once the audit has been completed, a letter is sent to the IC manufacturer granting facility approval or outlining any required corrective actions.

- After corrections have been made, the manufacturing facility is audited again and granted facility approval.

Facility certification must be renewed on a periodic basis, typically, every two years. The IC manufacturer must qualify a device for Class B status or begin qualification testing for a Class S device within one year after certification. In either case, failure to meet this requirement is cause for the revocation of the facility certification.

To requalify a manufacturing facility that has lost certification, the IC manufacturer must prove to DESC that certification requirements (process control, facility cleanliness, documentation, and equipment calibration) are still being met.

DEVICE QUALIFICATION
- Once product line certification has been granted, a specified lot size of the required IC is manufactured for qualification testing. The sequence includes screening and conformance to the specific sections of MIL-M-38510, referred to as Groups A, B and C. These tests (described later in this chapter) are performed on a randomly selected sampling from the lot.

- After submission of the required test reports to DESC showing that all tests and inspections have been satisfactorily completed, the manufacturer and the approved IC will be listed in the Qualified Parts List (QPL) - 38510 for monolithic ICs. Unlike product-specific monolithic ICs, hybrid ICs are facility and process specific. After hi-rel approval, hybrid IC manufacturers are listed in the Qualified Manufacturer's List (QML) - 38510, in accordance with MIL-STD-1772.

- To maintain the QPL or QML listing, the manufacturer must submit a yearly summary of the quality conformance testing that has been performed for a new lot of the approved IC or for an IC that is structurally identical.

- DESC, and not the final user, must be notified by the qualified manufacturer of any change in the product or its product assurance plans if that change might affect performance, quality, appearance, reliability or interchangeability.

- DESC will then inform the manufacturer regarding the steps, if any, that must be taken to retain qualification. After reviewing and approving the new data, DESC can reinstate the approved IC (or IC hybrid manufacturer) to the QPL or QML.

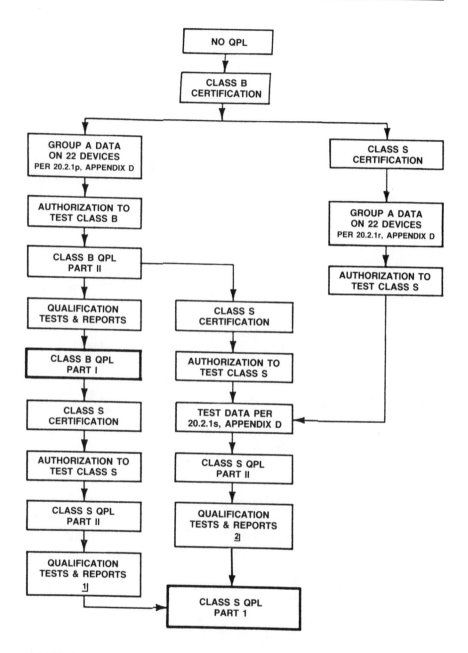

1 Qualification using MIL-STD-883, method 5005, tables I and IIa only.
2 Qualification using MIL-STD-883, method 5005, tables I, IIa and IV.

Qualification Procedure for Class B or Class S QPL-Listing
Figure 40

There are two levels of QPL listings, Parts I and II, with Part I requiring the more extensive qualification testing. Part II was established by DESC to expedite QPL listing of approved monolithic ICs. All product line certifications must be complete with significant test data, IC design and process information submitted to DESC before Part II listing on the QPL is granted.

Since additional Part I qualification procedures require considerably more time, manufacturers listed on the Part II QPL are able to ship standard JM38510 ICs (qualified to Part II), while their Part I qualification is being completed. The ICs processed to either Part II or Part I listings are identical.

Only monolithic ICs on the QPL, or hybrid IC manufacturers on the QML, can be specified for use in equipment intended for military or aerospace applications. If a condition exists where a desired monolithic IC, or hybrid IC manufacturer, is not listed in the QPL, or QML, permission must be obtained from the prime contractor to use the unlisted IC or unlisted hybrid IC manufacturer. DESC must then approve the transaction.

Since the requirements for Class S certification are much more stringent than those for Class B, the manufacturer of Class S devices is also qualified to produce Class B devices. Before shipment of the Class B QPL ICs, however, the manufacturer's ICs must be on the Class B QPL.

QUALITY CONFORMANCE TESTING
All levels of reliability require continual testing to be sure that the device conforms to the requirements of the military specification, MIL-M-38510, and to any additional details that may be covered in the slash sheet.

Requirements for each of the screening levels vary from class to class and are specifically detailed in MIL-STD-883. Each of the three levels (Classes B, C and S) require 100% testing of some characteristics and sample testing of others.

Qualification and/or quality conformance inspection test sample selection is done on an Acceptance Quality Level (AQL) based on the reliability level and is specified in MIL-STD-883. Successful completion of a qualifying and/or quality conformance test sequence that is run on a randomly selected sample of devices from the inspection lot qualifies the entire lot.

THE ELEMENTS OF MIL-M-38510

GROUP A TESTING

- Group A specifies the electrical tests listed in the manufacturer's data sheet and in the applicable slash sheet. They are performed on a 100% basis on a randomly selected sample taken from each inspection lot. The sample sizes and the specified group of tests depend on the product class.

- Visual and mechanical inspection of the package and its leads are performed according to the requirements of MIL-STD-883.

- Depending on the screening level required, different sampling sizes are listed. Some of the tests for the Class S level are performed in a specific sequence within a particular sub-group test procedure.

These tests are considered non-destructive and ICs that qualify may be shipped after being subjected to Group A tests.

GROUP B TESTING

Group B specifies a die and package stress test sequence performed on a randomly selected sampling of each inspection lot. The tests are often called "shake, rattle and roll" tests and are used to verify the quality of wafer fabrication, chip assembly, lead bonding, and package sealing. As with the Group A tests, each class level has its own limits and methods that are specified in MIL-STD-883. Each test is classified under a different MIL-STD-883 sub-group and include the following:

- Testing of lead solderability and resistance to solvents.

- Thermal shock test (temperature cycling) - Temperatures and cycle time are specified for each reliability level. Devices are initially placed in an oven at +125° C. When stabilized at that temperature, they are plunged into a cold (-55° C) environment. This test is used to verify lead bonding quality.

- Hermetic seal test - Verifies the seal between the open package and its cover. Depending on the required reliability level, gross and/or fine leak tests are performed.

- Stabilization bake - A preconditioning procedure done at a specified high temperature and duration which serves to stabilize the electrical parameters of the device. Generally, all ICs (military and commercial) undergo this procedure.

• Power burn-in - Devices are placed in an oven at a specified temperature and duration and operated at 80% of their maximum power capability. The values of the temperature and time are determined by the required reliability level.

A burn-in procedure discloses parts that have been improperly processed during wafer fabrication and serve to eliminate latent chip failures during this early period of device preconditioning. At the completion of power burn-in, changes are recorded from the results of the Group A tests of the specified electrical characteristics of the device. The slash sheet specifies the maximum changes allowed by burn-in.

• Decapping and internal visual examination - A random sample group of the inspection lot is decapped and visually examined to verify the structure of the device. When specified, a scanning electron microscope (SEM) test is performed. Lead bond and die shear tests are also performed when so indicated on the slash sheets.

Group B testing and the related documentation are very extensive and expensive. When required, they are specifically referred to in the purchase order for the required parts.

GROUP C TESTING
These tests are used for qualification data to verify package integrity and include testing of the device under mechanical, thermal and environmental stresses. All tests are run on a randomly selected sample with identical tests done for all three reliability levels. In accordance with the methods specified in MIL-STD-883, the following items are tested and verified:

• Electrical parameters of the device as specified on the manufacturer's data sheet

• Physical dimensions of the package

• Mechanical shock, vibration, acceleration and corrosion in a salt atmosphere.

• Terminal strength and hermetic seal for gross and fine leaks.

The last three tests may be done on electrical rejects from the same lot. Lot integrity may be confirmed by decapping defective ICs after the tests are performed. Depending on the reliability level (Class B, C, or S), Group C tests, despite being specified in a device slash sheet, are often waived by the contractor.

QUALITY CONTROL PROGRAMS

By establishing standardized test methods and preconditioning processes, MIL-M-38510 and MIL-STD-883 have provided an extremely effective technique for obtaining highly reliable ICs. To standardize quality and inspection criteria, DESC has established the following procedures:
- Quality Specification: MIL-Q-9858
- Inspections Specification: MIL-I-4520
- Calibration Requirements: MIL-C-45662

These specifications deal with the principles of maintaining a proper quality control system to assure compliance with the requirements of a military contract. The program used to implement these specifications is developed by the contractor and must include proper documentation, with the contractor's program subject to review by the Department of Defense.

QUALITY CONTROL AT THE IC MANUFACTURER'S FACILITY

A satisfactory quality control (QC) program must be used to ensure adequate monitoring of the quality of all aspects of IC manufacturing, including:
- Design and photomasking
- Packaging and sealing
- Electrical testing
- Sorting and branding
- Storage, packing, and shipping
- Fabrication and assembly
- Visual inspection
- Equipment calibration
- Facility maintenance
- Site installation

QUALITY CONTROL AT THE EQUIPMENT MANUFACTURER'S FACILITY

Despite careful control at the IC manufacturer's facility, some percentage of all devices shipped may be defective. Variances in the production process may occur during IC manufacture, testing, sorting and handling, resulting in an inordinate percentage of defective parts being shipped to the OEM.

The electrical characteristics of the device may also change after production testing, even when done on a 100% basis. This shift in characteristics is particularly critical in devices being used under conditions close to specification limits. A carefully planned incoming inspection program is a necessary step prior to any assembly stage. Incoming inspection of all parts, and especially ICs, will serve to minimize failure in subassemblies, subsystems, final products and, even more important, failures in the field. Preferably, incoming inspection of all ICs should be performed on a 100% basis. At the very least, it should be done on an appropriate sampling basis.

CAUSES OF IC FAILURE

MONOLITHIC IC PROCESS-RELATED FAILURES

Implementation of proper process control and quality control techniques and adherence to MIL guidelines will serve to minimize or eliminate any defects that are primarily due to any deficiency within the monolithic IC manufacturing process.

Wafer processing can be divided into distinct stages of the basic IC production, with the possibility of failures occurring at any stage of the manufacturing process. The stages include:

• Wafer fabrication   • Assembly and packaging   • Testing

FAILURE MECHANISMS	DETECTING OR CORRECTING METHODS
WAFER FABRICATION	
Metallization and oxide defects	Pre-cap visual, including Scanning Electron Microscope (SEM)
Surface contamination	inspection will detect defects
Photolithographic misalignment	Power burn-in is used to eliminate defective devices. Check mask alignment process
ASSEMBLY AND PACKAGING	
Poor die attach	Pre-seal visual required
Bad lead bonds	Thermal shock test will separate leads from pads
Sealing defects	Gross and fine leak tests for hermeticity
TESTING	
Uncorrelated test data	More frequent inspection and calibration of equipment
Frequent testing errors: Improper marking/branding Incorrect test results Grading errors	Replacement of test equipment or improved personnel training programs and/or supervision

HYBRID IC PROCESS-RELATED FAILURES

Because a hybrid IC consists of many purchased components (not produced by the hybrid IC manufacturer), the layout, mounting, soldering and handling of the hybrid IC is secondary in importance to the reliability of purchased components. For hi-rel hybrid ICs, a carefully monitored vendor qualification program and rigorous incoming inspection and quality assurance programs at the hybrid IC facility are absolutely necessary.

Strict adherence to the product requirements of MIL-M-38510 and to the certification of the IC hybrid facility (in accordance with MIL-STD-1772), will help to provide the assurance that the IC has been properly processed.

- The failure mechanisms inherent in the processing of discrete passive components (intended for use in hybrid ICs) are controlled and corrected by the manufacturers of these components. See PASSIVE COMPONENTS (VOLUME ONE - Part TWO) of this series for a detailed discussion of passive component failure mechanisms.

- The failure mechanisms, detection and corrective techniques for monolithic ICs are essentially the same as for the discrete semiconductor components used in the production of hybrid ICs.

USER (OEM)-RELATED IC FAILURES

The failure of a hi-rel IC can occur because of many reasons, both predictable and unpredictable. If the IC has been processed properly and the equipment manufacturer had implemented an incoming inspection and a required quality control program, the IC could be assumed to be ready for its intended application in a system. After assembly, however, some conditions can still result in failure of the IC, which, in turn, can cause other components in the circuit, or system, to be stressed to the point of failure.

Many of these failure-inducing conditions can be prevented by controlled equipment production techniques and competent equipment design practices, including: proper circuit design and PC board layout and knowledge of the required ratings and characteristics of the selected components of the system. In addition, having as much information as possible about the equipment's design requirements is essential. This information includes knowledge of the end-product's intended application and the expected stresses to which it may be subjected.

The following conditions may cause IC failure:

- The maximum voltage rating of an IC may be exceeded because of an inadvertent voltage transient, lightning, sudden increase in line voltage, or the discharge of electrostatic energy (ESD). An IC with a marginal maximum voltage rating for its application is susceptible to this type of failure; by adding fast-acting protective devices to the circuit, the IC can be protected.

- If the polarity of the system supply voltage is accidentally reversed, the polarity-sensitive IC and other polarity-sensitive components may fail without proper protection.

- Excessive current (beyond the maximum current rating of the IC) can be caused by failure of another component in the circuit or by the breakdown of insulation in the circuit. The IC can be protected by adding fast-acting protective current-limiting devices to the circuit.

- At a case (package) temperature substantially above 25°C, the maximum allowable power dissipation of an IC can be exceeded, resulting in permanent damage to the IC (and possibly other components in the circuit). The increased temperature may be due to one, or several factors, such as: insufficient heat transfer from the IC because of a poor thermal interface between its package and heat sink, an inadequate heat sink, an inadequate fan or blower (or no fan), inadequate or no hot-air venting holes in the system enclosure.

- The external terminal leads of an IC package can be damaged (or broken) when there is excessive bending of the leads and/or the improper insertion of the package into its socket.

- Mishandling of the package or the application of excessive strain on its rigid terminals can result in a cracked seal between case and leads. Penetration of deteriorating agents can cause contamination of the chip(s) inside the IC package.

- Because of mechanical distortion of its package, fracture of the IC chip can often occur. Generally, the surface of a package will distort if excessive torque is used in mounting the package to a heat sink or other rigid surface.

- Insertion of an IC package into a socket intended for another IC type may result in the IC failure.

THE HIGH COST OF
OMITTING INCOMING INSPECTION

DESC-approved ICs are in compliance with all required military specifications and standards. They undergo careful process and quality control at the IC manufacturing facility (including all confirming documentation). Since it is often assumed that there are no defective DESC-approved ICs, it also can assumed that it is not necessary to have an incoming inspection program at the user's facility. Despite these assumptions, extensive IC failure analyses have shown that with all the tests and control procedures instituted by DESC and the IC manufacturer, there may still be some defective units that have slipped by the IC manufacturer's final tests in any given IC lot that is shipped.

After acceptance of a shipment from an IC manufacturer, it is the responsibility of the end-user (usually, the OEM) to find and return these defective parts for credit or replacement, unless otherwise noted in a purchase order. It has also been established that after years of comprehensive investigation by the quality control community that, generally, for each level of testing that is omitted, the cost of replacing a defective IC increases by a factor of about ten.

At the OEM facility, when using automatic test equipment (ATE), the cost of visual inspection and electrical testing of an IC is about $.01 per device. To find a defective IC in an incoming lot of 10,000 units, incoming inspection, **on a 100% basis**, is absolutely necessary. The testing costs will be about $100.00.

If the policy of an OEM is to assume that there are no defects in any DESC-approved lot of ICs, then in all probability, no incoming inspection is performed on the 10,000 ICs; they will be stored directly into inventory and eventually assembled onto PC boards. If a defective IC is found at the PC board level of production, the original lot of 10,000 ICs becomes suspect and the completed PC boards are tested on a 100% basis. The cost of testing the 10,000 ICs increases to about $1000. If this procedure is extrapolated to final test, the testing cost to find a defective IC from the 10,000 IC lot is now about $10,000. If the system fails in the field because of a defective, untested IC, the implications could be disastrous, particularly, in military and aerospace applications.

Although, what may have appeared at first glance to be a costly practice, 100% incoming inspection of hi-rel ICs is a highly effective and, in the long run, an economical procedure.

RELIABLE ICs
FOR COMMERCIAL APPLICATIONS

The demand for dependable (high-quality), relatively low-cost electronic circuits (needing little or no maintenance) for use in medical equipment, public transportation systems, computers, telecommunications systems and other commercial applications, have encouraged hi-rel IC manufacturers to initiate "in-house reliability" programs. These programs eliminate some of the high costs inherent in the processing, preconditioning, testing, inspection, control and documentation requirements of DESC-approved hi-rel ICs while still offering highly reliable, low-cost components to the public.

To produce high-quality commercial ICs, it is necessary to maintain relatively high standards of reliability when compared with the ordinary standards of low-cost, commercial, industrial and consumer devices. The specifications and related standards of MIL-M-38510, MIL-STD-883, etc. provide the necessary hi-rel guidelines for processing, testing, inspection and quality control programs used to successfully produce a high-quality, functionally-equivalent, non-military IC.

These commercial hi-rel ICs may (or may not) be as dependable as the DESC-qualified hi-rel ICs since they are **not** subjected to **all** the tests, scrutiny, control and documentation essential to becoming a DESC-qualified part. According to the manufacturers of these ICs, they are "made to meet equivalent 38510 specifications" and are priced at about one-third to one-half the cost of functionally-equivalent JM38510 ICs.

Users of DESC-qualified ICs should be aware of some pitfalls in purchasing these devices. Since these lower-cost, in-house, hi-rel programs have been introduced, there has been a proliferation of hi-rel ICs that have been branded and sold as if they are DESC-qualified parts. They are referred to as: "M38510" ICs, "JAN-processed ICs" and "JAN-equivalent ICs".

Regardless of the reliability levels of these devices, none of them are QPL ICs; "JM38510" is the only designation of a QPL IC. The use of any other number or group of numbers, similar to the approved QPL designation, may give the impression that this device is on the QPL. This practice is expressly forbidden in the specifications of MIL-M-38510.

CHAPTER
SIX

INTEGRATED CIRCUIT TECHNOLOGY TRENDS

INTRODUCTION

PHOTOLITHOGRAPHIC
TECHNIQUES

IC WAFER MATERIALS

SEMICUSTOM ICs

GENERAL COMMENTS ON
IC TRENDS

INTEGRATED CIRCUIT
TECHNOLOGY TRENDS

INTRODUCTION

Integrated circuits are becoming more and more complex while using less power and taking less space; they are being used in just about every application of electronic circuitry. Perhaps, even of greater significance, ICs are becoming more dependable and less costly per function as technology improves. This situation has always been inherent in the development, production and application of semiconductor products since the industry began. Although hybrid IC technology has substantially advanced along the same lines, more dramatic progress has been made with monolithic ICs, enhancing the use of electronics in every industry at an ever increasing rate.

During the past two decades, the chip density of a monolithic IC has almost doubled every eighteen months, providing a rate of increase of more than a hundred times per decade. Semiconductor scientists are predicting that this rate of increase will continue well into the next century. This is not merely a figment of a science-fiction writer's vivid imagination; it is based on the vigorous, spectacular history and continuing achievements of semiconductor technology.

Most monolithic IC manufacturers are confidently forecasting that by 1992, a single silicon-based monolithic IC chip, about the size of a human thumbnail, will contain about 16 million component functions. Obviously, at this rate, by the onset of the next century, chip density capability will be about one hundred million component functions per chip.

When examining the implications of this extrapolation, it is evident that as monolithic IC technology becomes more sophisticated and chip density of a monolithic IC chip is increased to its projected value, these larger and denser chips will contain more functions, more complex circuitry, handle more work and have greater responsibility in electronic systems.

With this technical capability within reach, it is easy to envision that future single IC monolithic chips will be structured to provide systems that will include: an office on a chip, a library on a chip, a factory on a chip, test equipment on a chip and similar "systems on a chip" applications.

TRENDS IN
IC PHOTOLITHOGRAPHIC TECHNIQUES

Using an optical mask-making process described in CHAPTER TWO - SILICON-BASED MONOLITHIC ICs, the practical limit to the thinness of a line in the pattern of a monolithic IC layer is about one micron (40 millionths of an inch). With this technique, productivity and reliability levels are severely reduced as the limit of the thinness of a line is exceeded. Other, more advanced photolithographic techniques are being developed to achieve thinner lines and higher chip density than the first generation VLSI chips.

Some of the emerging photolithographic technologies that will eventually provide economic feasibility to the production of monolithic IC submicron line widths include: scanning projection aligning methods, wafer-stepping systems, "direct-write" electron-beam (E-beam) technology and improved X-ray exposure techniques.

SCANNING PROJECTION ALIGNERS
This technology offers a higher *wafer throughput* (defined as the number of wafers produced in one hour), compared with the wafer-stepping process. The poorer resolution and overlay capability inherent in the scanning projection aligning process, however, restricts this technique to chip geometries having line widths of one micron (one micrometer) or greater. Although this technique does provide for some degree of monolithic IC wafer production efficiency, it is not helpful in increasing monolithic IC chip density.

WAFER-STEPPING SYSTEM
This process is currently providing better than one micron line width capability with a resulting increase in chip density. With the use of "deep-ultraviolet" techniques, automatic alignment and focus, half-micron widths are now being achieved. Despite these obvious advantages, the relatively low wafer throughput of the wafer-stepping technique is considered to be a factor inhibiting general industry acceptance.

DIRECT-WRITE ELECTRON-BEAM TECHNOLOGY
This monolithic IC processing technique is not intended for a mass-produced, batch-process approach, but is generally used to minimize the cost of producing special-purpose, monolithic IC chips. (It is quicker and less expensive to store data for the photographic IC layout patterns in a computer's data-base than

to fabricate photomasks.) These photographic patterns are written directly onto prepared wafers from information that is part of a computer program, with no photomasks used on the wafer. It creates an IC layout pattern by rapidly turning an electron beam ON and OFF as the beam scans a photoresist-coated wafer. The degree of turn-on and turn-off, referred to as *modulation*, is controlled by the computer program.

Although E-beam photolithography is a relatively slow process, it does ease the problems inherent in other systems using multiple photographic overlay patterns on successive levels of a monolithic IC wafer. By sensing the four corners of a layout pattern written on one level of a wafer, and using these corners as guides in writing the next level, etc., it offers excellent resolution and overlay capabilities. E-beam technology is capable of writing lines that are 0.2 to 0.5 microns wide, providing considerably increased chip density ordinarily achieved with more conventional techniques.

Sometimes, E-beam technology is used to create high-resolution mask patterns that are used in the conventional ultraviolet mask-making process.

X-RAY PHOTOLITHOGRAPHIC TECHNOLOGY
This monolithic IC wafer processing technique will eventually become the major method for mass production of monolithic IC wafers consisting of submicron width resolution microchips. Although an X-ray technique was initially developed in 1982, because of technical problems and the high cost of equipment, it has not been a commercial alternative to more conventional photolithographic methods.

By the early 1990s, the existing X-ray photolithographic equipment is expected to be modified to include an improved, lower-cost, readily available X-ray beam source that will be about one hundred times the strength of conventional X-ray systems, providing the following advantages:

• The X-rays will neither diverge nor converge (parallel radiation), permitting the use of conventional optical steppers. As a result, optical masks (less expensive and easier to produce than X-ray masks) can provide higher resolution (thinner lines) in less time and at lower costs.

• High resolution patterns can be created simultaneously, providing improved wafer throughput and higher yields.

The wavelengths of X-rays (about one-thousandth that of ultraviolet waves) offer extremely fine resolution. By using a modified X-ray photolithographic system, achieving 0.2 micron width lines will be possible; it will also be possible to apply high density patterns to 1" x 1" (25mm x 25mm) areas on forty wafers per hour, each being 8 inches in diameter.

IC WAFER MATERIAL TECHNOLOGY

GALLIUM ARSENIDE-ON-SILICON

The relatively recent capability to grow gallium arsenide crystal lattices on a silicon substrate has prompted monolithic IC manufacturers to combine the best features of the two materials on a monolithic IC chip. This new technique promises to provide high-performance ICs at a lower cost by combining the lower processing cost, durability, and abundant supply of silicon with the higher speed, radiation resistance, and optoelectronic features of gallium arsenide material.

With the capability of growing gallium arsenide on a silicon wafer, instead of cutting a wafer from a small GaAs ingot (normally only 3" in diameter), the new material can be made on silicon wafers cut from 4", 5" and 6" diameter ingots. Larger size wafers are easier to handle, reduce production costs and increase yields. GaAs-on-silicon wafers, ready to be processed into completed monolithic ICs, are purer and more uniform than the GaAS material presently being used, further increasing yields. Since production equipment used for silicon technology can be used for GaAs, manufacture of these newer devices require no new major instruments or huge investments.

By integrating GaAs optoelectronic and digital circuitry on the same chip, some monolithic IC manufacturers have demonstrated that laser diodes created on a silicon wafer layered with GaAS and AlGaAs (aluminum gallium arsenide) can be operated for several hours at room temperature, a feat not previously possible. Although the laser diode current in this new approach is presently three times the normal laser diode current in an equivalent GaAs IC, the feasibility of producing a lower-cost laser system on a high quality monolithic IC chip is verified.

Other research efforts have produced GaAs-on-silicon wafers that combine light emitting diodes (LEDs) with advanced VLSI circuitry, resulting in electrically-isolated data links between different parts of a high-performance monolithic IC.

Because of the crystal lattice mismatch between GaAS and silicon, and the different thermal properties of these two materials, several technical problems must first be solved before GaAs-on-silicon products can be brought to commercial realization. Particularly, if laser technology is to be successfully combined with silicon-based monolithic IC technology, additional research efforts must be made to appreciably reduce the technical difficulties still existing.

In addition, and despite any technical problems that may exist, final acceptance of this new wafer technology largely depends on potential opportunities in the market-place. At present, the major areas for these new products are in high-speed, high-frequency (microwave) military and aerospace applications. It is anticipated that commercialization of these high-performance products is about three years away.

SEMICUSTOM IC TECHNOLOGY

With the increase of standard cell libraries used with CAD, development of complete systems on a monolithic IC chip is becoming prevalent. Previously limited to a fully custom design, an ASIC (Application Specific Integrated Circuit) chip can now include analog and digital circuits on a chip, providing lower-cost, higher-performance for "system-on-a-chip" ICs. In combining analog and digital functions in this "mixed-mode" manner, semicustom ASICs offer much higher real estate efficiency and faster circuit design (turnaround).

Larger standard cell libraries offer considerably greater design choice and flexibility by including familiar analog and digital circuits: op amps, timers, counters, logic gates, voltage references, A/D and D/A converters and other compatibile interface circuits. Because distances between the mixed-mode circuits have been appreciably reduced, the advanced ASIC chips are capable of operating at improved performance levels (higher switching speed, higher frequency response, etc.), previously not technically possible in a semicustom IC.

In addition to the choices made feasible by this mixed-mode approach to ASIC design, other performance features are being offered by several monolithic IC manufacturers. These include: low-power capability using CMOS technology, greater choice of a variety of monolithic IC technolgies, programmable components and programmable chip size, all influencing unit costs.

GENERAL COMMENTS ON IC TRENDS

At the present time, semiconductor manufacturers are producing microcomputers on a single chip, needing only a power source and necessary peripherals, i.e.: keyboard, monitor and printer, to complete the entire computer system. Although physically small (almost invisible to the naked eye), these chips are extremely versatile and capable of performing countless tasks at lightning-like speeds. IC applications appear to be limitless.

Even with present day production capabilities and the use of advanced processing techniques for very large scale integration (VLSI) ICs, the complexity of monolithic IC production procedures necessitates extreme care in process control, quality control and the utilization of state-of-the-art production and testing equipment to create acceptable production yields.

Present-day production control and quality control standards that have been considered acceptable until now are being discarded and new techniques, procedures and quality standards established to reach the ideal "zero defect" level that must become the norm for commercially-competitive devices. The vital factors necessary to achieve the successful mass production of relatively low-cost, reliable, super-density monolithic IC chips must include more efficient inspection procedures, more accurate and faster production and test equipment, and perhaps, most important of all, well-trained personnel on all levels.

The concept of "well-trained personnel on all levels" has a powerful implication, impacting on the educational systems and training methods now in existence. To motivate, train and maintain a competent, dedicated work force and to provide a creative environment for the continued development and advancement of this extraordinary technology, dramatic changes in the creation, administration, and implementation of more successful technical educational methods have become important priorities.

 ANSWERS TO REINFORCEMENT EXERCISES - PART I

CHAPTER ONE -
HYBRID INTEGRATED
CIRCUITS

CHAPTER TWO -
SILICON-BASED
MONOLITHIC ICs

CHAPTER THREE -
GALLIUM ARSENIDE-BASED
MONOLITHIC ICs

CHAPTER FOUR -
INTEGRATED CIRCUIT
APPLICATIONS

CHAPTER ONE
HYBRID INTEGRATED CIRCUITS

1. True

2. True

3. True

4. False - Ceramic materials used as the substrate material for hybrid ICs, such as alumina (aluminum oxide) or beryllia, withstand temperatures above the melting point of solder and resist chemical reactions from solvents and other chemicals. Silicon is used as a substrate material for monolithic integrated circuits.

5. True

6. False

7. False - Tantalum oxide has the highest capacitance per unit volume of any dielectric used for capacitors.

8. False - An unprotected tantalum chip will degrade in the presence of moisture; an epoxy-resin coating is used to protect the chip prior to final testing and shipping.

9. False - A silicon diode chip will act as a capacitor if a reverse D.C. voltage (plus voltage to the cathode) is applied across the chip terminals. As the reverse voltage increases, the capacitance of the chip decreases, allowing a silicon chip to be used as a variable capacitor (varactor).

10. False - Chips with three or more bonding pads are often mounted in a package with terminals suitable for mounting to the substrate surface. These packages include: Flatpacks, SOIC, LCC, and Leaded Chip Carriers.

11. False - These advantages are only true for back-bonded semiconductor chips.

12. False - Back-bonded semiconductor chips are more commonly used for hybrid ICs.

13. True

14. True

15. True

16. False - SMD packaging technology is very useful in applications that have low-profile, small-space requirements, enhancing the performance and desirability of hybrid ICs. In many cases, however, choosing SMD assembly methods depends on availability of specific SMD components, system quantity requirements, and cost considerations.

17. False - Hybrid IC technology has evolved into a mature, cost-effective choice for many circuits and systems. The growing availability of passive and semiconductor components, suitable for hybrid IC use, has resulted in reduced production costs, improved circuit and system performance and increased system reliability.

CHAPTER TWO
SILICON-BASED MONOLITHIC ICS

1. True

2. False - Either packaged or unpackaged, a monolithic IC is often called a "chip", or "microchip".

3. True

4. True, however, as monolithic IC technology advances, the area of a chip will increase to some practical level above its present value.

5. False - In those applications where silicon is not suitable, gallium arsenide (GaAs) is receiving serious consideration as substrate material to replace silicon because of recent improvements in processing techniques. GaAs, a compound of gallium and arsenic, offers higher switching speeds and lower power requirements than silicon.

6. True

7. True

8. True

9. False - As a rule of thumb, bipolar technology is capable of switching approximately 10 times faster than CMOS technology for comparable circuit functions. As CMOS technology is improved to increase its switching speed, its characteristics should be compared with a similarly improved bipolar device. Unlike bipolar technology, a CMOS device provides a built-in input capacitor as part of its structure. With CMOS monolithic IC technology, no additional processing steps are required to provide coupling capacitors between switching or amplifying stages and offers higher chip density capability.

10. True - The power dissipation of CMOS circuitry is considerably less than the power normally required for bipolar technology performing equivalent functions.

11. False - As power dissipation for either a bipolar or CMOS IC is increased, switching speed is increased.

12. False - The J-shaped terminals on a Leaded Chip Carrier can be soldered to metallic pads on a PC board and are suitable for soldering to the surface of a PC board.

13. True - Since gull-winged leads soldered to a PC board are more accessible for inspection than J-shaped terminals, packages with gull-winged leads may be preferred when PC board space is not critical.

14. False - A Leadless Chip Carrier (LCC) is not made with gull-winged leads.

15. False - The value specified for a specific IC chip density varies among different monolithic IC manufacturers, particularly, in the LSI and VLSI classifications. Until industry standards are set, designation of the chip density of a monolithic IC chip will depend on the manufacturers' marketing approach. As with any non-standard parameters, variations in their designations will exist until standards are established and achieve industry acceptance.

16. False - Large, successful semiconductor companies are moving in the direction of using automated production equipment (robotics) in all stages of the manufacturing process. Although the initial outlay for this capital equipment is extremely high, the effective use of robotics can be a vital factor in reducing manufacturing costs while producing a high yield that is consistent with the manufacture of good quality, low-priced ICs. Automated production equipment costs can be readily amortized over the huge production quantities that are normally basic to successful semiconductor manufacturing.

17. False - The final price of a monolithic or hybrid IC is determined by such costs as: packaging (including sealing), maintenance and calibration of processing and test equipment, labor, material, sales, marketing, and capital investments. A major consideration in the final price is a competitor's price for an equivalent component.

CHAPTER THREE
GALLIUM ARSENIDE-BASED MONOLITHIC ICs

1. True

2. False - Despite some better performance characteristics than equivalent silicon-based monolithic ICs, if there is no need for improved performance, the more readily available, lower-priced silicon-based ICs are being used instead.

3. True

4. False - Gallium arsenide has been used as a substrate material for discrete microwave diodes and LEDs since the early 1970s.

5. True

6. False - Gallium arsenide-based monolithic ICs are very specifically applicable for telecommunications and satellite systems working at microwave frequencies (above 1 Gigahertz) and fiber optic systems operating at even higher frequencies (the infrared regions).

7. True

8. False - GaAs devices offer much higher radiation hardness than silicon. Typically, radiation hardness values for GaAs are as high as 10^8 rads versus 10^4 rads for silicon.

9. False - Single-crystalline GaAs ingots, from which blank wafers are sliced, are more expensive and more difficult to process because arsenic is toxic and volatile at the high temperatures used to produce these ingots. A 3" diameter GaAs wafer is about $175, compared with a 6" diameter silicon wafer (4 times the area) that typically costs $30.

10. True

11. True

12. True - When in an ON state, the channel resistance of a GaAs switching component is lower than that of a silicon MOSFET. With less resistance, less power (I^2R) is dissipated.

13. False - Each system must be analyzed in terms of the operating temperature of all components in the system. If these components are dissipating more power than the maximum allowed at the operating temperature, to protect the devices, the system design must include some means of removing the generated heat efficiently.

14. True

15. True

16. True

17. True

CHAPTER FOUR
IC APPLICATIONS

1. True - Integrated circuit manufacturers have provided extensive catalogs and data sheets of their "product line" in their attempt to furnish the necessary technical information to the users of these devices on their features, electrical, mechanical, and thermal characteristics.

2. False - Although many IC manufacturers generally lump their non-digital ICs into a "linear" category, a valid general heading for non-digital ICs is "analog". Under "analog", there are "linear" and "non-linear" categories.

3. True - The output signal of a linear amplifier is an amplified version of the input signal and since its output signal is proportionate (a straight-line relationship) to its input signal, it has little or no discernible distortion in its waveshape.

4. True

5. True

6. True

7. False - Digital ICs, performing essentially equivalent functions, generally use less power itself for use in low-power, battery-operated, portable equipment. Although analog circuits have the capability of achieving precise levels of accuracy, a storage and/or transmission medium may inject errors into the system.

8. False - An operational amplifier is used for applications considerably broader than those for which it was originally designed. As a low-cost, extremely stable, monolithic IC is frequently designed into many analog systems as a special and general purpose linear amplifier.

9. False - In an op amp, common-mode voltages (generally electrical noise or other undesirable voltages), when amplified by a differential amplifier, are 180° out of phase with each other at the amplifier's output section. This produces zero common-mode voltage at the differential amplifier output.

10. True

11. True

12. True

13. True - These voltage regulators in monolithic IC form provide high performance capability in both hermetically-sealed and non-hermetic sealed packages. They are available as singles, duals and quads in a variety of output voltage and output current ratings.

14. True

15. False - With an 8-bit D/A or A/D converter, the resolution is 1 out of 256 (2^8), for an accuracy of 0.39%.

16. False - One-time mask design and tooling charges for the photomasks used in a custom monolithic IC design are usually paid by the purchaser, not the custom IC manufacturer, unless other arrangements have been made between the two parties.

17. True

18. True

19. False - Although most ASIC chips being manufactured at the present time are digital in nature, there are also requirements for analog and interface ASICs, but to a lesser degree. In addition, systems designers are combining analog and digital circuitry on the same ASIC chip to provide improved performance characteristics for the system, instead of using two separate ASIC chips, one analog and the other digital.

GLOSSARY
PART I

POPULAR INTEGRATED CIRCUIT TERMS

GLOSSARY OF INTEGRATED CIRCUIT TERMS

ALUMINA - Aluminum oxide pressed in molds and fired at high temperatures to produce a ceramic material used substrate for hybrid IC substrates.

ACTIVE SUBSTRATE - A substrate into which component functions are formed. Silicon and gallium arsenide are active substrates for monolithic ICs.

ANALOG CIRCUIT - A circuit that can process electronic signals (voltages or currents) that are linear in nature, within a specified dynamic range. The terms "Analog" and "Linear" are interchangeable. See LINEAR CIRCUIT.

ANALOG SWITCH - A digitally-controlled switching circuit that allows an analog signal to pass through its low-resistance switching section during its ON state.

ANALOG-TO-DIGITAL (A/D) CONVERTER - A circuit or component that converts an analog signal into a binary digital signal whose binary value is proportional to the numeric value of the analog signal. For example, refer to the table below:

Analog input	Digital output
2 volts	00101 (binary 5)
4 volts	01010 (binary 10)
8 volts	10100 (binary 20)

APPLICATION-SPECIFIC INTEGRATED CIRCUIT (ASIC) - A hybrid or monolithic IC that has been designed for a custom or specific use. See CUSTOM IC.

ARRAY - A group of similar devices in one chip or package, not necessarily connected in a specific pattern, such as: a resistor array, diode array, transistor array, logic or gate array. An array could be either in hybrid IC or monolithic IC form.

ARTWORK - The topographical pattern of a portion of a monolithic IC chip, accurately dimensioned for use in mask making as part of the basic manufacturing process . Generally, it is a greatly enlarged (200 to 500 times) version of the final mask size. Final reduction of the artwork is often accomplished with a step-and-repeat camera.

ASIC - See APPLICATION-SPECIFIC INTEGRATED CIRCUIT and CUSTOM CIRCUIT.

AUTOMATIC TEST EQUIPMENT (ATE) - Computer-controlled test equipment used to sequence and co-ordinate tests on electronic components and monitor, record and analyze the results of these tests.

BACK-BONDED CHIP - In a hybrid IC, the bonded surface of a chip is the side attached (bonded) to the metallized areas of a substrate. The inactive surface of a chip is considered to be its "back".

BALL BOND - A type of thermal-compression bond in which a gold wire is flame-cut to produce a ball-shaped end which is then bonded to a bonding pad on the surface of an IC or a header terminal by pressure and heat. Also called NAIL-HEAD BOND.

BATCH PROCESSING - A technique of processing many wafers simultaneously, to mass produce semiconductor chips. Generally up to 100 wafers are processed at the same time and are considered to be a "production lot" or "batch".

BEAM-LEAD CHIPS - Also called Beam-tape devices. See FACE-BONDED CHIPS.

BIMOS - A monolithic IC that uses both bipolar and MOS technology in the manufacture of the chip to provide the advantages of both technologies on a single chip. See BIPOLAR and MOS.

BINARY - Two-state or two-condition. It defines a numbering system, called "base two", which consists of only two digits, 0 and 1, as contrasted with "base ten", or the decimal system, consisting of ten digits, 0 through 9. In electronics, "binary" and "two-state" are synonymous.

BIPOLAR - An integrated circuit technology that uses bipolar transistors as he switching and/or amplifying devices in the structure of the circuit. Bipolar ICs can switch faster and operate at higher frequencies than MOS or CMOS ICs, but consume more power, take up more chip space use additional components and cost more to manufacture than do MOS technology circuits.

BONDING PAD - The metallized conductive area of a chip to which a gold, silver, or aluminum wire is connected.

BREADBOARD CIRCUIT - A circuit simulation using discrete components or partially integrated components to prove feasibility of a circuit or system.

CAD - See COMPUTER-AIDED DESIGN

CHARGE COUPLED DEVICE (CCD)- A semiconductor storage device in which an electrical charge is moved across the surface of the semiconductor by electrical control signals. Sometimes referred to as a BUCKET BRIGADE device.

CHIP - A section of semiconductor material, (silicon or gallium arsenide), on which a monolithic IC is formed by the use of a series of metallurgical, chemical, and photolithographic processes. Common usage of the term "chip" also refers to a monolithic IC chip enclosed in an IC package. The term "chip" also refers to a single

passive or semiconductor component in unpackaged (chip) form, made for use in hybrid ICs. Also referred to as DIE.

CHIP-AND-WIRE-HYBRID TECHNOLOGY - The use of back-bonded chips, interconnected conventionally to a hybrid substrate.

CHIP DENSITY - The term describing the level of complexity (the number of component functions per chip). The greater the chip density, more component functions on that single chip. (See SSSI, MSI, LSI and VLSI).

CMOS (COMPLEMENTARY METAL-OXIDE SEMICONDUCTOR) - A technology that uses both NMOS and PMOS FETs connected in a complementary switching configuration. When the NMOS FET is switched ON by a positive digital input pulse, the PMOS FET is switched OFF, acting as the high resistance load for the turned ON NMOS FET. When the input pulse is removed, a complementary action takes place - the PMOS FET turns ON and the NMOS FET turns OFF, acting as the high resistance load for the PMOS FET. A CMOS circuit is normally implemented as a monolithic IC and is characterized by its low power dissipation, high chip density, high noise immunity and relatively slow switching speed, when compared to the characteristics of bipolar ICs.

COMPUTER-AIDED DESIGN (CAD) - A computer-based technique to assist in the design of engineering projects, such as: photomasks for monolithic ICs, PC boards, logic arrays, etc. The computer has access to a library of modules, cells or elements of the desired project, which are manipulated on the computer monitor, tested and evaluated to complete the design.

CONFORMAL COATING - The application of a protective layer of material that conforms to the shape of the unit it is protecting.

CUSTOM IC - A non-standard hybrid or monolithic IC designed and produced as a unique product, based on the specifications established by the purchaser of the circuit. See ASIC, FULLY CUSTOM IC, SEMICUSTOM IC AND GATE ARRAY IC.

DERATING FACTOR - All semi-conductors, packaged in discrete or IC form, are rated at a maximum power dissipation at a temperature of 25 C. This is done to compare the power capability of similar devices at a reference temperature. During operation, the case temperature of the device generally increases. To avoid exceeding the maximum power dissipation at the normal operating temperature, a derating factor must be used to determine the decrease in allowable power dissipation from the 25 C value. It is given in watts (or milliwatts) per C increase in case temperature.

DEFENSE CONTRACT ADMINI-STRATION SERVICE (DCAS) - An arm of the Dept. of Defense with the authority to monitor and impose controls on the facilities and procedures of IC manufacturers of DESC-approved ICs.

DEFENSE ELECTRONICS SUPPLY CENTER (DESC) - An arm of the Dept. of Defense responsible for all specifications of electronic components and equipment used in military and aerospace applications and for procurement of same. DESC operates in close cooperation with DCAS.

DEVICE GEOMETRY - This term refers to the size and configuration of the patterns that are used to make up the circuits and interconnections on a monolithic IC. Generally, the narrower line widths, the denser the integrated circuit and the faster are its switching characteristics.

DIE - See CHIP

DIE ATTACH - In hybrid circuits, the operation of permanently mounting chips to a pre-wired substrate. In monolithic circuits, the operation of attaching a completed monolithic chip to an appropriate header (lead frame) prior to the wire bonding operations. Also called DIE BOND.

DIELECTRICALLY-ISOLATED INTEGRATED CIRCUITS (DIIC) - A monolithic semiconductor structure with integrated circuits electrically isolated from each other by a layer of dielectric insulation, usually glass, rather than by the more conventional reverse biased PN junction. This "insulated substrate" structure is far more radiation-resistant than junction insulated units, making DIIC the preferred approach for military and aerospace applications. (Sometimes called DIC).

DIFFUSION - A thermally induced process by which one chemical, in gaseous form, permeates another. In monolithic IC processing of silicon, elements such as boron or phosphorus, called dopants or impurities, are diffused layer by layer into a silicon wafer at elevated temperatures in a series of steps, to form a desired integrated circuit. See MONOLITHIC IC.

DIGITAL-TO-ANALOG (D/A) CONVERTER (DAC) - A circuit or component that converts a digital (step-function) signal to an analog (or linear) signal. The voltage or current of the analog signal is generally proportional to the numeric value of the digital signal. See table below:

Digital input	Analog output
00101 (binary 5)	2 volts
01010 (binary 10)	4 volts
10100 (binary 20)	8 volts

DIGITAL CIRCUIT - A circuit that processes electrical signals having only two states, such as ON/OFF, HIGH/LOW or POSITIVE/NEGATIVE voltage. In electronics, "digital" implies *binary* or a two-state technique of operation.

DIP - See DUAL-IN-LINE PACKAGE

DISTORTION - An unwanted change or addition to a signal or waveform. This definition excludes any extraneous electrical noise that is superimposed on a desired signal.

DOPING - The process of doping a controlled amount of a different element into a crystalline substrate material, such as silicon or gallium arsenide, to produce a layer of specific resistivity and/or polarity-sensitive material. The elements are called dopants or impurities. See DIFFUSION.

DUAL-IN-LINE PACKAGE (DIP) - A package made for enclosing a hybrid IC or a monolithic IC chip. A DIP is characterized by two rows of external metal terminals which can be inserted into an appropriate socket on a PC board. By proper bending of its terminals, it can be attached to the surface of the board. A hermetic DIP is made of Kovar, ceramic and glass materials and is suitable for use in military and aerospace applications. A lower-cost nonhermetic DIP is made of plastic (except for the metal leads) and is intended for use in commercial, industrial and consumer applications.

ELECTRON-BEAM (E-BEAM) PHOTOLITHOGRAPHY - An alternate, and advanced technique of producing photomasks compared to the more conventional optical approach. Using this method, it is possible to eliminate two photographic steps by writing the photographic pattern directly onto the working mask from the information stored in computer memory, offering the capability of producing higher-density ICs. A more advanced E-beam method allows the wafer pattern to be directly

written onto a properly prepared wafer surface, but is not intended for a mass-produced, batch-processed approach.

ENCAPSULATION - The process of coating or embedding a hybrid IC in a mechanically protective material, such as epoxy. The term is sometimes used to describe a package that encloses a hybrid or monolithic IC.

EPITAXIAL LAYER - Semiconductor junctions extend into a silicon device less than one-one thousandth of an inch. Silicon wafers, however, must be several thousandths of an inch thick to avoid excessive breakage in handling, but a thick wafer adversely affects component characteristics. A practical solution is to use a heavily doped thick wafer onto which is grown a thin, precisely doped monocrystalline layer of silicon into which are diffused the semiconductor junctions. This layer is called the epitaxial layer. In conventional IC processing, the thick layer is P-type material and the epitaxial layer is N-type.

EPOXY - A family of thermosetting resins used to package and protect discrete semiconductor devices and hybrid circuits. Epoxies form a chemical bond to many surfaces, including metal, and may be dipped, cast, or molded.

ETCHANT - A chemical capable of removing a solid material. In semiconductor processing, highly selective etchants are used to dissolve the unwanted silicon, silicon dioxide or hardened photoresist material to provide a proper pattern on the surface of the silicon substrate.

FACE-BONDED CHIPS - In a hybrid IC, the bonded surface of a chip is the side soldered to the metallized areas of the substrate. The top of the chip is considered to be its "face". These chips are inverted and attached to the metallized areas of a hybrid substrate by aligning and soldering the chip's bonding pads to the appropriate contacts on the substrate.

FLATPACK - A small slab-shaped, very low profile package, either square or rectangular-shaped, with a row of evenly spaced terminals extending horizontally from opposite sides of the package body. The terminals are welded or soldered to the appropriate bonding pads on the surface of a PC board. This package is generally used for military IC applications.

FLIP CHIPS - See FACE-BONDED CHIPS

FRONT-END PRODUCTION - In the fabrication of a monolithic IC, that part of the cycle commonly referred to as the production process that includes a completed, probed and unscribed monolithic IC wafer.

GALLIUM ARSENIDE (GaAs) - A chemical compound made of gallium and arsenic that is used as the active substrate for GaAs-based monolithic IC chips.

GATE ARRAY - A preprocessed array (or group) of logic elements on a monolithic IC chip, interconnected with one or more diffusion or metallization layers, as required. Also called LOGIC ARRAY.

GATE OXIDE - For a MOS FET gate to be effective in forming a conductive channel beneath it at relatively low input voltage, the gate must be as close to the conducting channel as possible. Therefore, the oxide under the gate material, e.g. silicon oxide, is extremely thin, typically about 50 microns (50 millionths of a meter).

HEADER - The mounting section of a package to which a chip is attached and which includes the external metal terminals of the package.

HEAT SINK - A metal device or structure used to conduct heat away from a component that generates heat.

HERMETIC SEAL - A characteristic of the closing of an electronic component package used for military and aerospace applications. This type of seal protects the chip(s) inside a sealed package from being penetrated by external moisture or other contaminants. A glass-to-metal seal provides the hermeticity between the Kovar leads and the ceramic body of the package.

HIGH-RELIABILITY (HI-REL) - The establishment of a predetermined level of assurance that the hi-rel ICs, and the equipment in which they are assembled, will function at a specified performance level over an estimated length of time, according to their specifications.

HYBRID IC - A combination of several different components in chip or packaged form, mounted on a pre-wired ceramic substrate to produce a circuit or sub-assembly, or several circuits or several sub-assemblies and enclosed in a single package. Despite the complexity of the hybrid circuit, the single package is treated as a single component.

INTERDIGITATED - A structure used to make a multi-layer ceramic capacitor chip for use in a hybrid IC. Alternate layers of ceramic and aluminum are connected to form the chip.

INTERFACE CIRCUIT - A circuit that is neither purely linear nor purely digital in nature, but, by including both types within the same circuit, provides compatibility between linear and digital circuits within a system. It provides the link or interaction between two circuits having different power levels, voltage levels and/or modes of operation. They are generally used between analog and digital ICs. See A/D and D/A CONVERTERS.

KOVAR - An alloy of iron, nickel and cobalt having thermal expansion properties similar to glass, silica, and alumina. Kovar/glass construction is used in IC packages to provide glass-to-metal hermetic sealing.

LARGE-SCALE INTEGRATION (LSI) - A category of the density, or level of complexity, of a monolithic IC chip having between 100 and 1000 component functions per chip. (See CHIP DENSITY).

LEADLESS-INVERTED DEVICES (LIDS) - See FACE-BONDED CHIPS

LCC - See LEADLESS CHIP CARRIER

LIDS - See LEADLESS-INVERTED DEVICES

LEADED CHIP CARRIER - A plastic or hermetic package, suitable for SMD packaging, used for enclosing a high density monolithic IC chip. The terminals, tucked under the package, are bent in the shape of the letter "J", providing more compliance than the gull-winged terminals of the LCC, avoiding the problems of a mismatch in coefficient of expansion between the package terminals and the PC board, to which they are soldered.

LEAD-FRAME - A metal structure holding the external in-line leads of a plastic package. Component chip(s) are soldered onto the structure prior to epoxy encapsulation.

LEADLESS CHIP CARRIER (LCC) - A package having no external leads but capable of being mounted to the surface of a hybrid IC substrate or the surface of a PC board. A hermetically sealed LCC is made of ceramic and Kovar used to enclose a high chip density monolithic IC intended for military and aerospace use. A plastic LCC (PLCC) cannot be hermetically sealed and is intended for commercial, industrial, and consumer applications.

LEADLESS INVERTED CHIP - See FACE-BONDED CHIPS

LINEAR CIRCUIT - A circuit in which a linear or straight-line relationship exists between output and input signals. Ideally, the output signal of a linear amplifier is an undistorted, amplified version of the input signal.

LOGIC - A mathematical approach used in the solution of problems, based on Boolean Algebra in which the operations are defined in terms of logic functions, such as : "AND", "OR" and "NOT".

LOGIC ARRAY - See GATE ARRAY

LONGEVITY - The period of time a component or system will operate as specified, under defined electrical, mechanical, and/or environmental stresses and conditions.

LSI - See LARGE-SCALE INTEGRATION

MASK - An optically flat plate used to reproduce the photographic pattern of a part of a desired circuit onto a semiconductor wafer.

MEDIUM-SCALE INTEGRATION (MSI) - A category of density (level of complexity) of a monolithic IC chip having between 30 and 100 component functions per chip. See CHIP DENSITY. MSI is the lowest chip density category for MOS monolithic technology.

MESA TRANSISTOR - One of the first transistors commercially manufactured. Because of its plateau-shaped geometry, it was called a mesa device.

METALLIZATION LAYER - A film of conductive material, generally gold, selectively deposited on the surface of a completed monolithic IC to permit connecting the elements of a monolithic IC to internal terminals on a package, or to the metallized connecting points on the substrate of a hybrid IC.

METAL SEMICONDUCTOR FET (MESFET) - A semiconductor manufacturing technology used in a

GaAs monolithic IC that incorporates a metal gate electrode in its structure. The gate makes direct contact with the surface of the GaAs substrate to form a junction (*Schottky diode*) - a diode that eliminates the need to use a silicon dioxide insulating film between gate and channel.

MICROCHIP OR MICROCIRCUIT - See CHIP and MONOLITHIC IC.

MICROELECTRONICS - Another term for implementation of the monolithic IC process.

MIL-M-38510 - The general military specification for monolithic integrated circuits used in military and space applications.

MIL-STD-883 - The military standard governing the test methods and procedures for integrated circuits (microelectronics) including both hybrid and monolithic ICs.

MONOLITHIC IC - An integrated circuit (as compared to a hybrid IC) that is manufactured completely on a single chip and contains no thin film, thick film or discrete components. The substrate material of a monolithic IC is either silicon or gallium arsenide, into which passive and/or semiconductor component functions have been created and metallurgically connected to produce a complete circuit or system.

MOS (METAL-OXIDE SEMI-CONDUCTOR) - A semiconductor manufacturing technology used to produce both discrete MOSFET semiconductors and monolithic MOS integrated circuits. MOSFETs are *unipolar* in structure, as compared with *bipolar* transistors, however the term "unipolar" is rarely used. The term "MOS", which implies unipolar is generally used in its place. For example: "MOS devices are slower than bipolar devices." MOS ICs have greater chip density, consume less power and cost less to manufacture,

but switch slower and operate at lower frequencies than do bipolar technology ICs.

MSI - See MEDIUM-SCALE INTEGRATION

MULTIPLE CHIP CIRCUIT - Another name for HYBRID IC.

MULTIPLEXING - A technique used to connect several transmission lines or channels to a common transmission line in a sequenced or timed manner. Conversely, multiplexing is also a technique of connecting a single transmission line to several channels in the same manner. Multichannel analog switches are frequently used for this application.

OPERATIONAL AMPLIFIER (OP AMP) - A versatile and stable, negative feedback amplifier, in either monolithic or hybrid IC form, used extensively in amplifier, control and measurement applications.

NMOS IC - A MOS monolithic IC structure in which N-channel MOSFETs are the active devices.

NOISE - Random, undesirable electrical signals that can cause unwanted and false output signals in a circuit. For example, noise may trigger a random electrical pulse in a digital circuit to produce a binary "1" at the circuit output where a binary "0" should be present.

PASSIVATION - A coating of an electrically inert material, such as silicon dioxide, used to protect ICs from environmental contamination.

PHOTOLITHOGRAPHY - The technology by which a microscopic photographic pattern is transferred from a photomask to a layer of a monolithic IC.

PHOTOMASK - See MASK.

PHOTORESIST - An ultraviolet

sensitive organic coating that is selectively deposited on an active monolithic substrate and hardens when exposed to ultraviolet light.

PLANAR - A transistor geometry that overcomes the production problems inherent in the mesa transistor structure.

PMOS IC - A monolithic MOS IC in which P-channel MOSFETs are used as the active devices.

POLYMERIZATION - One step in the photolithographic process used in the manufacture of a monolithic IC. By exposing photoresist material to ultraviolet light, the photoresist is hardened (fixed) so that it could not be etched away from the surface of the silicon wafer and so maintain the required photographic pattern on the wafer.

PURPLE PLAGUE - The term applied to an intermetallic gold-aluminum compound formed when gold wires are bonded to aluminum bonding pads. As the compound forms, aluminum migrates from the bonding pad, ultimately causing bond failure. The name stems from the purple color associated with the compound.

QUALIFIED MANUFACTURERS LIST (QML) - The list that contains all DESC-approved facilities of hi-rel hybrid IC manufacturers, in accordance with MIL-STD-1772.

QUALIFIED PARTS LIST (QPL)-38510 - The hi-rel monolithic IC parts list that contains all DESC-approved monolithic ICs, in accordance with MIL-M-38510 and the manufacturers of these ICs.

QUALITY - The degree of excellence of a component, circuit, or system that contributes to reliability. See RELIABILITY.

REAL ESTATE - The term referring to an area on a monolithic IC chip or the area on a wafer used in the basic monolithic IC process.

REFLOW SOLDERING - A soldering process used in the manufacture of hybrid ICs and surface mounted device (SMD) packaging techniques. By heating vapors around the assembled hybrid IC or SMD substrate and melting the solder paste that was previously applied to the metallized areas of the ceramic substrate, the component chips, that have been placed on the solder paste are permanently attached to the substrate, after the solder cools and solidifies. The solder is applied more uniformly and under more controlled conditions than by using a wave-soldering technique.

RELIABILITY - The combined **quality** and **longevity** of any component, circuit or system. See QUALITY and LONGEVITY.

RESOLUTION - The smallest measurable change in the variable output of a system. The level of resolution of the system depends on the number of levels that can be accurately determined.

RETICLE - The photographic pattern for a single layer in a monolithic IC chip.

SCRIBING - A scratching of the brittle surface of a silicon or gallium arsenide wafer or alumina substrate to ensure a clean cleavage along the scratch line. Monolithic IC wafers are scribed with a laser beam after wafer probe and then broken to produce integrated circuit chips.

SEMICUSTOM CIRCUIT - A monolithic IC chip designed mostly from precharacterized functional standard logic cells that are stored in a computer's data bank and used to optimize a custom IC circuit design. See CUSTOM IC.

SINGLE-IN-LINE PACKAGE (SIP) -

A hybrid IC package characterized by a single, in-line row of external terminals, or pins, that are inserted into the appropriate socket or holes of a PC board.

SINTERING - A process of cold-pressing ceramic powders and then bonding them under high heat into a desired shape.

SLURRY - A mixture of a ceramic powder and an organic powder. This mixture is used to make MLC chip capacitor for hybrid circuits.

SMALL-SCALE INTEGRATION (SSI) - A category of density (integration level) of a monolithic IC chip having up to 30 component functions per chip. See CHIP DENSITY.

SOLID-STATE - Description of a material that allows electrical conductivity within its solid crystalline mass. This term is used compared to the structure of a vacuum tube that allows current to flow through a vacuum across its metallic elements.

SPUTTERING - A process used in the production of thin-film resistor chips in which material for the film is ejected from the surface of the bulk source of the film when the source is subjected to ion bombardment.

SSI - See SMALL-SCALE INTEGRATION

STANDARD CELL - A building block for a semi-custom circuit. Standard cells do not exist as real entities until the IC is designed. Their parameters are stored in computer data banks (standard cell library) and the circuit elements that these parameters represent are placed into a final circuit layout with the use of computer aided design (CAD) techniques.

SUBSTRATE - In hybrid circuits, the non-conductive pre-wired material (comparable to a printed circuit board)

onto which the component chips and other devices are mounted. Hybrid substrate materials include ceramic, alumina (aluminum oxide), silicon, beryllia and sapphire. In thin-film and thick-film technologies, the non-conductive material onto which resistive films of various metallic content are deposited.

In monolithic ICs, the non-conductive element (silicon) or compound (gallium arsenide) into which dopants are diffused. See ACTIVE SUBSTRATE.

SURFACE MOUNTED DEVICE (SMD) TECHNOLOGY - A packaging technique using both passive and active components either in chip or pellet form, or these components packaged in very small multileaded enclosures. SMD components are structured so that they can placed on the PC board by automatic placement equipment and their terminals attached to either or both surfaces of a PC board by reflow soldering techniques. The resulting configuration is a very small, low profile, completely assembled PC board.

THERMAL-COMPRESSION BOND - The joining of metals by the combined effects of temperature and pressure. Also called THERMO-COMPRESSION BOND. (See BALL BOND and WIRE-BONDING).

THICK-FILM - The technology used to manufacture resistors in chip form for hybrid ICs and/or SMD packaging. Thick-film resistors are produced by using pastes to form resistive elements thicker than .01". They are screen-printed onto a substrate and fired at temperatures of 800° C to 900° C and are less expensive than thin-film, thick-film resistors.

THIN-FILM - A processing technology used to produce high reliability chip resistors for military and space applications in hybrid ICs and surface mounted device packaging techniques. See SPUTTERING and VACUUM EVAPORATION.

TRIMMING - A method for adjusting the value of a thick or thin-film resistor by using either lasers or abrasives.

ULTRASONIC BOND - The joining of two metals achieved by the scrubbing action and energy transfer of a tool vibrating at an ultrasonic frequency. This is one technique used to attach leads to bonding pads on silicon devices. See WIRE BONDING.

VACUUM EVAPORATION - A process in the production of thin-film resistor chips in which the thin-film material is vaporized and the vapor is deposited through openings in a mask onto a substrate to form a thin-film. See THIN-FILM.

VARACTOR - A semiconductor diode used as a voltage-variable capacitor in hybrid ICs, or diffused into part of a monolithic IC structure. A varactor exhibits a change in capacitance with a change in applied voltage.

VERY LARGE-SCALE INTEGRA-TION (VLSI) - A category of the density, or level of complexity, of a monolithic IC chip having 1000 or more component functions per chip. (See CHIP DENSITY).

VIA - The term used to designate the connection from one side of a PC board to another. (From the Spanish for "road" or "conduit".)

WAFER PROBING - Electrical testing of a finished monolithic IC wafer before it is broken into individual chips. A "bed of nails" microprobe contacts the chip bonding pads to test each identical circuit on the wafer and roughly determines the quality of each finished chip. Defective chips are marked with an ink dot to eliminate them from further processing. Only low current DC tests are feasible by wafer probing.

WEDGE BOND - A metal-to-metal lead bond formed with a wedge-shaped tool.

WIRE BONDING - The technique of connecting leads between bonding pads on the surface of a monolithic IC chip and terminals on an IC header, or from the monolithic chip bonding pads to bonding pads on the surface of a hybrid IC substrate.

PART TWO
COMPUTER CONCEPTS

INTRODUCTION TO COMPUTER CONCEPTS

Since the 1950s, a profoundly significant technological development in the industrialized world has been the emergence of the *electronic digital computer*. The modern computer has influenced the operation, productivity, and profitability of companies, not only in practically every industry, but in almost every area of human activity. Computers are used in applications that range from the relatively simple digital wrist-watch to the complex application as a tool in probing the secrets of outer space. With each application suggesting other applications, the uses of computer technology are virtually limitless.

The effect of computers as an aid in education has yet to be completely evaluated, but initial findings have been very impressive. In the entertainment world, computer technology has been used to produce startling and imaginative results in the creation of innovative sounds and graphics. In providing an accurate means of diagnostic testing and new life-saving medical procedures, computers have helped prolong human life. Computerized prostheses and implants are replacing, or by-passing, worn-out, or injured, human parts. As exciting as these applications have been, only the "tip of the iceberg" has been explored and the journey into new technology has just begun.

Some people are intimidated by these machines and others feel that their use will result in an impersonal, automated society that will control rather than benefit humanity. Unfortunately, the anxiety that a new technology may be abused is justified and the avoidance of these abuses requires constant vigilance. Fears have been expressed that the universal use of computers may result in the dehumanization of society. History has shown, however, that the uses and abuses of any new technology depend on human values, aspirations and, eventually, human decisions.

For example, the use of the newly invented telephone was initially considered to be "an invasion of privacy", however, modern society could not function without this significant communications system. After the automobile was invented, many were critical of this new machine with its ensuing noise, air pollution, and the inconvenience of relocating to make room for roads and highways. Despite the drawbacks of automotive technology, in most parts of the world, its use has become an essential element of normal living.

In considering the capabilities of a modern electronic digital computer, merely calling this amazing machine a "computer" does not describe its many uses beyond its ability to compute. Even though its original developers intended it to be a numerical computing device, a modern computer is more than a fast and accurate calculator. It has been more aptly referred to as an "all-purpose machine" capable of accomplishing any function, provided it has the appropriate capability consistent with the applicable set of instructions to control its operation. This description offers a more comprehensive meaning of the word "computer", the term that has become universally accepted through common usage.

The advance in modern computer technology is inexorably tied to the advance in monolithic IC technology and both have become symbiotically related; the two sciences depend on and enhance each other's growth and success. Most, if not all, of a modern computer's electronic circuitry is implemented with monolithic IC (microchip) technology, making the dynamic growth of computers possible. In turn, the remarkable growth of IC technology is mainly due to its use in computer circuitry.

The *microcomputer*, the newest and smallest of the computer "family", has dramatically changed the nature and direction of the computer industry. It is "pound-for-pound" the most powerful and versatile of the computer family and has made possible such electronic "marvels" as: computerized toys, video games, hand-held calculators, digital wrist-watches, household appliances, automatic cameras, low-cost word processing systems, and on-board computers in modern means of transportation.

Microcomputer technology was used in creating the "personal computer", a relatively low-cost, compact machine that has brought the flexibility and power of computers to homes, libraries, schools, hospitals, small businesses, government offices, and any institution that did not require, or could not afford, a larger, more powerful *mainframe* or *minicomputer*.

These are but some of the products based on computer technology that the electronics industry has produced and will continue to produce. It is only through consistent efforts of a responsible and technically-knowledgeable society, dedicated to scientific growth, that even more significant scientific breakthroughs and new technologies can be expected to evolve.

A BRIEF HISTORY OF COMPUTERS

Since the time when great mathematicians first discovered the power in numbers, they have strived for an effective way to avoid the drudgery of manual calculations and the manipulation of long lists of numbers. According to the determination of many historians, it was about 450 B.C. when a wooden or metal frame with beads strung on parallel wires was developed in China to calculate quickly and accurately. The device, called an *abacus*, was capable of adding and subtracting and, in skilled hands, both the abacus and its Japanese version, the *soroban*, were exceptionally fast; they are still being used in many parts of the world as a mechanical means of adding and subtracting a group of numbers.

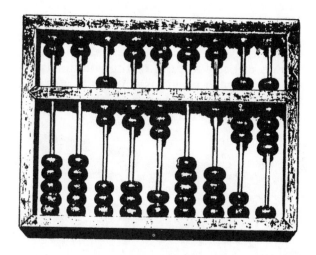

The Abacus

In 1594, a Scottish mathematician, **John Napier**, discovered that the process of multiplying and dividing could be no more complicated than addition and subtraction. He found that all numbers can be expressed in exponential form and, once written in that form, multiplication and division could be done by adding or subtracting exponents. In 1614, after creating a series of complex formulas to express the exponential equivalents of decimal numbers, Napier published his *Tables of Logarithms*, and except for some minor modifications, the same logarithm tables are still being used today.

In an attempt to mechanize the use of logarithms, Napier developed a device called *Napier's bones* - a movable multiplication table consisting of bone strips on which numbers were stamped. Multiplication and division were performed by appropriate movement of the strips. Logarithms and, to some degree, Napier's bones had a profound impact on the science of that time and eventually evolved into the *slide rule*, the device most commonly used for multiplication and division until microprocessor technology made electronic calculators available.

In 1649, **Blaise Pascal**, a French mathematician and physicist, invented the first automatic, mechanical calculator. This widely heralded calculating machine, capable of only addition and subtraction in the decimal system, was called the *Pascaline*.

This machine was based on operating a series of precision gears interconnected by a ratchet mechanism to cause a complete revolution of one gear to produce one-tenth of a revolution in the gear of the next higher order. This action is similar to that of a modern mechanical, decimal counter (automobile odometer) where the value of each column of the counter is increased in multiples of ten. As each previous column of a readout reaches the count of "9", the next count changes that column to "0" and adds an additional digit to the succeeding column.

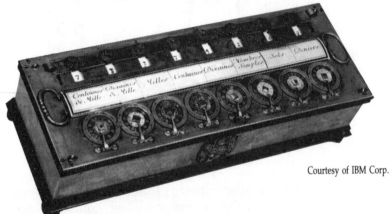

Courtesy of IBM Corp.

Pascal's Calculator - The Pascaline

The gears were activated by eight movable dials rotated in a manner similar to that of a telephone dial, producing a readout in the windows located on top of the box that enclosed the entire mechanism. The operation of most mechanical calculators that have been made since the introduction of the Pascaline is based on this same operating principle.

In 1666, **Sir Samuel Morland**, an English physicist, attempted to improve Pascal's mechanical caculator by including multiplication and division capabilities. He developed a device that attracted the attention of the noted German philosopher and mathematician, **Gottfried Wilhelm Leibniz**.

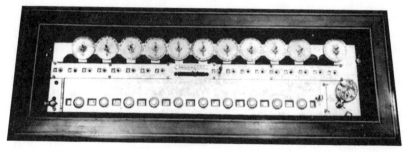

Courtesy of IBM Corp.

The Morland Calculator

In 1673, Leibniz perfected a general-purpose calculator capable of efficiently performing the basic four arithmetic functions - addition, subtraction, multiplication, and division. It was the first mechanical calculator that was successful in meeting the needs of most mathematicians and bookkeepers of the time. Since this first successful calculator was widely accepted, Leibniz attempted to develop more complex calculating devices. It was not until the 19th and 20th centuries, however, that the manufacture of these more advanced machines were made possible because of improved engineering design, new production techniques, and the availability of new materials.

Courtesy of IBM Corp.

The Leibniz Calculator

In 1833, **Charles Babbage**, an English mathematician and inventor, heralded the dawn of the digital computer age with the design of his "Analytical Engine". His idea was to develop a mechanical machine to automatically compute numerical tables which would be faster and more versatile than the calculators built by Pascal and Leibniz.

The Analytical Engine was steam-driven, used binary arithmetic, and contained the mechanical forerunners of some sections of modern digital computers. It had an area (MEMORY UNIT) that used punched cards to store information for future use, a mill (ARITHMETIC UNIT) to perform the basic four arithmetic calculations, and a section (CONTROL UNIT) that controlled the machine's operation using information specified in punched cards. It used metal pins for binary digits and had a series of gears and levers (SYSTEM BUS) to mechanically transmit information throughout the machine. A set of punched cards was used for external programming.

The development of the Analytical Engine caught the interest of **Lady Ada Lovelace**, a brilliant, British mathematician. She joined Babbage's staff and dedicated the last ten years of her life to working with and clarifying the machine's complexities and refining its operation. In 1843, on recognizing that a complex calculation might contain many repetitions of the same instruction, she improved the machine's program and, ultimately, its performance, by preparing only a single set of punch cards for recurring instructions. In so doing, she developed those parts of its final program that are now called "loop" and "subroutine". Despite some question on whether Ada Lovelace is considered to be the first computer programmer, there is no question that her contributions significantly influenced future computer developments.

In 1854, **George Boole**, a relatively unknown, self-taught British mathematician, published a paper, "An Investigation of the Laws of Thought", in which a set of symbols were applied to logical operations (rules of "cause" and "effect"). The set of symbols he developed, resembling algebraic symbols, could be manipulated according to fixed rules and could result in logical conclusions.

Although his theories initially attracted the attention of the mathematicians of his time, Boole's symbolic logic lay unused for many years because practical applications of his theories had not been developed. Even into the very early 1900s, many distinguished mathematicians belittled symbolic logic as a "philosophical curiosity without mathematical significance". Like those of Leibniz, Babbage, and Lovelace, Boole's contributions were finally understood and were used effectively by the scientific community, providing the major foundation for the design of modern computers.

In 1879, **Herman Hollerith**, an American mechanical engineer was recruited into the U.S. Census Bureau after graduation from college at the age of 19. It was there that he learned to appreciate the need for an accurate, fast, statistical tabulating machine for census taking. His idea to develop a machine that used punched-card data to sort and record census information was said to be inspired by observing a train conductor hand-punching specific areas of passenger tickets to permanently identify and record the cost and description of a trip.

Between 1884 and 1889, Hollerith devoted his engineering efforts to design a series of automatic, electromechanical, tabulating machines. He accumulated a total of 31 data processing patents using punched cards as the recording medium and succeeded in revolutionizing census taking procedures.

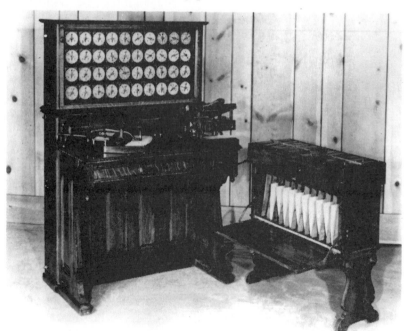

Courtesy of IBM Corp.

An Early Hollerith Tabulating Machine

One of Hollerith's listing and tabulating machines was used for the first time in the U.S. census of 1890. It took about half the time to enter data and ran about ten times faster than other competing systems using other methods. Hollerith's machine confirmed the need for fast and accurate census tabulation and was a major step toward the eventual use of modern computers for similar applications.

In 1896, Hollerith recognized the commercial value of his machines and founded the Tabulating Machine Company. When used again for the 1900 census, an added improvement featured automatic feeding of punched cards rather than manual insertion. Realizing that faster sorting of punched cards was required, Hollerith invented the first electric sorting machine. In 1911, the Tabulating Machine Company merged with the International Time Recording Company, the Dayton Scale Company, and the Bundy Manufacturing Company to form a holding company, the Computing-Tabulating-Recording Company (CTR). In 1924, this company was renamed the International Business Machines (IBM) Corporation. In 1933, IBM reorganized into an operating company, eventually evolving into the international computer giant of today.

In 1937, while doing research for his Master's degree in electrical engineering, **Claude Elwood Shannon**, a graduate student at the Massachusetts Institute of Technology, recognized that Boole's symbolic logic could be applied to solving switching circuit problems. His thesis, "A Symbolic Analysis of Relay and Switching Circuits", was credited for popularizing Boole's work and making Boolean Algebra the preferred mathematical technique for designing logic circuits - the heart of the modern digital computer. It is generally felt that Shannon was responsible for providing the impetus for using binary arithmetic (base 2) in modern computer logic circuitry, rather than using the more familiar decimal system (base 10).

In 1936, at age 24, **Alan B. Turing**, a noted British logician and mathematician, expanded on Ada Lovelace's work with the publication of a paper, "On Computable Numbers", that is considered to be one of the most important contributions to computer science. In his paper, Turing described the "Universal Turing Machine", a fully-specified, theoretical computer that was capable of doing any calculation a human being could do. It had design features that were later incorporated into actual digital computers. In 1938, he accepted a fellowship at King's College in Cambridge, England, where his work was instrumental in the development of modern digital computers.

In 1940, Great Britain, at that time at war with Germany, enlisted a group of distinguished mathematicians, scientists, and electronics experts to develop a digital computer to solve the code of "Enigma", Germany's captured code machine. Turing was mainly responsible for the mathematical efforts behind the design of this machine, considered to be the first working electronic digital computer. Instead of using relatively slow electromechanical relays for its circuitry, about 2000 vacuum tubes provided the required switching and logic action. The newer, higher-speed machine, called the "Colossus", was specifically dedicated to code-cracking and was not modified for other uses. Before the war ended, nine other more advanced computers in the "Colossus" series were designed, resulting in the eventual success in revealing the secrets of the "unbreakable" Enigma code.

Meanwhile, in 1940, just before the United States entered the war, IBM began manufacturing computers in response to the needs of the military for machines that would be able to handle many calculations relatively quickly. The noted American engineer and inventor, **Howard Aiken**, then in the Navy but doing research at Harvard University in Cambridge, Massachusetts, approached IBM, at the request of the U.S. Government, with the idea of combining several of their successful calculating machines into a super-calculator to meet the Navy's technical needs. A group of IBM engineers were assigned to the project, not to combine existing machines, but to assist Aiken in the development of an entirely new machine.

Courtesy of IBM Corp.

The Mark I - The First Generation Modern Digital Computer

In 1944, an automatic, sequence-controlled, electromechanical calculator called "Mark I" was jointly completed by IBM and Harvard University. It was 51 feet long and 8 feet high, containing over 800,000 electrical and mechanical parts and over 500 miles of wire cable. It could handle 23-digit decimal numbers, do addition in three-tenths of a second, multiplication in three seconds, and a 20-decimal place logarithm calculation in 30 seconds. Like Babbage's Analytical Engine, Mark I used binary arithmetic and its structure had the same basic digital computer elements - MEMORY, ARITHMETIC, and CONTROL UNITS. Steam-driven power was replaced by electricity and the metal pins of Babbage's machine were replaced by electromechanical relays. An INPUT/OUTPUT UNIT was added to its basic structure to provide a convenient means of data entry and to return processed data to its output peripherals. With Mark I, the first generation of modern digital computers was born.

In 1946, **John von Neumann**, an American mathematician at the Institute of Advanced Study at Princeton University in New Jersey, introduced the concept of "stored memory" to overcome the cumbersome programming techniques being used at the time. This new idea was to create a group of program instructions that are internally stored in a computer's memory bank. It could then be used by the computer's CONTROL UNIT to provide a wide variety of operations and computations. The instruction repertoire, eventually called the "instruction set", became part of a computer's built-in "software" program. Von Neumann's concept was instrumental in launching the software industry.

Before completion of a new project at IBM that was intended to improve on the Mark I, the first general-purpose, electronic digital computer was co-invented in 1946 at the University of Pennsylvania by **John Eckert, Jr.** *and* **John Mauchly**, two American scientists. It was called the "ENIAC" (Electronic Numerical Integrator And Calculator) and used high-speed vacuum tubes to replace mechanical relays. It heralded the birth of a second generation of modern digital computers that offered more speed and flexibility than all previous electromechanical computers.

By today's standards, ENIAC was a huge, clumsy piece of equipment that weighed more than 30 tons, covered 1,500 square feet of floor space, and needed a great amount of cooling equipment. It contained over 18,000 vacuum tubes, 70,000 resistors, 10,000 capacitors, 6,000 mechanical switches, and 500,000 solder joints. It required 150,000 watts of electric power and featured electronic operation, sub-routines, and a stored program. Although initially designed for military ballistics applications, the ENIAC worked on wind tunnel and weather forecasting problems and the study of cosmic rays. It had the ability to do over 5,000 additions and 1,000 multiplications per second.

To compete with the ENIAC, in 1948, IBM built the "Selective Sequence Electronic Calculator" (SSEC), however, neither machine was in active use for very long.

Courtesy of IBM Corp.

IBM's SSEC

In 1947, Eckert and Mauchly left the University of Pennsylvania to form the Electronic Control Company, later to be known as the Eckert-Mauchly Computer Corporation. Because of insufficient financial support, they were forced to sell their company to the Remington Rand Corporation in 1950. It was there that Ekert and Mauchly completed the design of the UNIVAC (Universal Automatic Computer), specifically produced for the 1950 U.S. census. In 1951, Remington Rand introduced the UNIVAC I as the first, commercial, electronic mainframe computer and in the commercial new world of mainframe computers, "the competitive juices" began to flow in earnest.

To counter competition, IBM, in 1951, introduced the Model 701, a scientific mainframe computer that operated about 25 times faster than its own SSEC. Within a year, IBM introduced other improved versions of its mainframe computer product line to the marketplace, putting them into the leadership position in the computer industry.

Courtesy of IBM Corp.

IBM's Model 701 Scientific Mainframe Computer

During the early 1950s, both the IBM and Remington Rand mainframe computers had the ability to operate many thousands of times faster than Babbage's Analytical Engine. In their basic design concepts, compared with the Babbage machine, they were all amazingly similar.

Although speed and miniaturization have been, and still are, the goal of computer development, most computers of the 1950's required an inordinate amount of electrical power and huge areas of floor space, not just for the computer system itself, but for the cooling equipment required to maintain proper operation of the machine.

Until 1954, there were no commercially-available, lower-power, smaller electronic equivalents for the vacuum tube, the component that used the most power, generated the most heat, and took the most space in a system. In addition, the computers available at that time required constant maintenance, periodic replacement of burnt-out vacuum tubes and initial capital investments that did not encourage the universal use of computers for other than dedicated applications, such as: military use, census tabulation, and similar special-purpose demands of both industry and government.

By 1954, the semiconductor industry had arrived. Fast switching discrete diodes and transistors replaced the vacuum tubes of the first electronic digital computers. A third generation of modern digital computers was created that were smaller, used less power, generated less heat, were more reliable, and were considerably less expensive.

The need for a dependable, relatively low-cost, process control computer led to the development of the second member of the electronic digital computer family - the minicomputer. Although the first minicomputers had limited capability compared with their older counterparts, their design was simpler and production costs lower. The new minicomputers used less power, less space, satisfied the need of many industries for "computerization", and still remained within the budget limitations of many small to medium-sized companies.

In 1960, just three years after it was founded, Digital Equipment Corporation (DEC) introduced the first interactive minicomputer, often referred to as "the machine that changed computing forever". It was the company's first Program Data Processor (PDP-1), a term considered less threatening than "computer". It incorporated the semiconductor devices available at the time and was specifically designed for scientific inquiry and mathematical formulation. The PDP-1 was about the size of three large refrigerators and retailed for the "astonishingly low" price of $120,000. Other smaller, lower-cost minicomputers quickly followed and, in 1965, the first mass-produced minicomputer, the PDP-8, was introduced to the marketplace.

Courtesy of Digital Equipment Corp.
The DEC PDP-1 - The First Minicomputer

As semiconductor technology advanced into the monolithic high-density IC era of the 1970s, other companies emerged to compete with DEC in the extremely active minicomputer field. With lower cost microchips offering greater circuit capability and system reliability, the demand for minicomputers proliferated.

In the early 1970s, Intel Corporation, one of the pioneering companies in high-density microchip technology, led the other monolithic IC manufacturers in developing new and startlingly imaginative approaches to electronic computer chips. **Ted Hoff**, manager of applications research at Intel, conceived the idea of producing a general-purpose monolithic IC chip that could be programmed to function as a calculator. In 1971, Hoff and members of his design team completed two years of intensive work with the introduction of the 4004, the first single-chip processing unit. It was called a *microprocessor*, originally designed for use in hand-held calculators, digital watches, simple tape controllers, and similar products. Although its creators were not immediately aware of the powerful implications of this new IC chip, the microprocessor was the heart of the fourth generation of modern digital computers. Among his associates, Ted Hoff was later aptly referred to as "the father of the microprocessor".

This first microprocessor chip, Intel's 4004, was 1/8" wide by 1/6" long, contained 2300 transistors and performed 60,000 operations in one second - the processing power of the ENIAC, the first electronic computer. The ENIAC, however, filled over 3000 cubic feet of space and contained over 18,000 vacuum tubes. To compete with this new chip, Texas Instrument introduced the TMS 1000, its own widely accepted version of a microprocessor chip.

Microprocessors were destined to become the catalysts for the successful marriage of rapidly advancing monolithic IC technology and modern computer circuitry. The world was on the verge of reaping the benefits evolving from microprocessor technology. The *microcomputer*, and eventually, one of its key applications, the *personal computer*, were about to became a reality.

In 1972, Intel upgraded the 4004 with the introduction of the 8008, a larger microprocessor chip with greater capability and commercial potential. Motorola's 6800 and Texas Instruments' 9980 microprocessor chips were introduced within a year, and by 1974, there were nineteen semiconductor companies producing competitive microprocessor chips and related support chips for use in microcomputers.

By 1973, several equipment manufacturers began to investigate the possibility of designing small computer systems for commercial applications by incorporating available microprocessor chips and new monolithic IC memories. In 1974, the MITS Company was founded by **Ed Roberts**, an electronics engineer. The company produced a small computer in kit form for electronic hobbyists based on Intel's new 8080 microprocessor. The kit was called the ALTAIR, named after a fictional planet on the Star Trek TV series and met with instant acclaim.

In 1976, while working out of a friend's garage during his free time, **Stephan Wozniak** used spare electronic parts to design a computer circuit board crammed with IC chips and other components. To function as a computer, the board required connections to an external power supply, keyboard, video monitor, and cassette player. The entire unenclosed system was later to be called the APPLE I and because of its immediate appeal, Wozniak and his friend, **Steve Jobs**, founded a company called Apple Computer. The need for a small, relatively low-cost computer, ready to plug into an available A.C. voltage source, led, in 1977, to the development of a fully-assembled personal computer, offering a microprocessor, memory, keyboard, power supply and connectors all in the same enclosure. The machine was named the APPLE II, the first successful, commercially available personal computer.

By 1980, there were more than a dozen computer companies in the United States that were producing personal computers and software to satisfy the needs of industry and home users. One of the factors providing a strong impetus to their acceptance was the sudden availability of software programs for video games that had caught the imagination of the public. Primarily, however, the capability and low-cost of these machines met many of the computer needs of small to medium-sized companies.

In 1981, the Osborne Corporation, founded by **Adam Osborne**, a technical author and computer columnist, introduced a portable personal computer, the OSBORNE I. Adam Osborne recognized that a need existed in a mobile industry for a small, portable computer. A machine was designed to have the capability of being a serious tool and still maintain its original intent of being easy to carry. After the demise of the Osborne Corporation, lighter, more powerful, portable, battery-powered personal computers were produced by other computer manufacturers. Referred to as "laptop computers", they had as much capability as larger desktop units.

In August 1981, IBM announced the availability of their first personal computer, officially named the Model 5010, but more commonly called "the IBM PC". It was an immediate success, not only because it was backed by the IBM service and reputation, but because it opened the personal computer industry to many companies involved in the manufacture of both support hardware and software. Within a very short time, IBM was the leader in the manufacture and sales of personal computers.

In 1983, IBM introduced the higher performance Model PC/XT personal computer that had a capability of storing over 10.6 million characters, the equivalent of 54,300 double-spaced, 8½" x 11" typewritten pages. This version was followed shortly by an even higher performance IBM PC/AT that operated faster and was capable of handling and storing larger software programs. The latest IBM personal computers (the Personal System PS/2 series) were introduced in 1987 as updated versions of IBM personal computers.

Many other computer manufacturers, however, were not idly standing by. Apple Computer introduced a series of MACINTOSH personal computers that met with exceptionally wide approval for their excellence in graphics. In a bid for their market share, other computer manufacturers began producing competitive machines, publicizing their own unique features.

The evolution of modern digital computers appears to be without limit. Becoming more apparent to a watching world has been the progress of the closely interdependent digital computer and monolithic IC technology. Computers, considered extraordinary in 1970, were only capable of 60,000 operations per second. In barely twenty years, smaller, faster, more powerful, lower-cost computers that are capable of 100 million instructions per second (MIPS) have been made available to the public.

It is also worth remembering that none of these products could have been produced without the human creativity and dedication that preceded the modern digital computer. Historians have recounted that in 1676, Sir Isaac Newton, considered by many to be one of the greatest intellects that ever lived, wrote in a letter to an associate, "If I have seen further than other men, it is because I stood on the shoulders of giants".

CHAPTER
SEVEN

THE COMPUTER ALPHABET

INTRODUCTION

RULES OF EXPONENTIAL NUMBERS

THE DECIMAL (BASE 10) SYSTEM

THE BINARY (BASE 2) SYSTEM

BINARY WORDS

VARIATIONS OF PURE BINARY

REINFORCEMENT EXERCISES

THE COMPUTER ALPHABET

INTRODUCTION

Binary code, the language of "zeros" and "ones", is referred to as *machine language* and is the only language the circuitry of a digital computer understands. Within a digital computer, electronic circuitry consists of many thousands of digital logic gates that are operated only through the use of binary code.

Sometimes, information actually entered into a computer is not in binary code (machine language); the data is often entered in another language. When not in binary code, however, data must be translated into the appropriate machine language before entering a computer's input circuitry.

To perform basic arithmetic functions (addition, subtraction, multiplication, and division), people have generally been taught to only use the decimal system (base 10), consisting of the numerals 0 to 9. Within a computer's circuitry, however, these basic functions are performed by using binary arithmetic (base 2), consisting of only two numerals: 0 and 1.

Despite its awesome capability, the complex circuitry of a digital computer consists of many simple switches whose timing and sequence of operation are controlled by a set of individual instructions, called a "program" that responds only to binary code. In a digital computer, an electronic switch, or a mechanical relay, is either ON (1) or OFF (0). To explain how the binary system works, *exponential numbers*, called *scientific notation*, are used; all numbers can be expressed in this form. In addition, exponential numbers are particularly significant since they are used to simplify large number notation.

An exponential number consists of a base number (B) and an exponent (e), a small number placed next to the upper right hand corner of the base number. For example, one billion can be written as 1,000,000,000 or, in exponential form, as: 10^9.

The value of an exponent determines the value of an exponential number. In the exponential number 10^2, "10" is the base number (B) and "2" is the exponent (e). The exponent "2" indicates that base number 10 is multiplied by itself (10 x 10). The exponential number 10^2 is equal to 100.

RULES OF EXPONENTIAL NUMBERS

The rules of exponential numbers apply to all numbering systems: the decimal (base 10) system, binary (base 2) system, or in any base system, regardless of the value of the base number. Rules 1 and 2 are considered to be axiomatic; they establish the basis for the truth of all the other rules.

Rule 1.
- Any number multiplied by 0 is equal to 0. Base numbers must be whole numbers (integers) and have a value larger than 0.

Rule 2.
- Any base number, regardless of its value, with its exponent equal to 0 is **always** equal to 1. For example:

$10^0 = 1$ $5^0 = 1$ $3^0 = 1$ $325^0 = 1$ $2^0 = 1$; etc.

Rule 3.
- Any base number having an exponent equal to 1 is **always** equal to the base number. For example:

$10^1 = 10$ $5^1 = 5$ $3^1 = 3$ $325^1 = 325$ $2^1 = 2$, etc.

Rule 4.
- Any base number having an exponent equal to 2 is equal to the base number multiplied by itself one time. This process is also called "squaring" the base number, or, the value of the exponential number is the "square" of the base number.

$10^2 = 10 \times 10 = 100$ $2^2 = 2 \times 2 = 4$, etc.

Rule 5.
- Any base number having an exponent equal to 3 is equal to the base number multiplied by itself 2 times. This multiplication process is also called "cubing" the base number. For example:

$10^3 = 10 \times 10 \times 10 = 1000$ $2^3 = 2 \times 2 \times 2 = 8$, etc.

The rules for exponential numbers can be stated as follows:
An exponential number is equal to its base number, B, multiplied by itself e minus 1 times. Exceptions to this rule are:
- When e is equal to 0 the exponential number is equal to 1.
- When e is equal to 1, the exponential number is equal to B.

$10^3 = 10 \times 10 \times 10 = 1000$ $2^2 = 2 \times 2 = 4$ $2^0 = 1$ $2^1 = 2$

DECIMAL (BASE 10) SYSTEM

The decimal (base 10) system, uses 10 *digits,* numerals 0 to 9. As an example, when "324" is used, the three combined digits (3, 2, and 4) symbolize a number whose value is immediately recognized. This number is spoken as "three hundred and twenty four", although, it is actually being read in terms of its "positional values".

The positional value is derived from the placement of a digit in a multi-digit number, indicating that a different value exists for each digit's place. In positional-value form, decimal "324" would appear as: 300 + 20 + 4, with each digit placed in its proper position to designate its "significant digit" value. In number "324", the "4" is positioned so that it is the "least significant digit", the "2" is the "next significant digit", and the "3" is the "most significant digit". The digit furthest to the right is always the "least significant digit" and the digit furthest to the left is the "most significant digit".

Digit position	Most significant	Next significant	Least significant
Digit symbol	3	2	4

ANALYSIS OF THE BASE 10 SYSTEM
Each digit in any base system can be expressed as $N \times B^e$.
• N is the significant digit of a number
• B is the base number that identifies the numbering system
• e is the exponent value
In number "324", only the most significant digit, "3", will be used as an example of calculating its exponential value.
From the expression $N \times B^e$: N = 3; in base 10, B = 10; and the exponent, e = 2. Therefore, $N \times Be = 3 \times 10^2 = 300$.

The chart in Figure 41 provides a technique for analyzing the base 10 system and can be applied to converting (decoding) a number in any numbering system to its equivalent value in the base 10 system. This chart creates a sequence of column values changing in specific multiples, depending on the base system.

In Figure 41, the base number (B) is equal to 10 and the exponent (e) designates the significant position of each digit of a decimal number. Since any exponential number (B^e) with e = 0 is equal to 1 ($10^0 = 1$), the exponent "0" indicates the least significant position, or the "units" column.

Each succeeding column, moving from right to left, increases in multiples of 10 as each exponent value increases by 1. As shown in the chart, e = 1 denotes the "tens" column and e = 2, the "hundreds" column. Decimal digits "3", "2", and "4" are placed in their appropriate columns. If a decimal number was larger, succeeding column values would increase in multiples of ten.

	Hundreds	Tens	Units
Exponent (e)	e = 2	e = 1	e = 0
Decimal digit (N)	3	2	4
Column value (10^e)	$10^2 = 100$	$10^1 = 10$	$10^0 = 1$
Exponential value ($N \times 10^e$)	$3 \times 10^2 =$ $3 \times 100 =$ 300	$2 \times 10^1 =$ $2 \times 10 =$ 20	$4 \times 10^0 =$ $4 \times 1 =$ 4

300 + 20 + 4 = Decimal number 324

Analysis Chart of Base 10
Figure 41

BINARY (BASE 2) SYSTEM

The binary system operates with only two digits, 0 and 1, and it is called the base 2 system. If number "1011" is chosen as an example, it would probably be read as decimal number "one-thousand and eleven". When it is noted that "1011" is a binary number, it should be read as: "one, zero, one, one", the **only** digits available in this system.

CONVERTING A BINARY NUMBER TO ITS DECIMAL SYSTEM EQUIVALENT
To convert a binary number to its equivalent decimal number, the same conversion technique is used. This time, a conversion chart (Figure 42) is constructed by using base 2 (B = 2), allowing conversion of a binary number to its decimal equivalent.

As before, the exponent "0" (e = 0) designates the position of least significant digit (the "units" column). Moving from right to left, each exponent value increases by 1 and each column value increases by multiples of 2.

A sequence of columns is created; the "twos" column (e = 1), the "fours" column (e = 2), and the "eights" column (e = 3).

The binary digit in each column is multiplied by the column value and then totalled. This sum is the decimal system equivalent of the binary number chosen as the example. Note that even though the column under e = 2 is still the "fours" column, the value of the binary digit is "0". Since any number multiplied by 0 will always equal 0, the base 10 equivalent of the binary digit in the "fours" column is also equal to 0.

	Eights	Fours	Twos	Units
Exponent (e)	e = 3	e = 2	e = 1	e = 0
Column value (2^e)	$2^3 = 8$	$2^2 = 4$	$2^1 = 2$	$2^0 = 1$
Binary digit (N)	1	0	1	1
Exponential value (N x 2^e)	$1 \times 2^3 =$ $1 \times 8 =$ 8	0 0	$1 \times 2^1 =$ $1 \times 2 =$ 2	$1 \times 2^0 =$ $1 \times 1 =$ 1

Binary number 1011 = 8 + 0 + 2 + 1 = Decimal number 11

Conversion Chart - From Binary to Decimal
Figure 42

The columns, reading from right to left, are sequenced in the decimal values, 1, 2, 4, 8, for a 4-digit number in binary. Moving in the opposite direction, the column value sequence is read as 8, 4, 2, 1. In whatever way the column values are sequenced, each column value is multiplied by the appropriate binary digit in that column. The result is a sum that is the decimal system equivalent number of the binary number.

After sufficient practice, conversion from binary to decimal can be accomplished easily, and quickly, without the use of a conversion chart.
The process is as follows:
• Note the value of each digit's position.
• Multiply the "0" or "1" in that position by the position's value and **add** the resulting numbers to obtain the decimal number equivalent.

For example, converting the 4-digit binary number "1 0 1 1 " provides its decimal system equivalent digits: 8, 0, 2, 1. These digits must then be totalled to create the decimal number equivalent of binary number "1 0 1 1" (8 + 0 + 2 + 1 = 11). Just as with decimal numbers, binary numbers can have as many digits as required to construct the final desired value.

CONVERTING A DECIMAL (BASE 10) NUMBER TO ITS BINARY EQUIVALENT

If the 4-digit binary number "1111" is converted to its decimal equivalent, the result will be 8 + 4 + 2 + 1 = 15. That means that the largest 4-digit "pure binary" number can be no greater than decimal number 15, or, a 4-digit pure binary number can be used only for a decimal system equivalent from "0" to "15". For decimal numbers greater than 15, more binary digits are needed. With each binary digit placed to the left of an initial 4-digit binary number, the value of each additional digit increases by a multiple of two.

For example, decimal number 23 is converted into its equivalent binary number 1011 as follows:

Exponential expression	2^4	2^3	2^2	2^1	2^0
Decimal values	16	8	4	2	1
Binary equivalent of "23"	1	0	1	1	1

- The largest column value that will fit into 23 is 16. 1 is placed under the "16" column and the 16 is subtracted from 23 to produce a remainder of 7.

- Since 8 will not go into 7, 0 is placed under the "8" column.

- Since 4 will go into 7, 1 is placed under the "4" column and the 4 is added to the previous 16 for an accumulated value of 20. The remainder is now 3.

- Since 3 will go into 3, 1 is placed under the "2" column and the 2 is added to the previous 20 for a new accumulated value of 22. The remainder is now 1.

- Since 1 will go into 1, 1 is placed under the "1" column and the 1 is added to the previous 22 for a final accumulated value of 23. The binary equivalent is read as " 1 0 1 1 1 ".

Larger decimal numbers can be converted into equivalent, pure binary numbers by placing more decimal numbers at the left end of the sequence until the sum of all these numbers at least equal the desired decimal number. For example, number "47" is converted to its binary equivalent as follows:

- Decimal digit sequence ⟶   32   16   8   4   2   1

- Binary digits ⟶   1   0   1   1   1   1

- Totalling the decimal system digits having binary "1s" under each number, produces ⟶ 32 + 0 + 8 + 4 + 2 + 1 = 47.

- Sequencing the resulting binary digits from left to right creates the binary equivalent of "47", or, 101111 = 47.

Using pure binary to convert large decimal numbers becomes quite awkward and requires a different conversion technique. Variations of pure binary are examined later in this chapter.

BINARY WORDS

Every language consists of a group of letters (alphabet) used to construct the many hundreds of thousands of words used for communication. As with all other languages, a computer's language (machine language) consists of its unique "alphabet" to create its different-sized "words". Unlike English which uses 26 letters for its alphabet, machine language does not use letters, but uses only two numbers, "0" and "1". These numbers are used to construct the binary words of a computer for communication within its structure and its peripheral devices.

Although in the English language, the word "bit" usually means a small portion or fragment of something, in machine language, a "bit" has an entirely different meaning. The computer's "bit" is a contraction of "binary digit", the universally accepted term for either of the two elements of a computer's "alphabet".

No one single letter of the 26 letters in the English language is more significant than another; all its letters are equally important in creating many different-sized words. Similarly, each bit in machine language, either "0" or "1", is equally important in creating many different-sized binary words. It must be understood, however, that a computer's single bit is only one element of a machine language word and does not in any way correspond to a single letter of an alphabet of human language.

In combining a group of bits to construct a binary word, it is this group of bits that represents a desired character, letter, punctuation mark, machine instruction, operation, a piece of information, a specific address in a memory structure, etc. The size of a binary word is usually determined by the specific conversion code used and by the design of the computer structure. The design of the computer's structure is influenced by the required width of the binary words to be used with that particular computer.

Although no standards exist in terms of word width, the computer industry has, to some degree, standardized on calling an 8-bit binary word a "byte". Some manufacturers refer to a 16-bit binary word as a "double-byte" and a 4-bit binary word as a "half-byte. (A half-byte is sometimes called a "nibble").

In a pure binary approach, each different word width inherent in a computer structure affords a specific number of possible combinations of 0s and 1s. For example, a 2-bit system can provide four (2^2) different binary words: 00, 01, 10, and 11. A 3-bit system creates different groups of 0s and 1s, allowing up to eight (2^3) words: 000, 001, 010, 011, 100, 101, 110, 111. The chart shown in Figure 43 illustrates the possible number of combinations of different words for different computer sizes.

SYSTEM SIZE OR WORD WIDTH	POSSIBLE COMBINATIONS
4-bit*	16
5-bit	32
6-bit	64
7-bit	128
8-bit*	256
9-bit	512
10-bit	1,024
11-bit	2,048
12-bit*	4,096
13-bit	8,192
14-bit	16,384
15-bit	32,768
16-bit*	65,536
26-bit	67,108,864
32-bit*	4,294,967,296

* Indicates popular computer sizes

Figure 43

Note that the width of a word is designated by the system size. The larger the system size, the greater number of bits per word available to designate machine operations, instructions, keyboard characters, and memory addresses, etc. Although this relationship is generally true, the structure of the computer might influence the size of addressable memory in the system and the specific capability of the computer.

For several years, the scope of the different members of the computer family were easily identified. Microcomputers ranged from a 4-bit to a 16-bit word width. Mincomputers started from a word width of 12-bits to larger 32-bit machines. Mainframes began where the minicomputers left off (32-bit word width) and were generally no larger than a 64-bit machine. A 40-bit computer system has a capability of over 1 trillion (a thousand billion) different binary word combinations (still within the range of small mainframes). Extremely large mainframe computers, called *supercomputers*, had 128-bit word widths.

Computer sizes are no longer as clearly delineated. Boundary lines are very blurred, with microcomputers available with 32-bit words and the capability of a large minicomputer or small mainframe; microcomputers using larger words are on the horizon.

VARIATIONS OF PURE BINARY

Variations of the pure binary converting technique are used to increase the capabilities of possible combinations available in 4-bit and 8-bit computer systems.

BINARY-CODED DECIMAL (BCD) CODE

The *Binary-Coded Decimal Code* (BCD Code) is used in 4-bit system (4-bit word width) computer systems that require the handling of large numbers, more than the 16 possible combinations that a pure binary 4-bit system normally provides.

When a computer is designed to accommodate the BCD code, each digit of a decimal number is converted into a 4-bit binary number, providing the system with a capability of handling any possible combinations.

A 4-bit word width has a capability of handling sixteen (2^4) different words, even though a maximum of ten different 4-bit words are needed to accommodate the ten different decimal digits (0 to 9).

The BCD code uses a different 4-bit binary number for each different value digit of a decimal number. The process of converting decimal number 974 into its equivalent BCD binary number of 1001 0111 0100 is illustrated below:

- Decimal number "9" is converted into its equivalent 4-bit pure binary number of "1001"

- Decimal number "7" is converted into its equivalent 4-bit pure binary number of "0111".

- Decimal number "4" is converted into its equivalent 4-bit pure binary number of "0100".

Each 4-bit binary word would be moved within the computer (and between the computer and its peripherals), in its proper order, to maintain the correct sequence of the decimal number.

EXTENDED ASCII
Extended ASCII is the more commonly-used 8-bit version of the original 7-bit ASCII (American Standard Code for Information Interchange) keyboard code. It is a pure binary code that provides 256 different word combinations to include all 26 letters of the alphabet (upper and lower case), all ten decimal digits (0 to 9), punctuation marks, and standard graphic symbols and control codes. The original 7-bit ASCII provided only 128 different code combinations.

OTHER COMPUTER CODES
- Extended BCD Interchange Code (EBCDIC) - This code performs the same basic conversion process as the BCD code, except that it is used for an 8-bit computer system. Each character in a non-numeric language is changed into an equivalent 8-bit binary designation.

- Octal system (base 8) - this code has 8 digits (0 to 7). Each positional value changes in multiples of eight, creating the sequence: 1 (8^0), 8 (8^1), 64 (8^2), etc.

- Hexadecimal (Hex) Code - a 16-digit code, incorporating the ten decimal digits (0 to 9) and the six letters (A to F) to encode data.

REINFORCEMENT EXERCISES

Answer TRUE or FALSE to each of the following statements:

1. The electronic circuitry in a digital computer system is operated through the use of binary code, the language of "zeros" and "ones". This is commonly called machine language.

2. When an even number in the decimal system is converted into its equivalent binary number, the least significant digit in the binary number is "1".

3. Unlike the decimal system whose positional values are sequenced in multiples of ten, the positional values in the binary system is sequenced in multiples of two. In both systems, the first position on the right is the least significant digit (1).

4. The decimal number "1011" is read as number "one-thousand and eleven". In the binary system that same group of digits should be read as "one, zero, one, one".

5. In converting a binary number into its decimal equivalent, the resulting decimal number is read from left to right as the sequence of the resulting decimal digits in each column.

6. The decimal equivalent of the pure binary number "11011" is number "27".

7. In converting from a decimal number into its pure binary equivalent, the number of digits in the equivalent binary number will depend on the size of the decimal number - the larger the decimal number, the more binary digits.

8. Converting the decimal number 27 into pure binary creates the binary number 11011.

9. To convert all 26 upper case letters of the English alphabet, 15 special characters, and all 10 decimal digits into a pure binary code, only a 5-bit binary system (using a 5-bit binary word width) is required.

10. A 4-bit binary word is referred to as a "byte", a 2-bit binary word is called a half-byte, and an 8-bit binary word, the largest-sized binary word used in a computer, is called a double-byte.

11. Doubling the word width of a computer system from an 8-bit word width to a 16-bit word width only doubles the number of possible combinations of binary words in the system.

12. The BCD coded number "1001 0011 0111" is the equivalent of the decimal number "937".

13. Converting the decimal number "619" into the equivalent BCD coded binary number, produces "0110 0001 1001".

14. All information entered into a computer's input circuit, except for the information entered through a keyboard, is converted (encoded) into machine language by using the American Standard Code for Information Interchange (ASCII). Each keyboard manufacturer uses a coding technique other than ASCII for this purpose.

15. Hexadecimal (Hex) Code is a 16-digit code that uses the ten decimal system digits (0 to 9) and the six letters (A to F) to encode data.

Answers to these reinforcement exerises are on page 277.

CHAPTER
EIGHT

DIGITAL LOGIC

INTRODUCTION

LOGIC GATES

FLIP-FLOP CIRCUITS

BINARY COUNTERS

SHIFT REGISTERS

DIGITAL LOGIC FAMILIES

REINFORCEMENT EXERCISES

DIGITAL LOGIC

INTRODUCTION

Digital logic is a form of mathematics based on a two-state (binary) approach to solving a related series of intricate conditions. In electronic computers, logic gates and similar switching circuits are used in a systematic plan to perform decision-making functions described in truth tables. Each gate interacts with the system by influencing the action of other gates and associated circuitry in the entire system.

Although the science of logic was initially introduced in the 3rd Century B.C. by the Greek philosopher, Aristotle, its application to mathematics was described in detail in 1854 by the English mathematician, George Boole. The rules of logic, sometimes called "rational thought " or "cause and effect", evolved into Boolean algebra, the symbolic, mathematical language used in the design of computer circuitry.

The theorems of Boolean algebra can be applied to any logic that is based on the assumption that only two possibilities exist as far as any statement is concerned: a statement can either be "true" or "false", but never partly true or partly false. If a given statement is true, the symbol "1" is used; if a statement is false, it is designated by the symbol "0".

In electronic digital circuits, "0" and "1" are represented by two different voltage levels and the particular "logic convention" used must be specified. "Positive logic" (generally used in modern computer circuitry) is described as follows:
• Zero voltage represents binary "0", called the "low state" or "space" and is graphically shown as a base line "_____".

• A positive signal represents binary "1" and is called the "high state" or "mark". It is shown as a digital voltage pulse, " ", whose magnitude is equal to the power supply voltage. The power supply voltage (typically 5, 6, or 12 volts) is determined by the requirements of the system.

In "negative logic", "1" denotes the most negative voltage level and "0" designates the least negative voltage level.

LOGIC GATES

Logic gates (elements) are the basic building blocks of computer circuitry, interconnected to perform a system's function. A logic diagram contains symbols that represent the logic function of a gate or a group of gates, but does not indicate the specific components that make up the logic gate. The symbols for the most common logic gates are shown in Figure 44.

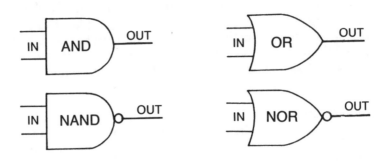

Basic Logic Gate Symbols
Figure 44

Boolean Algebra is based on the use of logic elements, commonly called: AND, OR, NAND (NOT AND) and NOR (NOT OR) logic gates and variations of these basic logic gates. All digital logic switching circuits use a two-state (binary) approach, either completely ON or completely OFF.

THE AND GATE
An AND gate is defined as follows: **If, and only if, all inputs are "True" (1), then the output is "True" (1).**

To present the function of any gate in an easily scanned tabular form, a *truth table* is constructed to indicate the conditions of the output under all possible conditions of input. See Figure 45. Note that the only condition in which the output is at logic "1" is when all inputs are at logic "1". If all, or any of the inputs is at "0", the output will be at "0".

The equivalent electrical circuit of the 2-input AND gate consists of two single-pole, single-throw (SPST) switches in series. When both switches are closed (1) simultaneously, the circuit is closed and the output is equal to the supply voltage, VCC, (1). If both, or either of the switches is open (0), the circuit is open and the output is at "0".

This 2-input AND gate can serve as a control element with one input acting to regulate the flow of data to the output. It provides a voltage pulse (logic 1) to a succeeding gate when all its input terminals are set to "1".

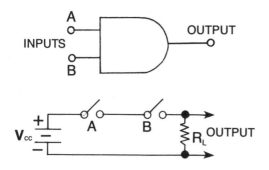

A	B	OUTPUT
0	0	0
1	0	0
0	1	0
1	1	1

Truth Table (above)

A 2-input AND Gate
Figure 45

THE OR GATE
An OR gate is defined as follows: **If one or more inputs are "True" (1), the output is "True" (1).** See Figure 46. The equivalent circuit of the 2-input OR gate has two SPST switches in parallel; the switches are in series with the load. If all the switches are open (0), the circuit is open and the output is at 0. When any (or all) of the switches are closed (1), the circuit is closed with the output voltage equal to the supply voltage and the output is at "1".

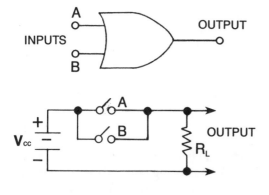

A	B	OUTPUT
0	0	0
1	0	1
0	1	1
1	1	1

Truth Table (above)

A 2-input OR Gate
Figure 46

THE NAND (NOT AND) GATE

The 2-input NAND gate shown in Figure 47 is the opposite (complement) of the 2-input AND gate of Figure 45 and is defined as follows: **If, and only if, all inputs are "True" (1), then the output is "False" (0).** The only condition in which the output is at logic 1 is when all inputs are at 0. If all, or any of the inputs are at 1, the output will be at 0. Note that the graphic symbol for a NAND gate is similar to the AND gate, except that the NAND gate has a dot at its output. This denotes that a gate with a dot at its output has the opposite, or complementary logic of the same gate without the dot, or "the dot is the NOT".

The equivalent circuit of the 2-input NAND gate in Figure 47 consists of an electrical circuit having two SPST switches in series, across (in parallel with) the load R_L. The supply voltage is protected by the series resistor R_s when all the SPST switches are closed (a 1 at each switch) simultaneously. In this condition, the output voltage is equal to zero and the output will be at "0."

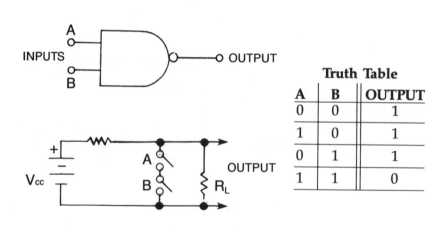

Truth Table

A	B	OUTPUT
0	0	1
1	0	1
0	1	1
1	1	0

2-input NAND Gate
Figure 47

THE NOR (NOT OR) GATE

The 2-input NOR gate shown in Figure 48 has a dot (NOT) at the output of its graphic symbol, denoting that this gate is the complement of the 2-input OR gate of Figure 46. A NOR gate is defined as follows: **If one or more inputs are "True" (1) the output is "False" (0).** Note that the truth table of the 2-input NOR gate is opposite to the truth table of the 2-input OR gate.

The equivalent circuit of the 2-input NOR gate consists of two SPST switches in parallel with the load. A series resistor is used to protect the voltage supply when either or both of the switches are closed (1) to produce zero voltage (logic 0) at the output.

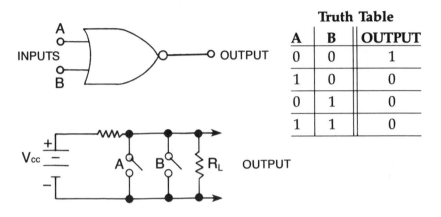

Truth Table

A	B	OUTPUT
0	0	1
1	0	0
0	1	0
1	1	0

A 2-input NOR Gate
Figure 48

In connecting logic gates to one another (output terminals to input terminals) to create a proper order of circuit logic, any input terminal of a logic gate has a specified capability of being connected to a maximum number of other logic gate output terminals. This specification is called *fan-in*. See Figure 49. If the maximum fan-in of a particular logic gate is exceeded, additional capacitive effects at the input terminal may act to delay the progress of a digital signal through the logic gate. To avoid any undesired delay, the design of the logic circuit may require some modification.

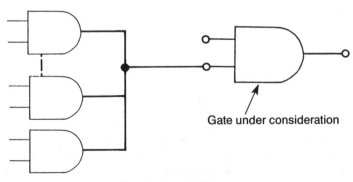

Gate under consideration

Fan-in Capability
Figure 49

THE <u>DRIVER</u> (NON-INVERTING)

The output of a logic gate has the capability of being connected to (drive) a limited number of other logic gates. This specification is called **fan-out** and indicates the power capability of the source gate. See Figure 50.

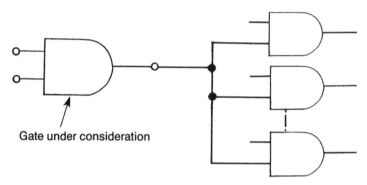

Fan-out Capability
Figure 50

The design of a logic circuit may require a logic gate to drive more input terminals of other logic gates that are beyond their specified fan-out capability. A power amplifier inserted between the output of the logic gate under consideration and the required input terminals will often be used to increase fan-out capability without changing the sense of the logic. This type of power amplifier, called a *driver*, or, more specifically, a *non-inverting driver*, is shown in Figure 51.

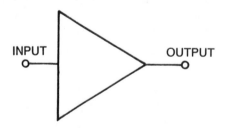

Truth Table	
INPUT	OUTPUT
0	0
1	1

Non-inverting Driver
Figure 51

Its truth table indicates that if a logic 1 is at the input, the same logic 1 will be at the output, providing power amplification for increased fan-out with no logic inversion. Non-inverting drivers are available with six individual drivers on a monolithic IC chip and are called *hex drivers*.

THE <u>NOT</u> GATE (INVERTER)

A NOT gate is defined as follows: **If the input is "True" (1), the output is "False" (0), and if the input is "False" (0), the output is "True" (1).** See Figure 52. Note that the NOT gate has only one input and one output and acts to invert or complement the input logic. Six individual inverters on one monolithic IC chip (each isolated from the other) is called a *hex inverter.*

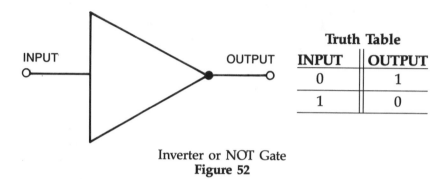

Truth Table

INPUT	OUTPUT
0	1
1	0

Inverter or NOT Gate
Figure 52

With the addition of a NOT gate, any logic gate can be changed into its complement function, for example:

- An AND gate and a NOT gate can create a NAND gate
- An NAND gate and a NOT gate can create an AND gate
- An OR gate and a NOT gate can create a NOR gate
- A NOR gate and a NOT gate can create an OR gate

THE <u>EXCLUSIVE-OR</u> GATE

This gate is defined as follows: **If one, and <u>only</u> one of the inputs is "True" (1), the output is "True (1).** See Figure 53.

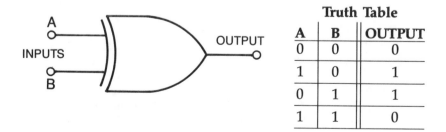

Truth Table

A	B	OUTPUT
0	0	0
1	0	1
0	1	1
1	1	0

A 2-input EXCLUSIVE-OR Gate
Figure 53

The EXCLUSIVE-OR gate is like a standard OR gate, except that its output is "0" if both its inputs are "1". Its truth table (Figure 53) states that its output is "1" only when the two inputs are different (one "0", the other "1"). When the inputs are the same, the output is "0".

The principle of the EXCLUSIVE-OR gate is used when two single-pole, double-throw (SPDT) switches are used at both ends of a stairway to allow the light at the stairway to be turned ON or OFF at either end. See Figure 54. This common electrical circuit is the equivalent of a 2-input EXCLUSIVE-OR gate.

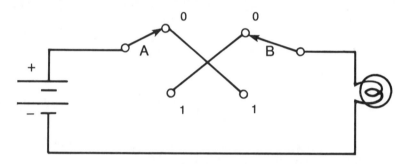

Equivalent Circuit of a 2-input Exclusive-OR gate
Figure 54

THE <u>INHIBIT</u> GATE

The INHIBIT gate is an OR gate with an "inhibiting" input. **The output is in its "1" state if, and only if, the inhibit input is at "0" and one or more of the normal OR inputs are at "1".** A 2-input INHIBIT gate is shown in Figure 55, with "B" designated as the inhibit terminal.

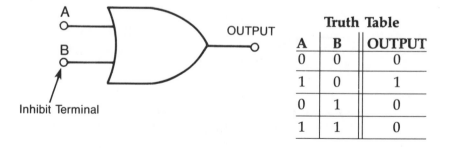

Truth Table		
A	**B**	**OUTPUT**
0	0	0
1	0	1
0	1	0
1	1	0

The 2-input INHIBIT Gate
Figure 55

The INHIBIT gate is useful for controlling the flow of signals applied to input "A".

• With an inhibiting signal (1) present at "B", the output is always OFF (0).

• With an inhibiting signal removed ("0" at "B"), the output is ON (1) when a signal (1) exists at the other input.

FLIP-FLOP (F/F) CIRCUITS

The operation of the logic gates discussed up to to this point contain no memory function, therefore, the state of the output of each of these gates, depends only on the logic state of the coexisting signals at their input terminals. These logic gates are sometimes referred to as *combinatorial logic elements*.

There are, however, other logic circuits whose operation is influenced by their previous condition or, by the sequential application of clock pulses that set the timing of all computers. These logic elements are referred to as *sequential logic elements*, the most significant of which are the *flip-flop circuits*, also called *bistable multivibrators*.

A flip-flop circuit is a logic circuit whose output state is stable in either a "0" or "1" condition (bistable). It remains in that state until a specific input signal changes its output state. It consists of combinations of some of the basic logic elements (AND, OR, etc.) interconnected to provide a desired operation. Because of its ability to store either a "0" or "1", a flip-flop is a basic element in a logic circuit structure.

Because the circuit action is such that an initial input signal will cause one of the outputs of the circuit to "flip" from a "0" to a "1" state, and a second input signal will cause that same output to "flop" back to its original state, the circuit is more commonly referred to as a "flip-flop".

A flip-flop circuit may have one, two, or three inputs and two complementary outputs (one output is "1" and the other "0" at the same time). The letter "Q" is used to designate one output terminal, with the second complementary output terminal designated with a line (bar) above the letter "Q" (called Q-bar). There are several different types of flip-flops, each having its own features and applications.

THE RS (RESET/SET) FLIP-FLOP

This flip-flop circuit has two inputs (SET and RESET) and two outputs (Q and Q-bar). See Figure 56.

- With a pulse (1) applied to the SET input, the output at Q flips to logic 1 (Q——▶"1"), and the output at Q-bar flips to 0 (Q-bar ——▶"0").

- The logic state at output Q (and at output Q-bar) will remain in its SET condition (regardless of further input pulses applied to the SET input) until a pulse (1) is applied to the RESET input.

- At this point, the outputs at Q and Q-bar will flop back to their initial logic states: Q——▶"0" and Q-bar——▶"1".

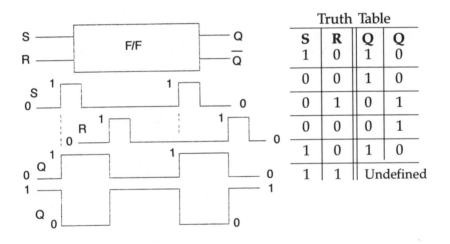

Truth Table

S	R	Q	Q̄
1	0	1	0
0	0	1	0
0	1	0	1
0	0	0	1
1	0	1	0
1	1	Undefined	

The RS Flip-flop
Figure 56

Since the RS flip-flop "remembers" which input was the last to receive a pulse, it can be used to store a specific bit (either a "0" or "1"). If, however, a "1" is applied simultaneously to both the SET and RESET inputs, the output at "Q" is undefined or ambiguous; its logic state is unpredictable (either "0" or "1"). The truth table shown in Figure 56 indicates this undefined output state, a condition that is unacceptable for proper operation of a logic circuit. Obviously, an RS flip-flop cannot be in a SET and RESET state at the same time.

THE JK FLIP-FLOP
This circuit is one of the most widely-used of the flip-flop family
in logic circuitry. Other than having a defined state, it operates
in the same manner as the RS flip-flop, with "J" being used as
the SET input and "K" as the RESET input. See Figure 57.

• When a pulse ("1") is applied to "J", the output at Q flips to "1"
  (Q ——➤ "1") and simultaneously, the output at Q-bar flips to
  "0" (Q-bar ——➤ "0").

• The logic state at output Q (and at output Q-bar) will remain
  in this condition (regardless of further input pulses applied to
  "J") until a pulse (1) is applied to "K".

• At this point, the outputs at Q and Q-bar will flop back to their
  initial logic states: Q ——➤ "0" and Q-bar ——➤ "1".

• When a "1" is applied to both "J" and "K" inputs at the same
  time, the output states at Q and Q-bar will reverse from their
  existing logic conditions, without any ambiguity.

This circuit was designated as a "JK" flip-flop by its inventor, Jack
Kilby, the Texas Instrument engineer who developed the original
concept of integrated circuits.

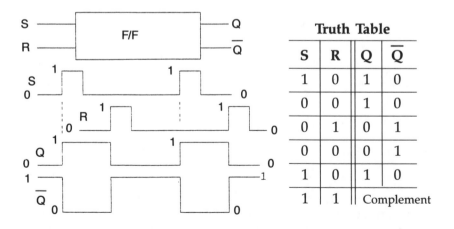

Truth Table			
S	R	Q	$\overline{Q}$
1	0	1	0
0	0	1	0
0	1	0	1
0	0	0	1
1	0	1	0
1	1	Complement	

The JK Flip-flop
Figure 57

THE D (DATA) FLIP-FLOP (LATCH)

A D flip-flop (Figure 58), also called a *latch*, operates on the rising (leading) edge of the clock pulses (generated within the computer at a specific frequency). It operates as follows:

• When a clock pulse (1) arrives at the CLOCK input and "1" is present at the DATA input, the output at Q is set, or remains at "1" and the output at Q-bar is set at "0". The Q output remains at "1" until the next clock pulse arrives.

• When a clock pulse (1) arrives at the CLOCK input and "0" is present at the DATA input, the output at Q is set, or remains at "0" and the output at Q-bar is set at "1". The Q output remains "0" until the next clock pulse arrives.

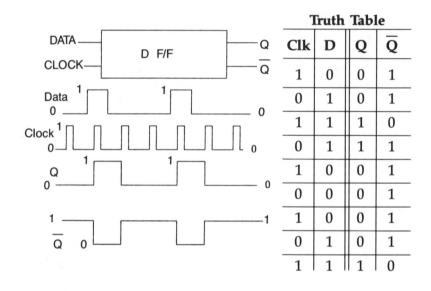

Truth Table

Clk	D	Q	$\overline{Q}$
1	0	0	1
0	1	0	1
1	1	1	0
0	1	1	1
1	0	0	1
0	0	0	1
1	0	0	1
0	1	0	1
1	1	1	0

The D Flip-flop
Figure 58

T (TOGGLE) FLIP-FLOP

The T flip-flop has two outputs but only one input, operating in a way similar to a simple SPST "push-on, push-off" switch. Assuming that the output at Q is "0", a pulse (1) is applied to the input to change the Q output to "1"; the output at Q-bar flips to "0". The output at Q will retain its logic "1" state until a second pulse (1) is applied to the input. At that point, the output at Q will change to "0". See Figure 59.

As with a mechanical SPST "push-on,push-off" switch, a disadvantage of a T flip-flop is that its output logic state is known only after an input pulse is applied, except if the previous state of the T flip-flop is known. In some systems, a designation of a "1" output is used (a visual or an aural signal) to provide output logic state information to an operator.

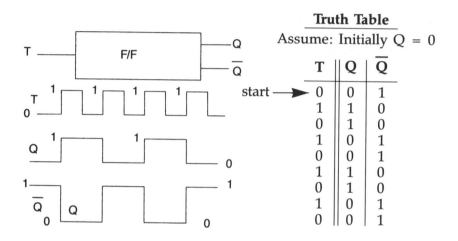

Truth Table

Assume: Initially Q = 0

T	Q	$\overline{Q}$
0	0	1
1	1	0
0	1	0
1	0	1
0	0	1
1	1	0
0	1	0
1	0	1
0	0	1

The T (Toggle) Flip-flop
Figure 59

The T flip-flop, or several interconnected T flip-flops, may also be used to provide several useful circuits that could be used as part of a computer logic circuit, as follows:

• Since two "1" pulses at the input are required for each "1" at the Q output (see the graphic presentation of the sequence of pulses in Figure 59), the T flip-flop acts as a "divide by two" circuit and is referred to as a *binary scaler.*

• A circuit that can count by twos is called a *binary counter.* Depending on the number of bits required, a group of properly connected T flip-flops can provide the necessary circuitry to create a multi-bit binary counter that can be operated as an "up counter", a "down counter", or as an "up/down counter" (set to function as an up counter or a down counter, as desired).

BINARY COUNTERS

BINARY UP COUNTER (FORWARD COUNTER)

By connecting three T flip-flops in series, a 3-bit binary counter is created. The counter circuit shown in Figure 60 is an *up-counter* or *forward counter*, since the output at Q of each T flip-flop is connected to the succeeding T flip-flop input. The "circle" at the input of each T flip-flop indicates that the flip-flop will toggle (change its output logic state) at the completion of the negative-going edge of the input pulse. If it is assumed that the flip-flop outputs at A, B, and C are initially set at "0", the up counter operates as follows:

- At the end of the first input pulse (1), the output at A (the input to F/F 2) changes to "1". The counter now reads "001".

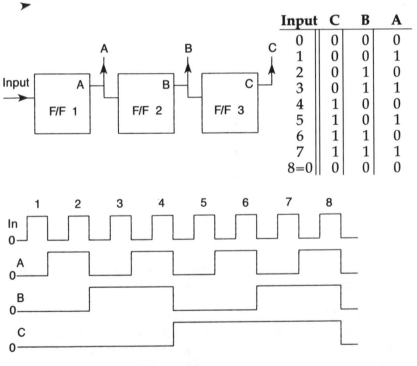

Input	C	B	A
0	0	0	0
1	0	0	1
2	0	1	0
3	0	1	1
4	1	0	0
5	1	0	1
6	1	1	0
7	1	1	1
8=0	0	0	0

A 3-bit Binary Up Counter
Figure 60

- At the end of the second input pulse, the output at A (the input to F/F 2) goes to "0", the output at B (the input to F/F 3) changes to "1", the output at C is still at "0". The counter now reads "010".

- At the end of the third input pulse, the output at A (the input to F/F 2) goes to "1", the output at B (the input to F/F 3) stays at "1", the output at C is still at "0". The counter now reads "011".

- At the end of the fourth input pulse, the output at A (the input to F/F 2) goes to "0", the output at B (the input to F/F 3) changes to "0", the output at C changes to "1". The counter now reads "100".

- The counting continues in the same manner through the end of the seventh input pulse and the counter now reads "111", the binary equivalent for decimal number 7.

- At the end of the eighth input pulse, the counter is automatically reset to read "000", and the process repeats.

If larger binary up counters are used, a negative-going edge is "carried-over" to the input of a succeeding T flip-flop to have the counter read "1000", etc. The input pulses "ripple through" the binary chain in a way that any binary flip-flop output cannot change its logic state until all the preceding flip-flops have done so. The truth table shown in Figure 60 illustrates the sequence of a counter display.

BINARY DOWN-COUNTER (REVERSE COUNTER)
In the binary up counter shown above, only the Q output of each T flip-flop is used so that each count **increases** the stored binary value by one bit. In a *down-counter* or *reverse counter*, only the Q-bar (complementary) output of each T flip-flop is used so that each count **reduces** the stored binary value by one bit. If a 3-bit binary down counter is started at "111", the counter sequence is: 111, 110, 101, 100, 011, 010, and 001.

BINARY UP/DOWN COUNTER
The only difference between a circuit made to operate either as an up counter or as a down counter, is the use of either the Q or Q-bar outputs of each T flip-flop in the counter circuit. A binary *up/down counter* (a counter that can be set to operate either way, when desired) is easily achieved. With the addition of a mechanical selector switch to choose between either of the complementary sets of flip-flop outputs, the circuit can be made to count either way. In a logic circuit, however, logic gates are generally used instead of mechanical switches.

SHIFT REGISTERS

A *general register* is a circuit that can store binary data and transfer it on command. The capacity of the register is usually small (one or just a few binary words) with its information very easily and quickly accessible. A *shift register,* a variation of a general register, has the ability to shift its contents from one of its elements (usually D flip-flops) to the next when a shift pulse is received. Shift registers can convert one data format to another and can also divide and multiply its binary number contents by two.

A shift register is constructed by connecting D flip-flops in series with the number of flip-flops to be used depending on the number of bits required in the register. When information in one flip-flop is shifted to the succeeding flip-flop, it is called a *forward shift register;* when information is shifted to the preceding flip-flop, it is called a *reverse shift register.*

FORWARD SHIFT REGISTER

The 4-bit forward shift register shown in Figure 61 contains four D flip-flops (designated as F/F 1, 2, 3 and 4) connected in series (cascade). The circuit operates as follows:

• When a "1" is applied to input D of F/F 1, with no clock pulse applied to the CLOCK input, the Q output of F/F 1 (and input D of F/F 2) is at "0". When the clock pulse appears at the CLOCK input, the output at Q of F/F 1 (and input D of F/F 2) is changed to "1".

• The next clock pulse shifts this "1" one place further, etc., until after the fifth clock pulse, the "1" is shifted out of the shift register. Note that the CLOCK inputs of all the D flip-flops are in parallel so that clock pulses are applied to each CLOCK input simultaneously.

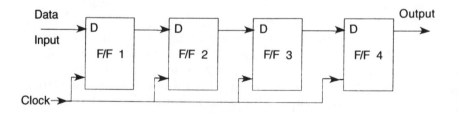

A 4-bit Forward Shift Register
Figure 61

One clock pulse at the input results in a shift of the "1" pulse at input D of F/F 1 to the right (input D of F/F 2). A shift of a "1" to the right in a binary number is the same as shifting one binary place to the right, or moving the "1" to the next lower significant digit value.

Each shift to the right is equivalent to **dividing** a binary number in the shift register **by 2**. For example: If the initial number was "1010" (decimal 10), after a single shift to the right, the new number in the register is "0101" (decimal 5).

REVERSE SHIFT REGISTER
The 4-bit reverse shift register, shown in Figure 62, operates in exactly the same way, in principle. The data applied to input D of F/F 4, however, is shifted to the left rather than to the right. Each reverse shift produced by each clock pulse moves the least significant binary digit originally in the units position to the next significant position, etc.

Each shift to the left is equivalent to **multiplying** the initial binary number in the shift register **by 2**. For example: If the initial number was "0111" (decimal 7), after a single shift to the left, the new number in the register is "1110" (decimal 14).

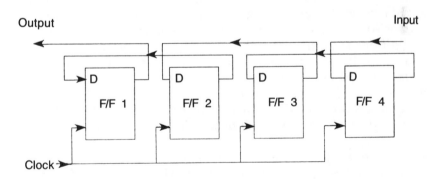

A 4-bit Reverse Shift Register
Figure 62

As with up/down binary counters, shift registers can also be structured to offer the forward or reverse shifting (dividing by 2 or multiplying by 2), when desired. With the inclusion of the necessary logic gates for direction switching, the same shift register can operate in either direction.

USING SHIFT REGISTERS TO CONVERT DATA FORMAT

As previously shown, a group of D flip-flops can be connected to form a forward, reverse or direction selectable shift register (using appropriate logic gate switching circuits). In each case, the circuit was configured to provide *serial-in, serial-out* data format. Shift register circuits can be modified to convert binary words D serial data format to parallel data format, or from a parallel d F/F 4 format to a serial data format. Depending on a computer's structure, some means of converting data format may be necessary. For example, the parallel format of BCD or Extended BCD codes may be desired for a computer that is structured for serial data transmission, or vice versa.

- *Serial data formatting* is the placement of a binary word on a single transmission line so that each bit of data follows one behind the other in time.

- *Parallel data formatting* is the placement of each bit of a binary word on a separate transmission line; each bit of a binary word is transmitted from one place to another at the same time. With parallel data formatting, the data rate and the computer's clock rate must be synchronized.

SERIAL-IN, PARALLEL-OUT (S/P CONVERTER)

Properly connecting four 2-input AND gates to a 4-bit serial-in, serial-out shift register (Figure 62) can create a 4-bit serial-in, parallel-out shift register. See Figure 63. Each Q output of the four D flip-flops is connected to the corresponding input of each AND gate, with the other inputs connected to act as common READ terminal. The circuit operates as follows:

- A 4-bit serial data word "a b c d" is applied to the shift register input, so that bit "d" (either a "0" or "1") is the first to enter the register. At the first clock pulse, bit "d" is at output Q of F/F 1.

- At the next clock pulse, bit "d" is shifted to F/F 2 and bit "c" enters F/F 1, etc., until, at the fourth clock pulse, the shift register contains the serial data word "a b c d".

- The original serial data word is now accessible in parallel data form at the outputs of the four AND gates and can be read out by providing a pulse (1) to the common READ terminal of the four AND gates after every four clock pulse intervals. If the four gates are D flip-flops (latches) and the READ pulse occurs every fourth clock pulse, the parallel output will remain in place for four clock periods.

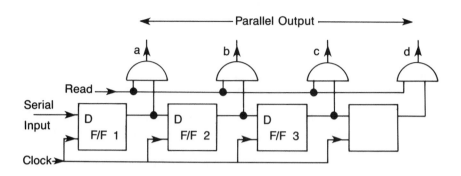

Serial to Parallel Converter
Figure 63

The capacity of the serial-in, parallel-out converter can be increased with the addition of more D flip-flops and AND gates.

PARALLEL-IN, SERIAL-OUT (P/S CONVERTER)
The 4-bit parallel-in, serial-out circuit, shown in Figure 64, operates in a reverse way compared with the S/P converter, as follows:
• The parallel data word is entered into the circuit through the four AND gate inputs by actuating its common ENTER input.

• With each successive clock pulse, each bit of the parallel data word is shifted through the register, and then, out in serial data form after the each clock pulse.

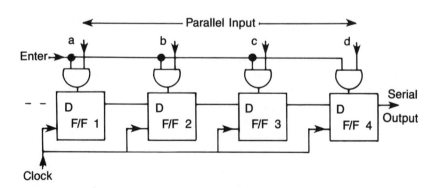

Parallel to Serial Converter
Figure 64

DIGITAL LOGIC FAMILIES
IN MONOLITHIC IC FORM

In the early 1960s, monolithic IC technology became commercially feasible. Several manufacturers began producing logic gates in monolithic IC form to meet the demand for compatible logic circuits at relatively high speed, low power and low cost.

The circuit specifications listed on a manufacturer's data sheet for these logic circuits (as with any IC data sheet) were not involved with the detailed parameters of individual circuit components but with the device as a complete entity. A data sheet listed the following details of the IC:

- Part number
- Function(s)
- Device technology
- Package size
- Pin designations
- Material
- Operating temperature range
- Specific features

In addition, it was necessary to provide information on:
- Maximum voltage and current capability
- Maximum power dissipation per gate
- Number of inputs per gate
- Number and different kinds of logic gates on a single chip.
- Propagation delay - length of time required for a gate to provide an output under a given set of circuit conditions
- Fan-in and fan-out characteristics

The variety of combinations proliferated in a very short time. Additional logic circuits, in monolithic IC form, became available in a diversity of configurations and included single, dual, triple, and quad logic gates on a monolithic IC chip. Each individual circuit was isolated from the others while using a common power supply and circuit reference. Other logic circuits included: flip-flops, counters, shift registers, converters, etc., in a variety of sizes, types, and combinations.

The first logic circuit series in monolithic IC form included over 150 different types, offering different combinations and options to provide a building-block method of interconnecting a complete logic system. This first logic circuit monolithic IC series was manufactured in bipolar technology and was called the *diode-transistor logic* (DTL) family. In terms of current, voltage, power capability, and propagation delay, all of the DTL series circuits were compatible. They offered ease and speed in logic system design and received wide acceptance throughout the industry. The need for faster circuits (shorter propagation delay) brought about improved logic circuits and newer logic circuit families.

By modifying the existing DTL series and still maintaining pin-for-pin interchangeability, a new series was developed called *transistor-transistor logic* (TTL). This series featured reduced propagation delay at the cost of increased power dissipation. See Figure 65.

LOGIC SYSTEM	SUPPLY VOLTAGE D.C.	PROPAGATION DELAY PER GATE	POWER DISSIPATION PER GATE
Bipolar DTL	$V_{cc} = 5.0\ V \pm 10\%$	30 nanosecs.	8 milliwatts
TTL		10 nanosecs.	15 milliwatts
TTL-S		5 nanosecs.	15 milliwatts
LP TTL-S		10 nanosecs.	2 milliwatts
ECL		1 nanosec.	35 milliwatts
*ALS		5 nanosecs.	1 milliwatt
*AS		3 nanosecs.	10 milliwatts

CMOS V_{DD} = 5.0 to 30 volts (Unregulated)

CD series		40 to 100 nanosecs.	50 microwatts
TTLC		40 to 100 nanosecs.	50 microwatts
*QMOS		20 to 40 nanosecs.	20 microwatts
*HCMOS		20 to 40 nanosecs.	20 microwatts

* Second generation series

Monolithic IC Logic Systems Comparison
Figure 65

Further improvements in the TTL series of logic circuits were initiated by using the characteristics of a Schottky diode that was diffused into the IC at the output of a logic gate and reduced propagation delay without the penalty of increased power. This new, improved logic circuit series was called *TTL-Schottky* (TTL-S), totally compatible and pin-for-pin interchangeable with the older series. The need for a lower power version of the TTL-S series led to the production of an improved performance *Low Power TTL-S* (LP TTL-S) series.

This new series was designed as a modification of the TTL-S logic circuits to provide the same desirable short propagation delay of the TTL logic circuit series with greatly reduced power dissipation. The *emitter-coupled logic* (ECL) family answered the need for a very low propagation delay series but improving speed of logic circuitry included the undesirable trade-off of increased power dissipation.

The first monolithic IC series of CMOS logic circuitry, called the *CMOS Digital* (CD) series, offered the extremely low power dissipation inherent in CMOS technology; it was used in systems that had no special low propagation delay or voltage regulation requirements. Because of their low power dissipation, CMOS logic circuits are specifically used for battery-powered, portable computer circuitry. Several semiconductor manufacturers produced pin-for-pin replacements for the bipolar TTL series in CMOS technology. This lower power series was called TTLC.

As monolithic IC technology improved, second generation logic circuit families were developed to provide improvements in both propagation delay characteristics and lower power dissipation parameters. These second generation logic circuit families included the *Advanced Schottky* (AS), *Advanced Low Power Schottky* (ALS), *Quick MOS (QMOS)*, and *High-Speed CMOS* (HCMOS) series.

REINFORCEMENT EXERCISES

Answer TRUE or FALSE to each of the following statements:

1. Digital logic is a form of mathematics based on a two-state (binary) approach to solving a related series of conditions. In computers, logic gates and similar switching circuits are used in a systematic plan to perform decision-making functions described in truth tables.

2. There is no interaction between the logic gates of a computer circuit.

3. Boolean algebra applies to a logic based on the assumption that the following possibilities exist as far as any statement is concerned: the statement can either be "true", "false", partly "true" or partly "false".

4. With positive logic, zero voltage represents the binary digit "0", often called the "low state" or "space". A positive signal represents the binary digit "1", often called the "high state" or "mark".

5. A binary "1" can be shown as a digital voltage pulse, whose magnitude is equal to the power supply voltage. The power supply voltage (typically 5, 6, or 12) is determined by the design of the system.

6. An AND gate can only have two input terminals and only two output terminals.

7. An NAND gate will produce a "1 " at its output when all its inputs, except one, are at "0".

8. The relationship between OR gates and NOR gates is exactly the same as between AND gates and NAND gates.

9. A NOT gate (inverter) can change the logic of an AND gate to that of a NAND gate, and vice versa. The same logic conversion can also be accomplished in using a NOT gate with an OR gate and to change its logic state to that of a NOR gate.

10. Non-inverting drivers having only one input terminal and one output terminal are used to increase the fan-in and the fan-out capability beyond the specified number in the logic gate data sheet, when required.

11. When a logic "1" is applied to the inhibiting input terminal of an INHIBIT gate and a logic "1" is at one or all of the other normal input terminals of the gate, the output will be at a logic "1" state.

12. A flip-flop is a bistable logic element with one or more input terminals and two complementary output terminals; when one output is "0" the other is "1" and vice versa.

13. Semiconductors, particularly ICs, must be used to design the logic gate circuits used in digital computers.

14. With an RS flip-flop, when a logic "1" is applied to both inputs simultaneously, the output logic state can be either a "0" or "1". This output condition is called an undefined state. When a defined or unambiguous output state is required, a JK flip-flop is used rather than an RS flip-flop.

15. A toggle (T) flip-flop, with one input and one output, is a common logic circuit that can be connected in series to design binary counters.

16. A data (D) flip-flop is used for processing data in a logic circuit and its action is independent of the clock pulses generated by the clock within the system.

17. A shift register is made up of a series of D flip-flops to store information and transfer data on command. Shift registers are often used to convert one form of data transmission to another, e.g.: serial-in, parallel-out or parallel-in, serial-out.

18. With compatibility between the different logic circuit families specified on a data sheet, the parameters that are critical in selecting a specific type in the design of a logic circuit are:
    • propagation delay per gate
    • power dissipation per gate.

Answers to the reinforcement exercises are on page 279.

 CHAPTER
NINE

COMPUTER MEMORIES

INTRODUCTION

MEMORY TECHNOLOGIES
  PAPER MEMORY
  MAGNETIC MEMORY
  OPTICAL MEMORY
  SEMICONDUCTOR MEMORY

REINFORCEMENT EXERCISES

COMPUTER MEMORIES

INTRODUCTION

A computer memory is a system, circuit, device or component into which digital data can be written and held (stored) for a specified length of time and then read out (accessed). The storage capability and access time depends on the particular technology and access method of the memory structure.

Accessing data on any memory medium includes the act of finding a desired location (address) in the memory structure and then reading out the information that has been written at that address. The method of finding a desired address is accomplished either by a serial access or random access technique.

SERIAL ACCESS MEMORY

In a serial access memory, a desired address is reached from any point of the memory structure by moving through the intervening data clusters until the desired address is found. The time required to access (find and read out) the stored information is **dependent** on the location of desired data within the memory medium. For data clusters located near the previous read out location, access time is very short. Even during a "fast forward" operation, it takes longer to find and read out (access) data stored some distance from the last read-out address. An example of a serial access memory is a magnetic tape (either "reel-to-reel" or "cassette") that contains prerecorded audio or video information.

RANDOM ACCESS MEMORY

In a random access memory, a desired address is reached by moving **directly** to that location. The length of time required to access the stored information is **independent** of the location of its data. A magnetic disk that stores digital, audio, or video data is an example of a random access memory. Regardless of the location of the next data address (either adjacent or far from the last read-out point), the access time will be the same. Although it is called a "random access memory", a more accurate phrase would be "direct access memory".

A computer memory is basically a place for storing data that can be retrieved at a later time. Most of the available memory media can be classified into the following commonly-used memory categories:

- Changeable (read/write) memory - volatile and non-volatile
- Permanent (read-only) table-storage memory

CHANGEABLE (READ/WRITE) MEMORY

NON-VOLATILE READ/WRITE MEMORY

These applications include data bases, such as: mailing lists, library listings, telephone directories, archival documents, and dictionaries; they must have random access capability. Data in this type of memory could include whole series of paragraphs or form letters to be read and kept for further use. Either serial or random access memory can be used as external "back-up" memory media to guard against the inadvertent loss of data by providing a means of replacing that data. This medium must be non-volatile, (data is not erased with power removed) and includes magnetic tapes, magnetic disks, and erasable optical disks. Although classified as changeable memory, because of its non-volatility, it has a high degree of permanence.

VOLATILE READ/WRITE MEMORY

This category of read/write memory consists of a semiconductor medium, called *Random Access Memory* (RAM) that is used to store a computer's working data. After the data is reviewed, or modified, it can either be erased or saved (copied to a non-volatile read/write memory) for filing or for future use. Data can also be removed from RAM at a computer operator's discretion to make room for new data to be reviewed, etc.

Other semiconductor memory, called *Scratch Pad Memory,* can contain from one to several hundred binary words of immediate interest and is used for temporary storage. Its most common application is for intra-system use and is conveniently located in the processing unit for quick access and easy reference.

PERMANENT (READ-ONLY) TABLE-STORAGE MEMORY

In this classification, fixed sets of values, data, or instructions are stored for frequent reference. It may contain software programs, conversion codes, "look-up" tables for conversion from temperature in °F to °C and vice-versa, and "look-up" tables for trigonometric functions and logarithms. The memories in this group are non-volatile, read-only, and unalterable.

MEMORY TECHNOLOGIES
PAPER MEMORY

From a historical aspect, it is worth noting the features of paper punched cards and paper tape (paper memory), although generally, they are no longer used. Both types of paper memory required electromechanical drive and control equipment. They had relatively long access times, consumed relatively high power, and were used for their bulk storage capability.

PAPER PUNCHED CARD

Each punched card was coded with holes in specific areas of printed rows and columns; each hole was used to represent a "1" bit and the absence of a hole represented a "0" bit. Mechanical or optical card readers were used to sense the presence or absence of the holes to record and sort the data. Since each card was physically separable from the other, it became a unit record in a file made up of sorted unit records. Small files were called *decks*, and some decks had thousands of cards (records). The cards allowed manual access and modification which provided some ease in preparing computer programs. Serially-accessed punched cards were used primarily for census tabulation, payroll, inventory, and mailing lists.

PAPER TAPE

Essentially, paper tape memory functioned as a narrow, unending punched card; a sprocket-wheel meshed with small holes in the tape and as the wheel rotated, it moved the pre-punched tape under a read/write head. As in the case of the punched card, the holes and spaces in the pre-punched paper tape represented patterns of zeros and ones to be read by either mechanical or optical readers. Its mechanical tape transport mechanism not only limited reading speed but also caused paper tape that was being continually used to wear out. This condition, plus the possibility of the paper tape tearing, presented a severe reliability problem for this type of memory.

Paper tape memory was first used in Teletype communications equipment and because of its low cost, ease of preparation, and availability, it was adopted by the machine tool industry as an inexpensive technique of quickly programming and changing control programs for automatic production processes. It was used to program the operation of lathes, presses, and automatic test equipment.

MAGNETIC MEMORY

Magnetic memories require electromechanical drives and suffer from similar speed limitations as all mechanical systems. Magnetic memory media consume relatively high power and have much longer access times than semiconductor memory. The main advantage of magnetic memory, however, is its high-density (bulk storage) capacity that is applicable for permanent file (archival storage) use.

Magnetic ferrite core, plated magnetic wire, and magnetic drum memories, once very popular memory media for bulk storage applications, have become obsolete. The only magnetic memory media still being used in computer systems are magnetic tapes and disks.

MAGNETIC TAPE
The surface of a plastic tape is permanently coated with a magnetic film. When the tape drive circuit is set to its "write" mode, with the moving tape placed adjacent to a read/write head, the magnetic particles on the surface of the tape are appropriately magnetized (oriented) to represent patterns of "zeros" and "ones".

With the tape drive set to its "read" mode, the moving programmed tape is set adjacent to the read/write head. By magnetic induction between the induction coil in the head and the magnetic particles on the tape, electronic pulses representing patterns of "zeros" and ones" are generated and transmitted to the computer's logic circuitry for processing.

Magnetic tape has long been used for data storage applications. It has the lowest cost per bit of all changeable memory media and is capable of efficiently storing huge amounts of digital data. Existing information can be easily and quickly erased, or changed (overwritten); it is non-volatile since its data is not lost when electrical power is removed.

Since magnetic tape is a serial access memory, finding the location of desired data requires moving through unwanted data clusters if the data to be read is not adjacent to a previous reading. The time expended in moving through unwanted data clusters make this memory technology undesirable for modern high speed data processing requirements. Its main use in modern computer systems is as bulk storage archival memory that serves as a means of backing-up vital information.

MAGNETIC DISK

Like magnetic tape, a disk's surface is coated with a magnetic film that stores digital data. The information is written by orienting the magnetic particles ("zeros" and "ones") on the surface of the disk. A magnetic disk is non-volatile and the information on its surface can be easily erased and quickly overwritten by the control of a read/write head. Unlike magnetic tape, however, magnetic disks use a random (direct) access technique to read and write the data.

There are two types of disk drives, each having its unique drive mechanism, connecting cable, and control circuitry.

HARD DISK

A hard disk unit, commonly called a *hard drive*, consists of a high speed motor, multiple rigid magnetic platters (disks), and an individual read/write head for each side of each platter. The entire assembly is sealed to protect against contamination and connected to an appropriate control circuit inside a computer enclosure. When energized and its speed stabilized, the motor will rotate at typically 3600 revolutions per minute (RPM), with each read/write head "floating" above the disk surface on a cushion of air, 15 to 50 millionths of an inch thick. Generally, a hard drive is not intended to be removable.

Courtesy of IBM Corp.

The First Magnetic Hard Disk Memory Unit (Winchester Drive)
Figure 66

WRITING DATA ON A MAGNETIC DISK
The disk's rigid aluminum material is coated with a nickel-cobalt magnetic film prior to having a hard, protective coating applied. Passing a current through one of the two magnetic coils of the read/write head on each side of the disk creates a directional magnetic field (flux) at the gap of the head; the particles on the disk surface directly adjacent to the head gap are magnetized. See Figure 67. To facilitate writing the appropriate binary code onto the disk, the magnetic field directions are designated as "0" or "1".

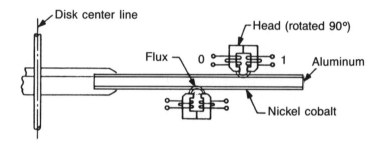

Cross-section of a Magnetic Disk
Figure 67

READING DATA FROM A DISK
By sensing different magnetic fields as the disk is rotated, the magnetic information written on a disk is read by the read/write head coils. As the magnetic fields on the disk surface are passed by the head gap, a voltage is magnetically induced in the coil of the "read" head, amplified, and then sent to the processing unit in the form of binary data. Hard disk access time is about 20 to 40 milliseconds.

Hard disk drives used in mainframe and large minicomputers are generally 14 inches in diameter and are capable of storing as much as one thousand Megabytes of data. (A thousand Megabytes are equal to one Gigabyte.) The hard disk drives used in microcomputers (personal computers) are 5.25 inches in diameter with some types capable of storing over 130 Megabytes of data. Newer hard disk drives are now available to accommodate smaller (3.25 inch diameter), rigid, multiple-platters with about the same storage capability as the older, larger drives.

FLEXIBLE (FLOPPY) DISK (DISKETTE)
Because the disk is flexible, compared with a hard disk, it is commonly referred to as a "floppy disk" or "diskette". The disk is protected by a non-removable, plastic jacket. The floppy disk, in its protective jacket, is inserted by the computer operator into an appropriate floppy disk drive compartment at the front or side panel of a computer. Since a floppy disk is a removable memory, it offers an easy way to physically transport data between computers equipped with compatible drives. The disk drive consists of a motor and two read/write heads, one for each surface of a disk, electronic circuits, and a cable connection to a control circuit.

When the drive's motor is energized and its rotation stabilized, its speed is maintained at typically 300 to 360 RPM. The read/write heads for floppy disks are designed to "land on" (touch) the disk's surface while reading and writing the information on the disk, rather than floating above the disk, as is the practice with hard disks.

Originally 8.5 inches in diameter, the floppy disk was used to provide a relatively inexpensive and convenient means of storing software programs for minicomputers and the first microcomputers. It also offered a means of creating "files" on magnetic disks without having to print hard copies for data that had been processed by a computer. A flexible, 8.5 inch double-sided disk is capable of storing 2.2 Megabytes of data.

As disk technology improved, a less expensive, easier to handle, double-sided, double-density, 5.25 inch diameter, flexible disk became the standard for floppy disk technology. It is capable of storing over 360 Kilobytes of information and has an average access time of about 400 milliseconds. Because of its smaller size, it is sometimes referred to as a "mini-floppy disk". Further improvements in recording techniques have made available a high-density 5.25 inch diameter, floppy disk with a storage capability of over 6 Megabytes of data.

State-of-the-art floppy disk technology uses a 3.5" diameter flexible disk enclosed in a hard plastic shell. This disk has a storage capability of 1.44 Megabytes. Although still called a "floppy disk", or "micro-floppy disk", its outer protective shell is rigid, providing a greater degree of protection for the enclosed disk. Its smaller size, hard outer shell, and automatic access window permit safer handling and afford the convenience of carrying a disk in a shirt pocket.

MAGNETIC DISK STRUCTURE

SECTORS, TRACKS AND SIDES

The collection of sectors that fits into a single ring on a disk is called a *track*. Unlike an audio or phonograph disk that has spiralling tracks, the tracks on a floppy disk (or the platters of a hard disk) are individual concentric rings; the outside ring is called Track 0 (the first track). The last track is the one nearest the center of the disk.

The binary data written on a disk is stored on *sectors*, the areas where information is physically recorded. See Figure 68. Typically, a single sector of one track is capable of storing 512 bytes with each byte denoting a specific character.

Most floppy disks are formatted to record on both sides of the disk and are referred to as *double-sided disks*; the first side is called Side 0 and the flip side called Side 1. A floppy disk, formatted to one of several disk formatting standards, has 40 tracks per side, or 80 tracks for a double-sided disk.

Both floppy disks and hard drives are structured in a similar manner, however, a double-sided floppy disk has typically 9 sectors per track, and each double-sided platter of a hard drive has typically 17 sectors per track.

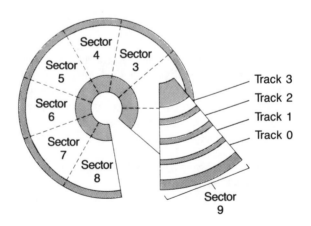

Tracks and Sectors on a Floppy Disk
Figure 68

- The disk's first sector is assigned to the *bootstrap loader* or "booting" section of the computer's operating software program (operating system). The booting section allows a computer to be started after power is applied. The *operating system* is the computer system's software program that supervises and controls its operation. For more detail, refer to CHAPTER ELEVEN — SOFTWARE CONSIDERATIONS.

- Sectors 2 and 3 hold the *file allocation table* (FAT) that keeps track of used and unused space on a disk. The FAT is also part of the computer's operating system.

- Sectors 4 and 5 accommodate the designated directories. The space in the remaining sectors are reserved for the data files stored on the disk. See Figure 69.

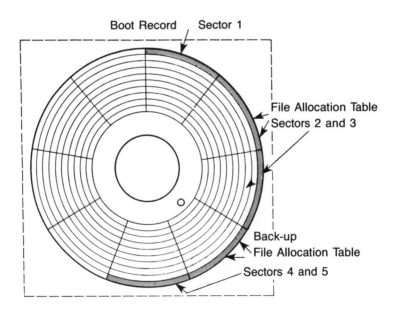

Allocation of Sectors on a Floppy Disk
Figure 69

CYLINDERS
Hard drives contain several platters with concentric tracks on both sides of each platter. Tracks that are the same distance from the center combine to form a *cylinder*. See Figure 70.

Since each platter has hundreds of tracks, the same number of cylinders are formed for a hard drive. Typically, a hard drive has 613 cylinders, regardless of the number of platters. Obviously, the more platters, the longer the cylinder, thereby providing a greater capacity in the hard drive.

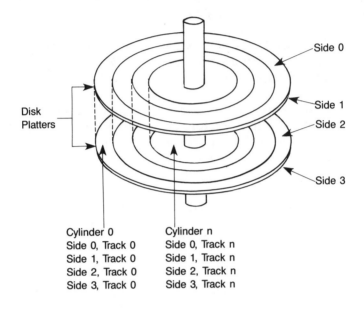

Cylinders on a 2-platter, 4-sided Hard Drive
Figure 70

A 6-platter hard drive, for example, has 12 tracks per cylinder with a read/write head for each side. Tracks in the same cylinder can be written and read without moving the read/write mechanism of the disk drive.

HARD DRIVE ORGANIZATION

DIRECTORY AND SUBDIRECTORIES
Like any organized document, a disk has a listing of its files which is similar to a table of contents in a book. This listing is referred to as a *directory* to which specific identifying label is assigned. A disk operating system (DOS) provides a *root directory*, to which other directories, referred to as the *subdirectories*, can be attached at the discretion of the computer operator. A subdirectory may have other subdirectories, often called *sub-subdirectories*. The number of subdirectories is only limited by the drive's capacity. See Figure 71.

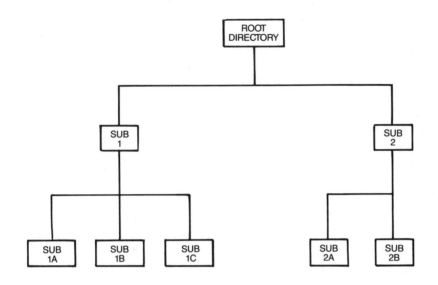

A Hard Drive Tree-structured Directory
Figure 71

FILE
The smallest unit of related information on a disk is called a *file* to which a specific identifying label has been assigned. Since there is no standard file size (within the allowable limits of the disk), the number of characters (bytes) in a file is left to the discretion of the computer operator. For example, a file can contain a single-page letter, a listing of names and telephone numbers, a single chapter or several chapters of a book, or the listing of inventory in a stockroom.

If a file is difficult to manage because the amount of related information makes a file very long, too much time is taken to move from one section to another. To avoid this inconvenience, it may be preferable to separate an extremely long file into two or more files.

In reverse, if no further processing is necessary on a group of related files, they may be merged to create a single file. The number of individual files that are created and the maximum number of files that can be created within any disk, is usually provided in a directory listing.

OPTICAL MEMORY

With recent improvements and cost reduction in laser technology and related production techniques, the CD-ROM (Compact Disk Read-Only Memory) has become a major optical memory alternative technology for computer mass memory storage, such as: large data bases for libraries, schools, hospitals and legal institutions. It is the logical extension of the highly successful compact disk digital audio technology, developed by Philips New Media Systems and Sony Corporation, providing high-quality audio reproduction for over a decade. This same technology using optics and a laser beam to read and reproduce the undistorted sound provided by a CD audio disk is being used to store programs and data in a format that allows retrieval by a computer.

A single, rugged, relatively low-cost, aluminized CD-ROM, 1.2 millimeters thick and 4.72 inches (120 millimeters) in diameter can store up to 660 Megabytes of data, the equivalent of more than 1800 standard 5.25 inch floppy disks formatted to hold 360 Kilobytes of data. That amount of data is equal to approximately 300,000 typewritten, single-sided, 8" by 11" pages.

The 3-layered CD-ROM consists of a substrate layer, a reflective film on top of the substrate, and a transparent plastic protective coating. See Figure 72. Information is first stored on the disk by means of microscopic pits that are burned into the disk's substrate by a laser beam. The pitted areas **deflect** rather than **reflect** laser light from the non-pitted areas, called *lands*, allowing reflected light from a laser beam to scan a rapidly spinning disk for translation into binary code.

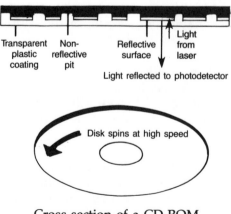

Cross-section of a CD-ROM
Figure 72

Unlike standard magnetic disk drives that store information on concentric tracks (Figure 73a), a CD-ROM has its data stored on a single, spiralling track (Figure 73b) that is divided into many sectors. The track length is approximately 3 miles long.

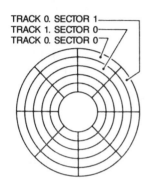

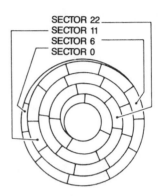

Standard Disk Concentric Tracks CD-ROM Single, Spiralling Track
Figure 73a   **Figure 73b**

ADVANTAGES
- Like a floppy disk, a CD-ROM can be removed from its drive and stored safely, conveniently transported, or mailed. The drive can be mounted in the same space usually occupied by a standard 5.25 " drive.
- Huge amounts of data can be stored on a CD-ROM, offering relatively low cost per bit for large data bases and archive information applications.
- Unlike mass density magnetic tape, a CD-ROM is a random access memory.
- With light being used to read the data, the read head can be placed much further away from the disk surface, essentially eliminating any possibility of a head crash.

DISADVANTAGES
- Access time of a CD-ROM is about 1 second compared with a hard disk's typical access time of 20 milliseconds.
- CD-ROM, being a read-only memory, is permanent and unalterable and cannot store the user's own data.

A Write-Once, Read Many (WORM), is another high-density optical disk memory available in a variety of formats ranging from 5.25" to 14". The WORM can be programmed once, permanently saving a user's data and then becomes an optical disk read-only memory having essentially the same features as the CD-ROM.

SEMICONDUCTOR MEMORY

The introduction of the first monolithic IC memory in 1969, by Intel Corporation, had a significant effect on the future design and use of computer systems. Semiconductor memory technology brought about dramatic and profound changes in hardware and software design with the concomitant increase in system performance and reliability levels. The scope of computer applications and end-user flexibility rose to unprecedented heights. The economic feasibility of the technology that led to the concept of the "microprocessor on a chip" and eventually, to the "microcomputer on a chip" was confirmed.

The diversion of different memories throughout a computer system has been made possible by the use of monolithic IC memory technology, replacing the traditional single system memory approach. This change in a computer's architecture resulted in the elimination of excessive "overhead" circuitry and higher power needs. It also influenced the design of a variety of printers and system networking methods.

Substantial amounts of semiconductor memory circuits are being used in new generations of computer-controlled consumer appliances, analytical instruments, process control systems, medical monitoring equipment, communications, automotive and other transportation systems. These new electronic machines offer improved performance, a minimum of maintenance, higher levels of reliability, greater adaptation to the user's needs, lower costs, and smaller packages.

FEATURES OF SEMICONDUCTOR MEMORY

• Has faster access time than other memory media - The access time of the slowest semiconductor memory is about 200 nanoseconds; it is about 100,000 times faster than the access time of a typical hard drive and about 1,000,000 times faster than a floppy disk drive.

• Requires no electromechanical drive - Uses only semiconductor drive and control circuits with its inherent reliability and mechanical shock-proof and vibration-proof characteristics.

• Uses less power, weight, and space and is easily replaceable.

• Has a higher density per unit area than other memory media, although, the total capacity per device is lower.

Semiconductor memories, like other monolithic IC devices, are available in a variety of processing technologies. The intended application, the availability of a specific type, and its immediate and long-term cost determine which memory is chosen.

For example, access time of bipolar technology is about one-tenth that of an equivalent CMOS memory, but a bipolar memory consumes several hundred times more power. If access time is not critical and low power is of prime importance (as in the case of a portable, battery-operated computer), CMOS memory chips would be chosen for that application. If, however, access time is the primary parameter, the application will dictate the selection of a memory technology with the lowest access time. CMOS technology produces memories with VLSI chip densities at a lower cost per bit than does a bipolar approach.

SEMICONDUCTOR MEMORY ORGANIZATION

Semiconductor memories can be visualized as structured with horizontal rows and vertical columns in a matrix of cells resembling post office cubby holes. Each row is used for a specific address, storing either a single binary digit (zero or one), a group of bits (a byte, half-byte, double-byte, etc.), or several binary words. Each group of bits in an address is the binary code representation of an instruction, machine operation, or a portion of data. Memory *organization* is the number of rows (addresses) and number of columns (bits per address).

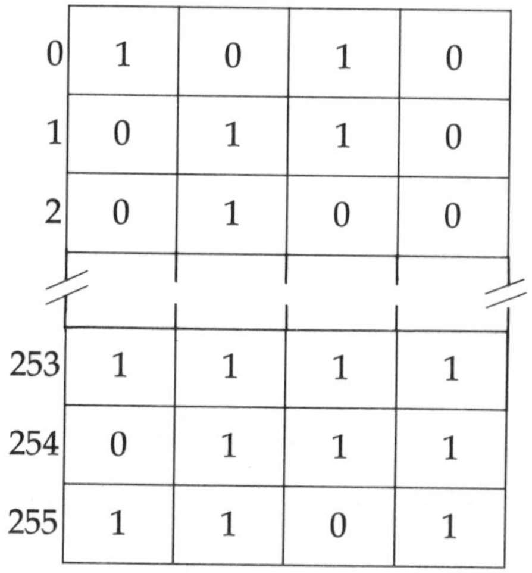

0	1	0	1	0
1	0	1	1	0
2	0	1	0	0
253	1	1	1	1
254	0	1	1	1
255	1	1	0	1

Semiconductor Memory
Organization

Figure 74

The semiconductor memory (Figure 74) is organized as a 256 by 4 structure. This means that this memory has a total capacity of 256 x 4 or 1024 bits. The "0"s and "1"s inserted in the blank spaces of the structure have no specific significance, other than to illustrate the different coded binary words that can be written in each address.

For ease in specification, memory capacity is normally referred to in increments of "K". The "K" in this case, unlike "k", the International Standard designating "1000", really means 1024, therefore, the memory structure shown in Figure 74 is called a "1K memory". When organized as a 256 by 8 structure, there are 256 addresses, with each address being 8 bits wide. Although the total capacity is 2048 (256 x 8), the size of the structure is referred to as a "2K" memory. When called a 64K-bit memory, it has a capacity of 65,536 bits.

An important consideration is whether the "64K" size is specified in **bits** or **bytes**. A byte is an 8-bit binary word, therefore, a 64K **bit** memory has only 8K **bytes**. Unfortunately, there is no standard designation of memory size, although the trend in the industry is to specify the number of bytes in a computer memory and the number of bits in a chip. The user should observe caution in noting this designation.

The structure of a semiconductor memory provides an extremely flexible approach when expansion is required. For example, connecting a 256 by 4 memory in parallel with another 256 by 4 memory, the new structure is now organized as a 256 by 8 memory structure as shown in Figure 75.

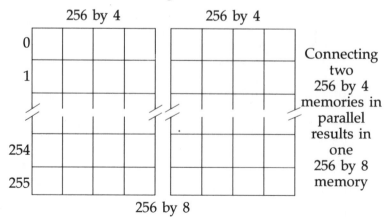

Connecting Two Semiconductor Memories in Parallel
Figure 75

If two memories, both 256 by 8, are connected in series, a 512 by 8 memory would result. See Figure 76.

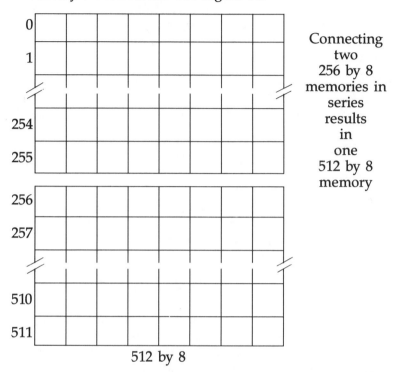

Connecting
two
256 by 8
memories in
series
results
in
one
512 by 8
memory

512 by 8

Connecting Two Semiconductor Memories in Series
Figure 76

TYPES OF SEMICONDUCTOR MEMORIES

RANDOM ACCESS MEMORY (RAM)

Although a random access memory is defined as a memory in which the length of time required to access the stored information is **independent** of the location of data, a semiconductor RAM is understood to be an erasable read/write memory. Using the acronym "RAM" merely signifies that this particular memory is a random access memory. Although all semiconductor memories are randomly accessed, different names are used for the other memories.

Semiconductor RAM has the fastest access time of all memories and is used as the computer's working memory. Its data can be read and written easily and quickly, however, a semiconductor RAM is generally volatile. Unless some backup power is incorporated in the circuitry, if power is turned off, the information in the RAM is lost and is irretrievable.

RAM data backup can be done by either of the following means:
- Data can be copied to a non-volatile memory, such as a floppy or hard disk. This is often done automatically every preset interval as a feature of a word processing program, or the data in RAM is "saved" by being copied to a disk at the discretion of the computer operator.

- A battery can be used as a back-up for an inadvertent loss of power. The battery must have sufficient capacity to hold the information in RAM until more permanent power is restored.

There are two types of erasable read/write memories - *static* RAM (SRAM) and *dynamic* RAM (DRAM). The individual cells of static RAM consist of JK flip-flops that will maintain their stable state as long as power is applied to the memory. The logic of each memory cell is changed by applying a reset pulse to the input terminal of the required JK flip-flops. Static RAM features high-noise immunity (less sensitivity to power supply and circuit noise), and simplicity of design.

Cells of a dynamic RAM consist of small capacitors that are charged to a logic "1" state by the application of a digital pulse. The charge will quickly dissipate, and the data lost, unless the capacitor cells are recharged (refreshed) periodically (about once every 2 milliseconds). Although, an additional circuit is required to apply refresh pulses to the memory cells, a dynamic RAM is faster to access, has greater chip density, uses less power, and cost per bit is less.

READ-ONLY MEMORY (ROM)
This non-volatile memory is mask-programmed during manufacture and serves as a means of storing data that must not be erased or changed. The information programmed in a ROM identifies the computer's uniqueness compared with all other machines. For example, it could include a program that dictates a computer's specific function, a unique operating system, a standard code converter, data that will translate one language to another, or other data that could be used to convert one technique of measurement into another.

The "modules" supplied with video games to be plugged into the appropriate video game assembly are preprogrammed ROMs containing data for a selected game only. Depending on which module (ROM) the operator inserts into the indicated compartment in the machine, it is the information in that chosen ROM that will dictate the particular game to be played.

Because of the uniqueness of the programs stored in ROM, only large production quantities of ROM can justify the high costs of a custom program set of masks. A PROM is an alternate, more cost-effective approach for small quantity requirements.

PROGRAMMABLE READ-ONLY MEMORY (PROM)
A PROM is a blank (unprogrammed) monolithic IC memory intended for end-user custom programming. With the use of a proper programming machine, the end-user can access the PROM structure and convert the original blank memory into a programmed ROM. Once the programmed patterns are "burned-into" the memory, the PROM becomes a non-volatile ROM; the data becomes a permanent part of the memory and cannot be changed.

PROMs are manufactured with all memory cells containing either:
• All "ones" in the form of fusible links that are selectively "zapped" by a programmer to change the "ones" to "zeros", or
• All "zeros" in the form of non-conducting diodes (PN junctions) that are selectively "shorted" to change the "zeros" to "ones", to create the desired memory pattern.

UV-ERASABLE PROGRAMMABLE ROM (UV-EPROM)
The UV-EPROM is enclosed in a package that has a fused, transparent silica lid positioned above a MOSFET chip. (Figure 77).

UV-Erasable Programmable Read-Only Memory (UV-EPROM)
Figure 77

The chip has no connection made to its gate and is often referred to as a "floating gate" or "isolated gate" EPROM. It is programmed by applying a sufficiently large voltage between the package terminals connected to the selected source and drain elements of the MOSFET cells in the circuit. An electrical charge is induced into the floating gate which, in turn, causes the selected MOSFET channels to become conductive. The presence or absence of conduction in each cell provides the desired programming for the memory matrix.

The window above the chip permits exposure to ultraviolet light radiation. Exposing the floating gate MOSFET to high-intensity ultraviolet light radiation causes the gate charge to leak off and restores the device to its original, unprogrammed state. As long as its transparent window is properly covered to prevent the chip's exposure to ultraviolet (UV) light, the memory will remain in its non-volatile, programmed state.

The main feature of a UV-EPROM is its ability to be erased "in the field" and then easily patterned with a different software program while still retaining its non-volatile characteristics. This procedure of programming, erasing, and then reprogramming can be repeated an unlimited number of times with no detrimental effects on the UV-EPROM chip.

ELECTRICALLY ERASABLE PROM (EEPROM or E2PROM)
Sometimes called an *Electrically Alterable PROM* (EAPROM), the EEPROM, like the UV-EPROM, is programmed by applying voltages across appropriate terminals of its package. As a result, the channel resistance of the memory cells' MOSFETs is decreased from infinite resistance (0) to zero resistance (1) to set the pattern of the memory matrix. Unlike the UV-EPROM, the EEPROM is not erased by UV light and therefore, needs no window in the lid of its package.

When installed in a circuit, the EEPROM's entire program, or selected addresses in the structure, can be erased as follows:

• When a voltage pulse is applied to appropriate package terminals, totally erasing all the data in the memory. The EEPROM is now ready for reprogramming.

• When a voltage pulse is applied across other specified terminals of the package, selective locations in the memory matrix can be addressed, erased and reprogrammed.

Although UV-EPROMs are generally specified to function only at normal room temperature, EEPROMs, particularly those intended for use in military or aerospace equipment, are specified to function over a wide operating temperature range.

REINFORCEMENT EXERCISES

Answer TRUE or FALSE to each of the following statements:

1. A computer memory is basically a means of storing data that can be retrieved at a later time. Generally, the different memory media are classified into commonly-used memory categories, as follows: changeable (read/write memory) both non-volatile and volatile, and permanent (read-only) table-storage memory.

2. Accessing data on any memory medium is the act of finding a desired address in the memory structure.

3. The time required to find and read out the stored information in a computer's serial access memory is dependent on the location of the desired data written in a memory.

4. In a random access memory, the time required to access the stored information is independent of the location of its data in that memory.

5. A semiconductor RAM is a memory that is considered to be volatile since its information can be changed or distorted because of the instability of the circuit technology.

6. When a memory medium is categorized as "non-volatile", it means that the stored data cannot be changed but will remain as a permanent record for read-only applications.

7. The memory media that contains the computer's working data is categorized as "volatile memory and is generally volatile memory.

8. Since magnetic tape is a random access memory, it is often used as a permanent storage memory, with its main advantage being its fast access time.

9. The data written on the surface of a computer's magnetic disk cannot be modified or overwritten but is part of the computer's permanent software program.

10. A hard drive consists of a high speed motor, multiple rigid magnetic platters (disks), and individual read/write heads that float on a cushion of air on each side of each platter. The assembly is sealed to protect against contamination.

11. Since a flexible (floppy) disk drive uses a random access technique, it has the same access time as a hard drive - about 20 to 40 milliseconds.

12. The plastic jacket on a floppy disk should be removed before the disk can be operated properly.

13. The semiconductor memory referred to as a RAM is the only semiconductor memory that is a random access memory. Other semiconductor memories use a different accessing method.

14. A ROM (read-only memory) is a non-volatile memory that is mask-programmed during manufacture. It serves as a means of storing data that must not be erased or changed. The information programmed in a ROM often identifies the computer's uniqueness compared with all other machines.

15. A PROM (programmable read-only memory) is a monolithic IC memory that has been programmed by the semiconductor manufacturer but can be changed by the end-user with the use of a proper programming machine.

16. An ultraviolet-erasable PROM (UV-EPROM) uses a bipolar monolithic IC chip that can be erased by exposing the chip within its package to high-intensity levels of ultraviolet light radiation.

17. The procedure of programming, erasing, and then reprogramming a UV-EPROM can be repeated an unlimited number of times with no detrimental effects on its chip.

18. An EEPROM is programmed by applying voltages across appropriate terminals of its package. Erasure of the entire EEPROM program is accomplished by applying appropriate voltage pulses to proper terminals while the EEPROM is mounted in a circuit. When a voltage pulse is applied across other specified terminals, selected locations in the memory matrix can be addressed, erased, and reprogrammed.

19. Both UV-EPROMS and EEPROMS are specified to operate only at normal room temperature.

Answers to these reinforcement exercises are on page 281.

CHAPTER
TEN

THE BASIC COMPUTER SYSTEM

INTRODUCTION

ELEMENTS OF A COMPUTER
  I/O SECTION
  MAIN MEMORY SECTION
  CENTRAL PROCESSING UNIT
  SYSTEM BUS

MICROPROCOMPUTERS AND VLSI

SUPPORT HARDWARE

REINFORCEMENT EXERCISES

THE BASIC COMPTER SYSTEM

INTRODUCTION

A modern, digital computer is made up of a group of related and interconnected electronic circuits that recognize and act on a predetermined set of instructions in a series of sequential steps. The aim of the computer's instructions is to accomplish a specific task with the use of its compatible hardware and appropriate software.

The basic purpose of a computer is to access data, or an instruction, and then, to perform the function specified by that data, or instruction, with total accuracy. Although many instructions may be necessary to complete a single machine operation, each instruction is accomplished at a very high speed.

Essential to the functioning of a computer are both *hardware* and *software*.

• The term, hardware, designates the physical elements contained in a computer structure which include all of its electrical, electronic, magnetic, and mechanical components, as well as, its interconnecting parts and enclosure.

• The term, software, designates the *program* (set of instructions), languages, codes, documentation, and other written information used with a computer to direct and supervise the operation of the equipment (hardware). The details of software are covered in CHAPTER ELEVEN - SOFTWARE CONSIDERATIONS.

When a software program is written into a hardware structure, the combination is referred to as *firmware*. For example, a ROM (read-only memory) is firmware. It is a hardware component containing a program or instructions stored in its cells for use by the computer. Although initially a hardware component when in a blank state, a PROM (programmable read-only memory) becomes firmware after it is programmed.

Whether a computer is classified as a mainframe, minicomputer, or microcomputer, in principle, the physical structure of all three consists of the same basic sections.

All computers are similar in their ability to provide accurate results, regardless of their speed and size. One difference, however, is in their *throughput*, the number of instructions per second a machine can handle. Although throughput can be influenced by other factors, a computer's clock frequency and word width contribute to increasing a computer's throughput. For example, a 16-bit computer generally has a higher throughput than an 8-bit computer if both are operated at the same clock frequency; when operated at a higher clock frequency, the throughput value will increase.

Other differences include: the comparative size of a computer's memory, as well as, the size and capability of its other sections to handle different size programs and/or tasks.

These differences are gradually being reduced as the rapid advance in computer circuit technology continues. With microcomputers developing into more powerful machines, it is becoming more difficult to clearly define the boundary lines among computer categories. In many cases, some of the new microcomputers have met, and exceeded, the performance capabilities of older minicomputers and are approaching the capabilities of older mainframe computers.

A computer is called a "powerful" tool because of the accuracy and speed with which it performs its assigned operations. A "more powerful" computer means greater speed, greater ability to store more information, and a greater facility to accommodate additional, peripheral (external) equipment. It is this capability of providing accurate results at high speeds that creates its remarkable appeal and universal acceptance.

ELEMENTS OF A COMPUTER

The diagram shown in Figure 78 illustrates the basic computer structure, regardless of its speed, size of memory, and size of its other sections. It consists of the following elements:

- Input/Output (I/O) Section
- Arithmetic and Logic Unit (ALU)
- System Bus
- Main Memory
- Control Unit

Each element is an interrelated part of a computer, with each element's size and capability contributing to its category designation - mainframe, minicomputer, or microcomputer.

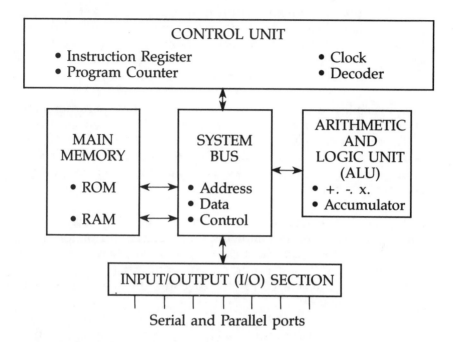

Below the diagram:

INPUT PERIPHERALS
- Keyboard
- Magnetic disk drive
- Magnetic tape
- Remote terminals
- POS equipment
- MO**DEM**
- Process sensors

OUTPUT PERIPHERALS
- Video monitor
- Magnetic disk drive
- Magnetic tape
- Printer/Plotter
- Remote terminals
- POS equipment
- **MODE**M

Basic Computer Structure with Input/Output Peripherals
Figure 78

INPUT/OUTPUT (I/O) SECTION
The entry and exit points of the computer, referred to as the Input/Output (I/O) *ports*, are the computer's interface with the outside world. Within this I/O section are the physical layouts of electronic circuitry, conducting paths, etc. that are provided in a computer to allow data to be transferred between the computer and its peripheral devices.

A computer must have at least one I/O port; generally, several I/O ports are available, even in small microcomputers. A large mainframe computer, for example, can have as many as several hundred I/O ports to communicate with its peripheral devices.

Each I/O port terminates with an appropriate socket with pin configurations to accommodate serial or parallel communications. The sockets are located at the back or side of a computer enclosure to accept an interconnecting plug and cable. The other end of the connecting cable is terminated at a peripheral device.

I/O ports allow a computer to access its different peripherals by referring to the specific ports commonly designated as: LPT1, LPT2, etc. for the parallel ports and COM1, COM2, etc. for the serial ports. The peripherals are connected to the designated ports to be accessed in a manner that is similar to the way a memory address is accessed.

A typical I/O structure allows a group of peripherals to be connected to a computer allowing it to receive information from, or transmit information to these different peripheral devices, as directed by a software program. An appropriate program can automatically direct a computer to communicate with several peripheral devices.

For example, at the direction of a typical program, a computer may receive information from a sensing instrument and a fraction of a second later, process that information and display the calculated results on its video monitor. Similarly, a program can direct the information being typed on a computer's keyboard to be instantly displayed on its monitor.

The logic circuits in the I/O section also perform the following I/O communications functions:

- The computer's timing is synchronized with its peripherals.

- Incoming and outgoing data is converted to an appropriate format, i.e.: serial to parallel or parallel to serial.

- Incoming language codes are translated into machine language and outgoing machine language into desired codes: ASCII, etc.

- Incoming and outgoing interrupts and pauses are controlled.

- With appropriate circuitry installed, direct access to the main memory data is possible without additional processing steps normally involved in accessing an address in memory. To provide this feature, a separate chip, called a *Direct Memory Access Controller* (DMAC) must be added to the I/O section.

MAIN MEMORY

The *Main Memory* of a computer contains both read-only memory (ROM) and random-access memory (RAM) in monolithic IC form.

READ-ONLY MEMORY (ROM)

Every computer is supplied with a set of software instructions developed by the manufacturer which allow it to perform its I/O output operations. These permanent instructions (routines) reside in ROM and are not erased each time the computer loses power or is turned OFF. The ROM contains the program that defines its uniqueness compared with all other type computers and is referred to the *basic input/output system* (BIOS).

Each time the computer is turned on, the ROM's system startup routines are invoked. The computer's operating system uses these startup routines (and other routines contained in its operating system) to create an area in RAM responsible for the computer's input/output operations. See Figure 79. Although the computer's operating system software could be part of the same ROM containing the BIOS, or supplied as a separate ROM, for convenience in upgrading an operating system intended to improve the machine's operation, the computer's operating system is generally contained on an easily transportable floppy disk.

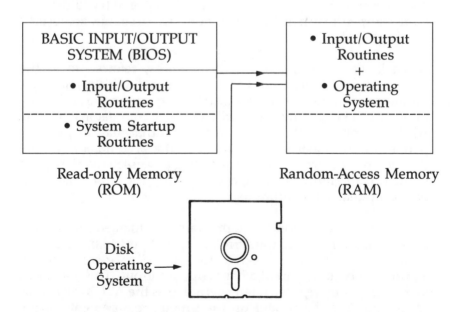

Installing the BIOS and Operating System into RAM
Figure 79

RANDOM-ACCESS MEMORY (RAM)
The amount of erasable, read/write, random-access memory
(RAM) available for use as its working memory depends on the
specific capability of a computer. Mainframe computers have
several hundred millions of bytes that can accommodate large
software programs. As computers are reduced in size from
mainframe to minicomputer to microcomputer, the size of available
RAM is also reduced. At the same time, a smaller computer's
capability is lessened. The amount of RAM available in the smallest
microcomputers ranges from 64K bytes, for the older machines,
to several million bytes in the newer microcomputers.

To provide more RAM capability, a computer can be designed with
the flexibility to expand its initial RAM capacity within the limit
of the system. More RAM chips can be added onto its existing
main memory printed circuit board, or plug-in boards, assembled
with compatible RAM chips, can be inserted into available slots
in the structure. The specified maximum RAM limit, however,
cannot be exceeded.

ARITHMETIC AND LOGIC UNIT (ALU)
Within the ALU, its logic circuits provide the basic four arithmetic
processes - addition, subtraction, multiplication, and division.
Large computers, generally, have additional circuitry to perform
more complex mathematical operations; these circuits are located
within the ALU.

A small, fast, volatile, read/write memory, referred to as the
accumulator, a temporary register that stores (accumulates) numbers
during an arithmetic process is also located within the ALU. Any
number can be stored temporarily in the accumulator while the
ALU is involved with another calculation that may, or may not
pertain to a number already stored in the accumulator. At the
direction of a program, the number being processed may be added
to the existing number in the accumulator or it can be placed in
the accumulator for future use.

Still under the direction of the program, the totalled numbers in
an accumulator may be tranferred to an I/O port to be displayed
on a monitor, sent to a selected storage device, or connected to
a printer to become part of a hard copy print-out. The actual size
of this temporary register, often referred to as the ALU's "electronic
scratch-pad", is dependent on the unique requirements of the
computer and can range in size from a single 4-bit register to several
16-bit or 32-bit registers.

CONTROL UNIT

The Control Unit is the "brain" of a computer. It coordinates and supervises all the sections of the system in a logical, timed sequence. The *clock,* located in the Control Unit, generates the digital timing pulses to properly synchronize the logic functions, flow of data, and instruction timing.

When a computer is turned ON, it must be set at an initial address in memory *(initialized)* to begin executing the program. To have a computer operate automatically, the binary code of the initial address is placed in a *program counter,* a register that is part of the Control Unit. The way in which the initial address is placed in the program counter varies from one computer type to another, but it must be done when a computer is turned ON. The program counter indicates the specific address in memory that must be accessed to allow the first instruction, and succeeding instructions, to be *fetched* and *executed.* A computer operates by performing a series of instructions. These programmed instructions and other information, collectively referred to as data, are contained in the computer's memory.

The computer's basic operations consist of two parts:
1. The *fetch cycle* - accessing an instruction
2. *The execute cycle* - executing the instruction or
    a sequence of instructions

The fetch cycle consists of finding the address of an instruction in memory which is specified in the program counter and placing it into the Control Unit. During the execute cycle, a *decoder* converts the binary code contained in that address and transfers the decoded word to the *instruction register* in which the computer's instruction set *(microcode)* is contained. When accessing a specific word in the instruction register, the microcode converts each word from the decoder into the corresponding machine operation. See Figure 80.

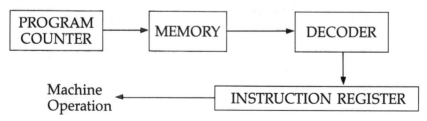

The Fetch and Execute Cycles
Figure 80

Each word in the memory has an address and, depending on the program being processed, the program counter will sequentially indicate a new memory address where the next sequence of instructions to be executed is located. When another address code is placed in the program counter, another sequence of instructions must now be executed. The process is repeated until the end of the program. The sequence of program counter codes will be established by the requirements of the program.

Although there are many instructions needed to complete a machine operation, each individual instruction is an extremely simple step when taken individually. The computer's lack of instruction complexity is compensated by the high speed by which the computer can fetch and execute each individual instruction.

Within the Control Unit, input information is examined to determine if the word patterns represent instructions for machine operations or temporary data. A small read/write memory circuit, called a *data register*, is located in the Control Unit to allow temporary data to be readily accessible for immediate processing.

CENTRAL PROCESSING UNIT (CPU)
The only sections in a computer structure where processing is done are in the ALU and Control Unit. When these two sections are combined, this single unit is called the *Central Processing Unit* (CPU). The drawing of the basic computer structure (Figure 81) illustrates the ALU and Control Unit combined as a CPU.

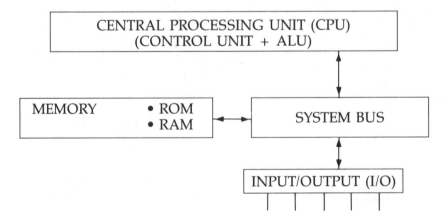

The Basic Computer Structure - CPU, Memory, and I/O
Figure 81

SYSTEM BUS

A computer "bus" can be compared to a timed, highly-controlled, multilane superhighway over which many vehicles are traveling at very high speeds. A computer bus is **not** a vehicle, but is the means by which information is transmitted and received throughout its internal structure. Buses are seen on a computer's printed circuit boards as a group of parallel, copper-foil lines (conducting copper traces), with the dimensions of the boards influenced by the bus structure and the type and configuration of the connectors used on each board.

Within a computer, the **channel** of communication used to transfer information throughout its structure is referred to as the *System Bus*, regardless of the complexity or size of the computer. See Figure 81. The system bus consists of three separate sections: the *Data Bus*, the *Control Bus*, and the *Address Bus*. In some computers, the three buses are timed-shared and, in some computers, they might be hidden; these buses, however, are always present in a computer.

A computer reads information from memory by placing the binary code for a desired location in the memory onto the Address Bus. After the access time inherent in a particular memory has elapsed, the data that has been read from the memory is placed on the bidirectional Data Bus and then transferred to its destination - the CPU. From there, the required processing is performed and the appropriate outbound data is placed on the Data Bus to be distributed to other sections of the computer. The timing and sequencing of data movement is controlled by signals sent from the CPU via the Control Bus.

CONTROL BUS

All digital computers are designed to operate in a synchronous manner. The Control Bus distributes timing signals derived from the Clock to synchronize the activities of its separate elements and to establish the timing needed to move data through the system. Control signals are used in the transfer of information on the Data Bus throughout the computer's structure by placing unique codes on the Control Bus to specify their timing and direction for execution of read/write functions.

The Control Bus also carries signals that indicate the status of an instruction cycle and similar activities, as well as determining whether the I/O devices, or the data in memory, are involved in any information transfer.

ADDRESS BUS
The Address Bus carries the signals that specify the destinations outside the CPU. When transferring information to a memory location, the CPU places the data on the Data Bus and then, specifically addresses the destination by placing its unique identity on the Address Bus.

This bus is structured to have as many lines as necessary for memory accessing with its size determined by the width (number of bits) in a single address of a memory structure.

DATA BUS
The Data Bus provides the path upon which data is transferred between any source and any destination inside a computer. In an 8-bit computer, an 8-bit Data Bus is needed to transfer 8 bits of data in parallel; a 16-bit computer needs a 16-bit bus, etc.

If a CPU is processing 16-bits at a time and its Data Bus is only 8 bits wide, two successive transfers are required, thereby slowing down the system. Since information being processed by a computer is moved on the Data Bus, a true 16-bit system would be structured so that both the Address and Data Bus are 16-bits wide. In comparing two computers, each specified as a 16-bit system and having the same clock frequency, the computer with the 16-bit Data Bus can potentially run 80 to 100 percent faster than the machine with an 8-bit Data Bus.

MICROCOMPUTERS AND VLSI TECHNOLOGY

THE MICROPROCESSOR UNIT (MPU)
If the huge amount of logic circuitry comprising a Central Processing Unit (CPU) is implemented in monolithic IC (VLSI) technology, this monolithic IC chip is called a *Microprocessor Unit* or MPU. Newer MPU chips generally have a large part of the System Bus included as part of its structure. See Figure 82.

MICROPROCESSOR UNIT (MPU) (CONTROL UNIT + ALU)	
SYSTEM BUS	• Data Bus • Address Bus • Control Bus

Microprocessor Unit (MPU) $ System Bus Implemented in VLSI
Figure 82

When a particular monolithic IC chip (MPU plus System Bus) is selected as the processing unit of a Microcomputer, its specific type number becomes the generic key to the selection of the other optional chips that comprise the entire computer circuit. The selected MPU and its System Bus dictates the selection of the memory chips (ROM and RAM), I/O chip(s), and other support chips for expansion of memory and enhancement of communications capability. The devices must be "bus-compatible" with the family type number designated by the MPU part number.

THE MICROCOMPUTER
The individual computer parts, in monolithic IC form, can be assembled on appropriate bus-compatible printed circuit boards and connected to a required D.C. power supply to create a complete *Microcomputer*, often referred to as a Microprocessor-based computer. The entire assembly can then be installed in an appropriate enclosure. See Figure 83. When peripherals are connected to the appropriate serial and parallel I/O ports, the hardware portion of a complete Microcomputer System is created.

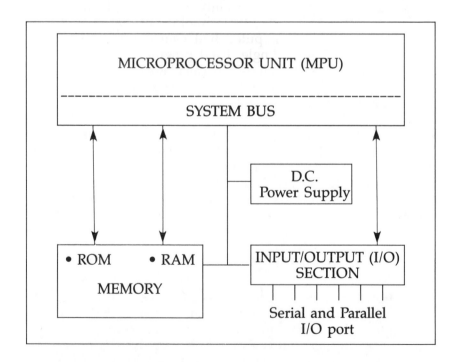

Microcomputer or Microprocessor-based Computer
Figure 83

BOARD-LEVEL COMPUTERS

Initially conceived as an assembly concept for minicomputers, *board-level* computers provided an entire computer on two or three pre-assembled printed circuit boards. As high-density monolithic IC technology became economically feasible, microcomputer manufacturers began producing *single-board* microcomputers (SBC) on a single, pre-assembled printed circuit board containing components required for a complete computer.

The boards are designed to connect to a "backplane" or "motherboard" that has a common system bus and a common power supply bus. Single board computers are assembled with connectors that attach to either serial and/or parallel I/O ports. Open sockets are also available on the boards for convenient addition of memory and other computer support chips.

SINGLE-CHIP MICROCOMPUTERS

The early 4-bit, *single-chip microcomputer*, containing the required CPU, memory and I/O section, merited the "computer on a chip" designation, however, its capability was constrained by the limitations of the monolithic IC technology of that time. Those early, single-chip microcomputers had a small word size, limited memory (ROM), and a single, fixed program. They served as dedicted computers for hand-held calculators, digital watches, electronic toys and games, and the simple controllers needed for tape recorders and home appliances.

With increase in chip density capability to very large scale integrated (VLSI) levels, 8-bit, and eventually, 16-bit single-chip microcomputers were produced with more memory (ROM and RAM) for general-purpose and customized applications. These applications include: automotive electronics, industrial process control, instrumentation, and sewing machine control.

SUPPORT HARDWARE

The optional complementary devices used to enhance computer performance and increase its power are called *support hardware*. Although a basic computer can be enhanced with "bus-compatible" support hardware, a careful analysis is needed to determine the technical and economic advisability of replacing an existing system. With the availabiity of newer, improved-performance computers, it may be more advisable to replace, rather than add to a system to achieve higher performance operation.

MAIN MEMORY SUPPORT HARDWARE

The main memory of a computer can be expanded with additional *add-in* and/or *add-on* memory. Functionally, both serve the same purpose and act to:

- Extend the computer's capability to operate larger programs

- Decrease memory access time, resulting in higher throughput characteristics

ADD-IN MEMORY - A bus-compatible memory that is added to the system **within** the computer's physical housing.
- Add-in memory can be supplied as individual RAM chips to be inserted into existing open sockets on a board. The added RAM chips can also be mounted on an additional PC BOARD (card) that is inserted into an "expansion slot" on the existing computer assembly. In the latter case, the frame of the expansion slot is already connected to the existing system bus and power supply.

- The addition of a floppy disk and/or hard disk drive to function as add-in memory is accomplished by assembling the new drive(s) in the designated space(s) inside the computer's enclosure. An appropriate cable connects the drive(s) to the existing computer circuit. For floppy and/or hard drive additions, it is also necessary to add a proper drive controller board or chip(s) to the existing computer circuit to accommodate the additional disk drive(s).

Advantages of using add-in memory:
- Relatively low-cost memory expansion is achieved without the need for an additional power supply and its connections.

- Existing memory can easily be replaced with denser and/or faster individual memory chips, cards, or disk drives without installng additional cables and connectors.

- Few system changes are required to accommodate higher performance memory.

Disadvantage of using add-in memory:
- An inadequate power supply may be a limiting factor in handling the increased memory. Changing the power supply may prove too costly to warrant the addition of memory.

ADD-ON MEMORY - "Plug-compatible" memory that is added **externally** to the computer. Add-on memory is connected with an external plug and connecting cable to a designated socket (at the rear or side of the computer cabinet) when provision has been made for external memory expansion. Add-on memory has its own power supply and controller circuit, with the entire assembly enclosed in its own housing, and is generally placed alongside the computer cabinet. Magnetic disk and tape drives are examples of add-on memory.

Advantages of using add-on memory:
• Memory expansion is not limited by the maximum power capability of the existing power supply. (The amount of memory that can be added, however, is limited by the maximum memory capability of the existing computer circuit, a condition that is true for both add-in and add-on memory.)
• Overall reliability of the system is enhanced by add-on memory serving as the back-up system for the internal memory.

Disadvantages of using add-on memory:
• Additional cables, connectors, interface circuits and software may be needed internally to accommodate the external add-on memory. Detailed documentation for the installation of the required interface circuits and software are required.
• Installation of add-on memory often requires a fairly high-level of technical expertise.

INPUT/OUTPUT (I/O) SUPPORT HARDWARE

Data communications between a computer and its peripherals can occur by a synchronous (clocked) method, coordinated by timed pulses, or an asynchronous method coordinated by random pulses.

SYNCHRONOUS COMMUNICATIONS
A synchronous system requires the transmission of clock pulses along with the data word to be transmitted from an I/O parallel port to establish coordination between a computer and a clocked peripheral. This technique is suitable for applications requiring high-speed data transfer and requires a peripheral device to have a parallel port. The parallel port at each end of the communications link is typically an 8-bit port with two extra lines per port to synchronize the clock at the computer with the clock at the peripheral. This synchronization step is referred to as "handshaking".

ASYNCHRONOUS COMMUNICATIONS

An asynchronous communications mode requires interfacing techniques that will coordinate incoming asynchronous data with a computer's clock, and conversely, convert the computer's clocked output into a string of randomly transmitted signals.

Typically, asynchronous communication operates as follows:
• An asynchronous line is left in an idle condition when data is not being transmitted.

• A START bit precedes each transmitted word to indicate that a new word is being sent.

• One or more STOP bits signal the end of the word, returning the line to the idle condition.

• When transmission is no longer required, an appropriate command from the transmitting end indicates the conclusion of the communication.

Asynchronous word widths vary from 5 to 8 bits, depending on the particular code used - ASCII, Baudot (Telex), etc. In addition, an extra bit is often used for checking errors, a technique called "parity". If a 7-bit ASCII word is being sent in an asynchronous mode, it consists of the 7 data bits, one START bit, two STOP bits, and one parity bit. The extra 4 bits are considered to be "overhead", an expense that is typical of asynchronous communication and limits this system to relatively low speed or irregular transmission applications.

Asynchronous communications is used when only one transmission line (standard telephone line) is available and requires the use of a serial I/O port at both ends of the transmission link.

ASYNCHRONOUS COMMUNICATIONS SUPPORT DEVICES
• Universal Asynchronous Receiver-Transmitter (UART) - The UART IC chip, generally mounted inside a computer enclosure, converts an 8-bit parallel input to a serial output and a serial input to an 8-bit parallel output. In addition, a UART automatically manages START and STOP bits and, if desired, can verify the correct transmission of data by using parity.

• MODEM (MODulator/DEModulator) - MODEMs, with appropriate software programs, are required to transfer digital information over a telephone line, with one MODEM and its software program used at each end of the line. A MODEM is available in the form of a plug-in board mounted inside a computer enclosure, or as a separate enclosed box placed alongside a computer. The external MODEM includes its own power supply, power line cord and connecting cable that is plugged into a computer's I/O serial port.

At the transmitting end, the outgoing digital information is "keyed" (modulated) onto a low frequency audio tone (carrier) by the MODulator section of its MODEM. At the receiving end, the transmitted digital data is removed (demodulated) from the carrier by the DEModulator section of its MODEM.

ADDITIONAL SUPPORT HARDWARE

• Direct Memory Access Controller (DMAC) - Provides access to the main memory without going through the processing unit.

• Numeric coprocessor chip - Provides the capability to speed-up complex mathematical operations that are not included in an ALU capability. Programs, such as: computer aided design (CAD), complex spread sheets, and intricate graphics programs can be operated very quickly and efficiently with the aid of this chip, however, appropriate software is also required.

• Data converters - Analog to digital converters (ADC) to convert analog information into digital form; digital to analog converters (DAC) to convert digital data into analog form.

Although electronics technology deals primarily with the physical elements (the hardware) contained within a computer system, the software that is used to direct, coordinate, and supervise the operation of the hardware is an equally essential part of the system. A computer system without one or the other is **not** a computer system. Knowledge of software, however general in scope, is fundamental to the understanding of the computer's mechanism. CHAPTER ELEVEN - SOFTWARE CONSIDERATIONS is provided to shed some light on the science of software.

REINFORCEMENT EXERCISES

Answer TRUE or FALSE to each of the following statements:

1. A modern, digital computer is made up of a group of related and interconnected electronic circuits that recognize and act on a predetermined set of instructions in a series of sequential steps. The aim of the computer's instructions is to accomplish a specific task with the use of its compatible hardware and appropriate software.

2. A modern digital computer can operate without software as long as it is produced with compatible hardware.

3. The term "firmware" is just another name for software and the two can be used interchangeably.

4. Computers have the ability to provide accurate results at very high speed and, in principle, the physical structure of all computers consists of the same basic sections, regardless of their speed and size.

5. One of the features that differentiate a mainframe, minicomputer, and a microcomputer is the "throughput", the number of instructions per second a machine can handle.

6. A computer's clock frequency and word width has no influence on its throughput capability.

7. Some other features that differentiate a mainframe, minicomputer, and microcomputer are the comparative sizes of their memory, as well as, the size and capability of their other sections.

8. A computer is considered to be an extremely "powerful" machine because it consumes more electrical power than other electronic equipment.

9. The basic computer structure consists of the I/O Section, the Main Memory, the Arithmetic and Logic unit, Control Unit, Central Processing Unit, and the System Bus.

10. The hardware of a computer system includes its basic computer structure, an appropriate power supply, an enclosure to house the hardware, peripheral devices, and compatible connecting cables, plugs and sockets.

11. Regardless of the size of a computer, the channel of communication used to transfer information throughout its structure is called the System Bus.

12. The System Bus consists of three separate buses, the Data Bus, the Address bus, and the Control bus. The Data Bus and Address Bus must have the same word width.

13. To improve a computer system's capability, the best approach is to add more support hardware to the existing machine to take advantage of the common power supply, enclosure, and other proven features of the older computer.

14. Single-chip microcomputers are generally used for dedicated applications, such as: on-board automobile computers, electronic sewing machines, and home appliance circuitry.

15. A serial port at the computer and at a peripheral device is required if a synchronous communication technique is used to transfer data between them.

16. Asynchronous communication techniques are used for the transfer of digital data over a 2-conductor telephone line between computers. This mode of communication requires a MODEM interface circuit at each computer.

17. A computer can function without any software, but if software is used, the computer's performance is improved.

Answers to these reinforcement exercises are on page 283.

 CHAPTER
ELEVEN

SOFTWARE CONSIDERATIONS

APPLICATIONS SOFTWARE
SYSTEM SOFTWARE
  THE OPERATING SYSTEM
  MULTITASKING OPERATING SYSTEM

COMPUTER PROGRAMMING
  ALGORITHMS AND FLOW-CHARTING

HIERARCHY OF COMPUTER LANGUAGES
  MACHINE LANGUAGE
  ASSEMBLY LANGUAGE
  MACRO-ASSEMBLY LANGUAGE
  HIGHER-LEVEL LANGUAGES

HARDWARE VS. SOFTWARE

SOFTWARE CONSIDERATIONS

> Computer software is the information that is written on any memory media, including: microchips, magnetic disks or tape. The information consists of programs, instructions, codes, routines, languages, documentation, and other data.

A modern computer cannot function without the software that has been created to automatically direct, supervise, and control its operation. With software, the computer can also automatically perform specific tasks that are accomplished with great precision and incredible speed. A major factor in determining the selection of a computer is based on its intended application, therefore, *the function of a computer is identified by its software.*

APPLICATIONS AND SYSTEM SOFTWARE

APPLICATIONS SOFTWARE

Referred to as a *computer program*, applications software provides the set of instructions, in sequenced form, that automatically directs the computer to perform specified task(s). Examples of typical applications areas that require externally entered applications software include:

- Word-processing systems
- Automotive electronics
- Traffic control
- Accounting procedures
- Filing systems
- Communications systems
- Computer-aided design
- Production control
- Chemical processing
- Inventory control
- Mailing lists
- Energy distribution
- Computer graphics
- General data bases

Some computers have applictions software included within their basic system. These applications software programs are referred to as "bundled programs".

To assist the applications software perform its assigned work, an additional category, the *system software* is required.

SYSTEM SOFTWARE

System software is part of the internal computer system and begins to function when the computer is turned ON. It assists in the successful accomplishment of an applications program by controlling the resources within the computer system. In addition to supervisory and control functions, the system software keeps track of time, verifies the correct sequence of events to be performed, and controls input/output (I/O) functions.

OPERATING SYSTEM

The collection of system software programs that supervise and control a computer's operation is called the *operating system*. Since it acts as the interface between the computer hardware and the applications program, the operating system is considered to be the software extension of the hardware. The operating system carries out those unique services for which the computer system has been designed.

For example, an applications program may include a request to send an instruction and/or data to a specific peripheral device, such as: the computer's monitor screen, disk drive or printer port. With the help of the operating system, the request is carried out, allowing the system to perform its required task quickly and accurately .

An operating system has a complex structure that is organized into a group of service sections performing specific functions.
• Basic data handling services are performed, for example, output data from an applications program is accepted for storage on a disk for later use.

• At the discretion of the computer operator, the operating system allocates a specified amount (*virtual memory*) of the system's RAM. A virtual memory is often called a *RAM disk*. Its purpose is to allow some, or all, of the data that would generally be on an external disk to be accessed at the inherent high speed of a semiconductor read/write memory (RAM) compared with the slower access time of a magnetic disk.

• The operating system acts to load applications software (computer program) into RAM and adjusts the location of the addresses in the program to correspond to their exact location in memory. The operating system will also act to recover from any program errors through its error handling capability.

- A *command processor* accepts and acts on commands entered by the computer operator. These commands are generally requests for the execution of some service routine, such as a copy command, a print command, or a screen clearing command. In most personal computer operating systems, the command processor is in a file named COMMAND.COM.

- The operating system's *Basic Disk Operating System* (BDOS) monitors the execution of the applications program instructions (Figure 84) and any commands the computer operator enters via the keyboard. BDOS allows the applications program (or the computer operator) to address and access devices (a specific disk drive or printer) without needing to be aware of the details of how the addressed devices actually work.

The BDOS section is the same for different computers that use the same operating system. Its characteristics provide compatibility between computers, making it possible for the applications software designed for a specific operating system to be run on different machines.

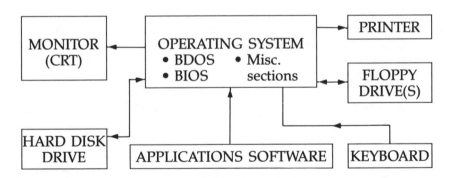

Operating System Interfacing Between Programs and Peripherals
Figure 84

- The *Basic Input/Output System* (BIOS) section of the operating system is "machine-specific" and can vary from machine to machine to accommodate different kinds of computers.

The BIOS is responsible for handling input/output operation details that include the tasks of relating any applications program's logical data to any peripheral device's physical characteristics. These BIOS routines are called *drivers*, or device handlers, and isolate the specifications and details of each peripheral from the rest of the operating system.

MULTITASKING OPERATING SYSTEM

Since a *task* is the basic unit of programming, each task performs a single function. A collection of tasks can be sequenced and assigned to specific operating priorities with the use of a *multitasking* operating system. The advantage of this technique is that it allows additional applications programs to run during the same time period the initial applications program is working. Although it may appear that more than one program is running concurrently, this time-saving approach is actually a high speed sequential sharing of the capabilities of a CPU.

Tasks that require responses to events as they occur are called *real-time applications* and demand immediate, and complete, access to the computer's resources at regular and irregular intervals. The computer's resources can be used to operate less urgent programs, such as data processing, between peak load times. A multitasking operating system can be used to evaluate the priorities of various programs and preempt the less urgent ones when a real-time event needs servicing.

Since the CPU is the only section in a computer that executes an instruction, it can control only one task at a time. A task operation, however, includes more than CPU involvement. With a multitasking operating system, a real-time event that starts a process and then waits for the operation to be completed will not use CPU time while it is waiting. While one task waits for the operation to be completed outside the CPU, a multitasking operating system can give control of the CPU to another task.

COMPUTER PROGRAMMING

To create a well-designed computer program, certain instructions called *routines* and smaller *subroutines* must be included that relate to specific tasks to be executed within a program. Each portion of a complete program may have many individual routines with their unique sequence. In the same manner, subroutines may exist within routines. Each program, routine and subroutine is developed by creating an *algorithm*.

ALGORITHMS

The procedure, or set of rules, describing a sequence of actions during an operation is called an algorithm. For example, a typical algorithm describes the act of opening a closed door as follows: "Turn the door knob in a clockwise manner until the door latch is released and then push the door forward".

This apparently simple procedure actually contains other, more minuscule, routines and subroutines which are necessary to properly specify the sequence of the movements of a door-opener's hand and arm, and in so doing, complete this program.

In a similar manner, a computer can successfully execute any program if provided with a clearly-defined, properly-sequenced group of algorithms, however, the design of "**clearly-defined, properly-sequenced** algorithms" may be more complex than what appears to be so very simple. Algorithms must contain **all** the necessary steps and procedures to fulfill the needs of a particular program and, in some cases, small, but important, details are overlooked or improperly sequenced.

FLOW CHARTING
One of a computer's programmer's major tools for creating a well-designed algorithm is the *flow* chart. It provides a means of observing a program's sequence, from its concept to its final operational state, by graphically illustrating each step of the program's movement. The use of a flow chart helps in avoiding inadvertent omission of steps and assists in establishing the interrelationship of individual instructions in the program. To denote the specific classes of computer operation, standard flow chart symbols are used, with the most commonly used symbols shown in Figure 85.

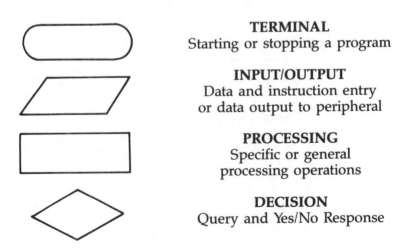

TERMINAL
Starting or stopping a program

INPUT/OUTPUT
Data and instruction entry
or data output to peripheral

PROCESSING
Specific or general
processing operations

DECISION
Query and Yes/No Response

Commonly Used Flow Chart Symbols
Figure 85

To create a flow chart, connecting lines are drawn between these symbols to indicate the sequence of the program to be executed. Conventionly, a flow chart is written from top to bottom and from left to right, unless otherwise indicated. Arrows drawn on the connecting lines clearly designate the direction of the program's flow, the routines or subroutines to be performed, and the start and completion of a program. Information inside the symbols identify the title of a specific instruction, or other required information.

To illustrate an example of a simplified flow chart, a general approach to an initial design of an electronic circuit is flow-charted in Figure 86.

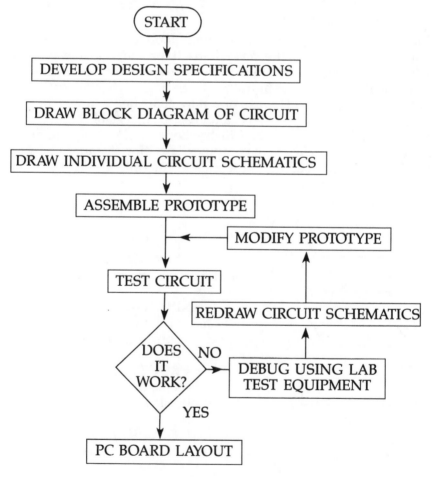

Flow Chart Approach to an Electronic Circuit Design
Figure 86

The flow chart illustrated in Figure 86 has several intermediate steps omitted, however, the inclusion of documented detail will help to minimize any possible errors.

A portion of a flow chart (Figure 87) illustrates a "fetch and execute" operation for a sequence of several operations.

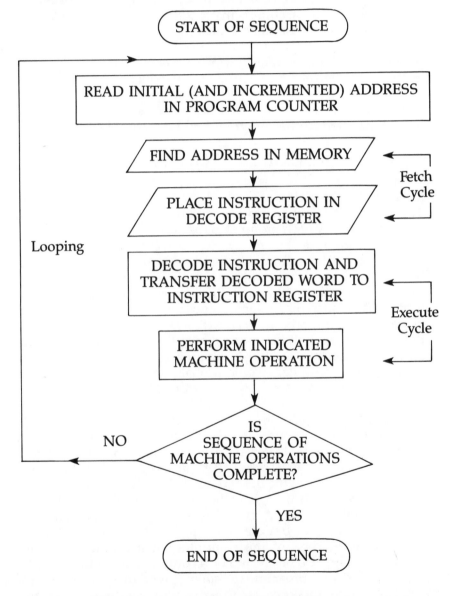

Flow-charting a Fetch and Execute Sequence
Figure 87

COMPUTER LANGUAGES

A computer can only execute commands that appear in the form of binary words (patterns of zeros and ones), more commonly called *machine code* that is referred to as the *object program*. The binary word for each command is generally provided in a listing by the computer manufacturer, or the CPU (or MPU) manufacturer, in the form of a machine's instruction set or microcode, the repertoire of the computer's capabilities.

A computer's input program (applications software) is referred to as the *source program* and consists of a sequence of instructions to be entered into the computer and arranged into the memory section, so that when each instruction is executed, the specific task(s) assigned to that program will be accomplished.

SOURCE PROGRAMS

MACHINE LANGUAGE
The most fundamental way of entering the data of a source program is to key each group of zeros and ones, representing the machine language binary words, directly into a keyboard connecting to the computer's input section. Each binary word instruction entered at the keyboard will result in a corresponding machine operation. Although this process maintains the most intimate relationship between a source program and the operation of a computer, this procedure is never followed since it is extremely time-consuming, tedious, and removes the advantage of fast data entry provided by a modern computer. If this was the only way to enter data, computers would probably not have been used for more than just an interesting laboratory novelty.

ASSEMBLY LANGUAGE
A more convenient approach to enter the instructions contained in a source program is to develop a set of simple, easy-to-remember symbolic names or labels, called *mnemonics*, that look like shorthand versions of the desired instruction. For example, "SHR" could represent "**SH**ift Logic **R**ight", or "CLA" could mean "**CL**ear the **A**ccumulator", etc. A complete set of these mnemonics is generally supplied by the microprocessor manufacturer to represent each code of the computer's instruction set. Other mnemonics can also be created by a computer programmer to be used for the source program. The source program is called *Assembly language* and is much easier to work with and is more clearly understood by programmers than Machine language.

Since a computer can only understand and respond to machine language (binary code), the program written in Assembly language must be translated (converted) into machine language. The process of converting from Assembly language to the binary words of machine language is called *assembling a program*.

To simplify and speed up this process, the tedious conversion can be accomplished by the computer itself. A listing (look-up table) containing the Assembly language mnemonics being used along with their equivalent microcode instructions can be placed into the computer's memory section. With a properly written algorithm, the computer can be directed to look up and convert each source program mnemonic into the appropriate machine operation. This conversion software program is called an *Assembler*.

Each instruction in an Assembly language source program will produce exactly the same result as if an instruction in machine language had been entered; the same one-to-one relationship will exist, as before. Each operation of the machine is apparent to the operator as each instruction is entered. This procedure may be desired by the computer operator, however, the process of translating Assembly language mnemonics to machine code is merely a matter of looking up the appropriate microcode in a table for each mnemonic to be entered.

MACRO-ASSEMBLY LANGUAGE
In using an Assembly language source program, each individual entry results in the performance of a single machine operation. If desired, a variation of the use of pure Assembly language source code could provide a time-saving data entry technique.

A coded *label* that represents a group of related source program instructions used during the data entry process is created by the computer programmer. Each coded label is called a *macro* and when converted, translates into several related and properly sequenced microcode instructions and addresses. A macro can contain many Assembly language mnemonics, each resulting in an instruction, with the actual number depending on the content of the source program, the relatedness of the machine operations assigned to that macro, and the discretion of the computer programmer. The source program, in this case, is written in *Macro-assembly language* or a combination of Assembly and Macro-assembly language. The software that converts the source program into the object program is called a *Macro-assembler*.

HIGHER-LEVEL LANGUAGES

A source program written in either Assembly or Macro-assembly language can only be used for a specific computer. It would be desirable to have a source program written in a language that removes the need to be involved with the intricate details of machine language programming. Creating mnemonics for each machine language instruction and its related binary code and writing individual algorithms to perform relatively routine operations can be avoided by using *higher-level languages*.

An important reason for using a higher-level language is that it is **not** unique to a particular computer, but can be used with any computer, regardless of computer variations. As long as a software translating program has been developed, standard, higher-level languages allow different computers to exchange programs and communicate with each other in a common language. Since different processing units exist in different computers, each with variations in its instruction set, the machine code performing specific operations will be different for each computer and if a common high-level language were not used, no interchange of information would be possible.

This incompatablle situation among computers can be compared with two people trying to communicate with one another, when each person can only speak a language the other does not understand. If a mutually understandable language existed, they could converse and exchange information in the common language. This analogy illustrates the need to use a mutually compatible higher-level language, instead of an incompatible Assembly or Macro-assembly language between computers.

There are many "standard" higher-level languages used for a variety of computer applications. Their differences relate to their intended use, the operations they can perform which are unique to an application, the syntax structure of each language, and other characteristic features. Some are specifically used for business needs, others to solve scientific and mathematical problems, others for military applications, etc.

Although there are many standard higher-level languages, new higher-level languages can be created for similar or totally different applications. By defining a different syntax structure and providing new meanings for its symbols, the newer languages become viable. Newer languages are constantly being created as the urgency increases for compatibility and ease in communication between computers.

A brief listing of some popular higher-level languages include:

- BASIC - Beginner's All-Purpose Symbolic Instruction Code - Because of its relative simplicity, it is the language most commonly used in personal computers for the non-programmer.

- FORTRAN - FORmula TRANslation - This language is generally used in scientific and mathematical applications.

- COBOL - COmmon Business-Oriented Language

- ALGOL - ALGOrithmetic Language

- PASCAL - The first language to be named after a person, the French mathematician, Blaise Pascal. Its particular advantage is that it has a highly structured format, making it easy to document and correct (debug), if needed. Some variations of PASCAL include: Pseudo-code (P-code) and C code (C) ,

- ADA - Named after Augusta Ada Lovelace, Charles Babbage's associate. She is considered to be the first computer programmer in history. The language is military-oriented and used for computer-control of "hi-tech" armaments.

- APL - All-Purpose Logic - A general-purpose language.

- FORTH - A mainframe language developed to overcome the deficiencies of some of the other higher-level languages. Variations of FORTH include: Mini-Forth (for minicomputers) and Micro-Forth (for microcomputers).

ADVANTAGES OF HIGHER-LEVEL LANGUAGES
- The commands and keywords resemble the English language, making computer programs easier to write, read, and debug.

- Programs written in higher-level languages are easier to modify, revise (up-date) and repair. The costs of program maintenance are reduced. Some languages, such as PASCAL and ALGOL, have a structured format that includes functional blocks (modules) as part of the language. Modules can be altered individually without upsetting the overall structure.

The major disadvantage of higher-level languages is that the computer is used less efficiently; higher-level languages require memory space much greater than that required with Assembly or Macro-assembly languages.

Some of the higher-level languages may also accommodate some Assembly language instructions to allow for optimization of a program. This technique is called *hand optimization* and offers saving of time and memory; it is often used with some of the newer 16-bit and 32-bit computers.

The hierarchy of computer languages is shown in Figure 88.

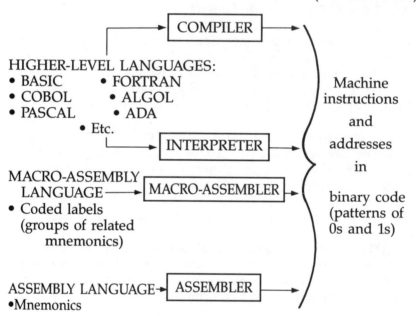

SOURCE PROGRAM   TRANSLATION PROGRAM   OBJECT PROGRAM
                                        (Machine Code)

COMPILER

HIGHER-LEVEL LANGUAGES:
• BASIC   • FORTRAN
• COBOL   • ALGOL
• PASCAL   • ADA
        • Etc.

INTERPRETER

MACRO-ASSEMBLY
  LANGUAGE ——➤ MACRO-ASSEMBLER
• Coded labels
  (groups of related
   mnemonics)

ASSEMBLY LANGUAGE ➤ ASSEMBLER
•Mnemonics

Machine
instructions

and

addresses

in

binary code
(patterns of
0s and 1s)

The Hierarchy of Computer Languages
Figure 88

INTERPRETER OR COMPILER
There are two kinds of higher-level language translators, each having unique features. Each translates the instructions of a high-level language program into machine code, but, unlike an Assembler, a high-level language translator provides output codes that invoke hundreds, and possibly thousands, of machine instructions. Interpreters and Compilers, however, are used in two completely different ways.

When a program is run using an Interpreter, the source program is translated into machine code, line by line, while the program is running.

When a program is run using a Compiler, the operator must first command the Compiler to translate the source program into an executable file; then the file is run as a separate step. Although compilation of the source program takes time, the final compiled program will run much faster and is preferred if the program is to be run many times.

COMMENTS ON HARDWARE AND SOFTWARE

Computer system hardware is made up of chips, wires, printed circuit boards, and peripheral devices whose costs and manufacturing time can be accurately evaluated. Finished products can be quickly and easily manufactured and warehoused as inventory. Traditionally, the electronics industry is hardware-oriented, with a comprehensive understanding of measurable test standards, production methods, and quality control.

Software, on the other hand, is not nearly as tangible nor is its production and quality easily controlled. In addition, there is a universally-accepted understanding that a software program does not work the first time it is written, nor the second, nor the third. It is extremely difficult to accurately assess its production and maintenance costs, or to precisely estimate the length of time required to complete a complex software program.

Computer software consists of programs, instructions, data, flow charts, computer languages, and documentation. The science of software engineering is a relatively young discipline that attempts to define a set of rules, which when implemented, will result in predictable, computer program code that minimizes the need for testing and inordinate time and cost overruns. Software engineering is involved with conceptualization and strategy for producing a software program; computer programming implements the program concept.

Testing software has a different set of problems associated with it than testing hardware. With hardware, there are clearly defined specifications that must be met and the methods and standards of testing hardware performance is straightforward. Software, generally, has no well-defined test specifications. If a program appears to work satisfactorily, the software program is assumed to be marketable, until some errors appear that require correction.

Although speed is a measurable parameter, there is a great deal of end-user subjectivity involved in the evaluation of software programs. Such subjective words and phrases as "elegant", "easy to learn", "intuitive", and similar, vaguely descriptive terms offer very little objective insight into a program's quality or desirability.

The performance and quality of hardware has dramatically improved during the past two decades. Miniaturization of components and changes in technology, particularly in the area of high-density, high-speed, lower-power monolithic integrated circuits, have revolutionized electronic packaging concepts, increased hardware productivity, improved circuit and system performance, and raised system reliability levels. At the same time, the cost of material, production, and testing have been reduced for most of the new hardware, including computers and their peripherals.

Software, however, has not benefited from advances in automated manufacturing technology as has its hardware counterpart. Since software is written by fallible humans, and not by machines, reliability of software has not been substantially improved. Software costs have increased to the degree that they have become a major element in the total cost of a computer system.

The selling price of a software program is not related to the direct costs of the disks it is written on, nor to the direct cost of the printed matter accompanying the program. The price is basically determined by the costs of **creating** the software program and the documentation, the anticipated size of the product's market, and the desired profit. Competitive prices also play a major role in influencing the final selling price. Because of the explosive proliferation of computer applications, the combined **development and production** costs of software are currently ranging between $35 billion to $40 billion per year, and that does not include the cost of maintenance.

It is estimated that software **maintenance** costs (updating and post-production program error correction) are about 70% of the total cost of software over the life of a software program. It is eminently clear that less expensive software programming and improved maintenance efficiency could have a significant impact on the economic health of a modern, industrialized world.

CHAPTER
TWELVE

COMPUTER TECHNOLOGY TRENDS

MEMORY
  SEMICONDUCTOR RAM
  ROTATING DISK MEMORIES

DATA ENTRY TECHNIQUES
  OPTICAL CHARACTER RECOGNITION
  GRAPHIC SCANNERS
  SPEECH RECOGNITION

COMPUTER STANDARDIZATION

COMPUTER TECHNOLOGY TRENDS

INTRODUCTION

There is increasing evidence that future computer systems will become more spectacular as the technology moves into the last decade of the 20th Century. A consistent, unbroken trend of significant improvements in computer hardware technology is being maintained, generally accompanied by the rapid reduction of manufacturing costs and end-user prices. The factors suggesting these continuing patterns include:

- Greatly expanded use of Very Large Scale Integration (VLSI) - Since the birth of monolithic IC technology, chip density has increased at the rate of about 100 times per decade. With chip density now over 1 million component functions per chip, all indications point to the availability of monolithic IC chips that will have a density of at least 100 million (and possibly higher) by the beginning of the 21st Century.

- Single-chip computer capability is expanding. Circuits are being produced on smaller pieces of silicon with more functionality designed into each chip.

- Improvements in semiconductor material processing, specifically, gallium arsenide and GaAs on silicon wafers, have provided improved performance characteristics at reduced production costs. These developments have offered the promise of inherently faster chip material regardless of clock speed and structural design of new computers.

- In the computer industry, there is a strong movement toward expanding existing technologies into improved-performance peripheral devices. They include:
  - Full-color flat panel displays

  - Inexpensive laser printers

  - Erasable (read/write) optical memories

  - Optical-character recognition (OCR) and graphic scanners

  - Voice-activated data entry devices made possible with automatic speech-recognition equipment.

SPECIFIC TECHNOLOGY TRENDS

MEMORIES

Computer memory technology that includes both semiconductor RAM and rotating disk memory is advancing at a rate faster than the other components of a computer system. These changes in traditional computer memory structures promise to provide more capacity, speed, and flexibility in future computer systems. The need to define the nature of future computer systems will present computer manufacturers with critical selection choices.

SEMICONDUCTOR RAM
Within the next decade, silicon chips will begin replacing magnetic disks as a more convenient means of storing information. Although floppy disks are still the most cost-effective way of storing and transporting software programs, semiconductor chips are gaining in storage capability and declining in cost per bit at a faster rate than that of magnetic memories.

• Semiconductor RAM chips with a capacity of one million bits of binary data are readily available. These chips are being packaged in wallet-sized cards for insertion into an appropriate slot, with data-protecting batteries included.

• IC manufacturers are starting to produce 4 Megabit memory chips and are developing experimental 16 Megabit chips.

• By the start of the next century, the availability of a semiconductor chip that is capable of storing one billion bits of data (at a cost per bit similar to that of magnetic storage) is a strong possibility. This is equivalent to 125 megabytes, six times the capacity of a 20 megabyte hard drive commonly used in many personal computers.

ROTATING DISK MEMORIES

Rotating-disk storage technologies are safe from being replaced by advancing semiconductor memory, if for no other reason than its advantage of having a relatively larger capacity and lower cost per bit. Although great strides are being made in RAM chip density, magnetic and optical disk storage are still in the vanguard of memory technology because of improvements in magnetic read/write heads, disk media to read and write on, and advances in accuracy and tracking ability.

MAGNETIC MEMORY - FLOPPY DISKS

Advances in floppy disk technology have kept in step with succeeding generations of personal computers. While the physical sizes of the disks have decreased, storage capacities have increased. The storage capacity of floppy disks has grown from an initial standard of 240 Kilobyte capacity in an 8" floppy disk to a 1.2 Megabyte capacity in the 5.25" disks. Relatively newer 3.5" micro-floppy disks are available with 720 Kilobyte capacity; a high-density version with a capacity of 1.44 Megabytes is also available.

Although there are still many dedicated word processing computers that use the original 8" floppy disks, the demand for this size disk has appreciably diminished. Since more advanced hardware is required for reading or recording on the higher-density 1.2 Megabyte capacity 5.25" floppy disk, the current standard of 360 Kilobyte capacity on the 5.25" disk will probably remain the favored size for the desktop personal computer and co-exist with the more advanced, more rugged 3.5" micro-floppy disks. Because of their low price, reliability, ease in handling, mailing, storing and loading of software programs, floppy disks are generally equivalent to paper files.

In 1989, a large-capacity 3.5" floppy drive has been introduced for market evaluation. It has the capacity to store over 11 Megabytes of formatted information on a metal disk that has 640 tracks on each side. It can read both the existing low-density and high-density 3.5" disks and has an average access time of less than 60 milliseconds. Although, at this time, this newer, more advanced, higher-capacity drive does not present a strong competitive stance to existing floppy disks, it indicates the direction being taken by floppy disk manufacturers in this highly competitive field.

MAGNETIC MEMORY - HARD DRIVES

The first hard disk drives measured 14" in diameter and were enclosed in cabinets that were 6 feet high. They could only store a few Megabytes of data, used immense amounts of electrical power, and required a dust-free, air-conditioned environment for their operation. In 1979, IBM introduced the 8" "Winchester" hard disk drive that eliminated the necessity for a controlled environment. As the need for greater storage and smaller drives increased, the 8" hard drive gave way to the 5.25" unit with a storage capacity of 5 Megabytes and then, to the 3.5" hard drives. A typical hard drive, with its "normally" sealed case open, is shown in Figure 89.

Typical 5.25" Hard Drive
Figure 89

Hard drive storage technology can now offer sealed 5.25" hard drives capable of storing over 900 Megabytes of data. The smaller hard drive, only 3.5" in diameter and about 1.5" high, has a capacity of 80 Megabytes. It can fit into a desktop computer, or into a small, portable laptop computer that can be easily carried; it can operate in a dusty environment with no specific need for climate control. As hard drive technology advances, higher capacity drives are anticipated.

OPTICAL DISK DRIVES

While disk drive manufacturers are successfully trying to squeeze more capacity out of magnetic disk storage, great strides are being made in the area of optical disk drives. Because of improved laser technology, the CD-ROM (Compact Disk-Read Only Memory) has finally come into its own as an effective high-density medium for large data bases and archival documents. At present, CD-ROM drives are available with 660 Megabytes of storage capability on a 4.72" disk or cartridge that can be easily inserted and removed from a drive compartment.

WORM (WRITE-ONCE, READ MANY) DISK

Although considered by many potential users to be a storage medium with limited applications, WORM (Write-Once, Read Many) optical disks are available in several formats, from 5.25" to 14". The user can enter data, **only once**, into the available space on the WORM; it then essentially acts as a CD-ROM. Any unused space on the disk can be written on until the disk is full, but the information already written is unalterable. It provides a high-density storage equivalent of a semiconductor PROM that can only be programmed once to become a non-erasable, non-volatile read-only memory.

WORM technology is best suited for creating large customized databases, such as: corporate documents, financial histories, and insurance policies. It provides a high degree of integrity for records that are intended to be permanent. WORM systems can easily outperform paper-based files. The files on a disk can be accessed more quickly than paper files and cannot be misfiled or lost. In addition, a WORM database in which the equivalent of 3 million 8" x 11" pages of information can be stored requires only about 16 square feet of space. The same amount of paper-based information stored in filing cabinets needs over 1700 square feet.

ERASABLE OPTICAL DISK

The major limitation in optical disk technology is its inability to be erased and re-written, however, high-density optical disks with read/write capability will be available in the very near future. The storage capacity of erasable optical disks will range between 60 to 500 Megabytes, with attention devoted to 3.5" and 5.25" drives for use in personal computers. Erasable optical disk technology will combine the storage capacity and reliability of optical disks with the erasability and flexibility of magnetic media. All projected erasable optical drives will probably use the magneto-optic technology illustrated in Figure 90.

READ/WRITE TECHNIQUE FOR
MAGNETO-OPTIC TECHNOLOGY

Unlike the structure of a CD-ROM that uses a laser beam to physically burn holes (pits) into a metal substrate and thereby make the data unerasable, the writing laser beam used in magneto-optic technology heats the substrate material in the presence of a magnetic bias field. The heated bit positions will then assume the polarization of the magnetic field and retain it after the substrate is cooled.

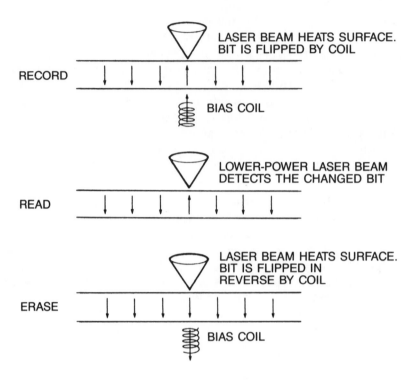

Magneto-Optic Technology for Erasable Optical Drives
Figure 90

To erase the bits, the substrate is again heated by the laser beam and the bias field at the appropriate position is reversed before the substrate cools.

To read the data, the polarization of the reading laser beam is rotated by the magnetic field. Polarization of the light striking the written bit positions will be opposite of that striking the rest of the media.

Overwriting data on a magneto-optic disk is inherently slower than with a magnetic disk, since one revolution of the disk is required to erase a bit and a second revolution is needed to write back to the erased location. Software drivers will also be needed to handle this characteristic.

Erasable optical drives may eventually replace floppy and hard disks as primary storage devices. Because of their greater capacity, they are suitable for replacing magnetic tape as a back-up system in personal computers. A typical magnetic hard drive used in a personal computer provides storage capability ranging from 20 Megabytes to 60 Megabytes. The more durable, easily replaceable, erasable optical disks can provide data storage up to 500 Megabytes.

Despite these advantages, there are some drawbacks to erasable optical disk technology, including cost and access time. Initially, like any new product, its biggest disadvantage will be the relatively higher cost for both the drive and disks, although, once available and tested favorably in the marketplace, these costs will drop dramatically.

Although still not specified, access time of an erasable optical disk will probably be substantially slower than a magnetic hard drive of comparable size and may deter initial acceptance of new products. As always, access time will eventually be improved as the technology matures.

DATA ENTRY TECHNIQUES

OPTICAL-CHARACTER RECOGNITION (OCR) AND GRAPHIC SCANNERS

The term *optical-character recognition* (OCR) refers to the equipment that looks at a page of text and uses optical techniques to determine which marks on that page are letters, numbers, or coded bars. It then converts that information into binary code for use by computers.

OCR equipment has been more commonly used in reading bar codes, such as the Universal Product Code (UPC) that is scanned with a laser beam at the check-out counter of a supermarket. Because of the ever-increasing costs of entering computer data, the business world is moving in the direction of OCR readers as an alternative way of managing and reducing these costs.

Compared with manually retyping printed or typed pages of text, the use of OCR equipment results in lower direct labor costs by providing faster and, in many cases, more accurate data entry. The pages of printed or typed text are then stored as digitized data. A dedicated word processor, or a personal computer using a word processing program, can then be used to edit, reformat, and print the data at a fraction of the previous costs.

Other data entry equipment, called *graphic scanners,* are used to optically scan images, such as: maps, photographs, and other artwork and then convert these images into digitized data for entry into a computer.

Although graphic scanners have been available for several years, new software is being introduced to use existing scanners in a more accurate, lower-cost approach to optical-character recognition techniques. Since printed text is another form of graphic symbols, configured to appear as letters and numbers, appropriate software can analyze each symbol, convert it into the standard ASCII code, and store it into a computer's memory as text.

A hand-held scanner, resembling an overgrown computer "mouse", can perform selective data entry as opposed to scanning an entire page and then editing unwanted material. It can recognize either typewritten or typeset proportionally-spaced and fixed-pitch text as well as letter quality (and near-letter quality) characters produced by a dot-matrix printer. Some of the new, more expensive scanners can also accurately read the normally poorer quality dot-matrix text.

When a graphic scanner system is set to automatically recognize type size and styles, there is no need to identify the particular typeface being scanned. It can work with a variety of source materials, including books, magazines, and typewritten pages with data being entered at speeds of 40 characters per second, and higher. Newer units offer faster data entry rates at correspondingly increased prices.

When scanning maps, drawings, photographs, and other artwork, the scanned material can be viewed on a computer monitor after entry. It can be electronically cropped, scaled, and positioned on a finished page when used in conjunction with any of the popular desktop publishing software programs that are presently available on the market.

SPEECH RECOGNITION
Although truly satisfactory speech recognition for computer entry applications is still not a practical reality, improved software techniques and declining semiconductor costs promise major breakthroughs. Current products have limited vocabularies and some difficult operating procedures. Newer, low-cost, software-intensive systems, incorporating 32-bit signal processing circuits will make speech recognition a cost-effective supplement to keyboard entry within a few years.

The human voice speaks in so many accents, dialects, and inflections that it presents an enormous standardization problem to speech technologists and software programmers. Present systems are available that offer continuous speech recognition application-specific vocabularies of up to 500 words, using predefined grammatical structures with better than 99% accuracy, high background noise tolerance, and with the ability to differentiate among most speech variations.

Despite present shortcomings, today's speech recognition systems offer several useful applications, including speed-up of materiel management, quality control, and computer-aided design and manufacture (CAD/CAM). These programs work particularly well when the operator has "busy-hands/busy-eyes", such as on a production line.

Future systems will provide improved human-to-machine voice data entry with large vocabulary capability. Before then, however, more technical advances are needed, such as: improved modeling of fine phonetic distinctions among letters and numerals, more efficient search-and-compare algorithms, enhanced noise-handling techniques, and faster processing speeds.

Speech recognition can play a major role in telephone communications, electronic banking, and access to centralized databases. Although, new developments are having a significant impact on some industries and occupations, natural-language recognition, similar to that used by the computer HAL in the movie "2001" will, coincidentally, probably not be available until that very date.

COMPUTER STANDARDIZATION

Any general discussion pertaining to computer technology trends should deal with the standardization of its elements to provide compatibility between various types of existing computers. At present, each computer has its unique characteristics, architecture, and its own set of timing rules and signals to perform its required functions. In the area of bus structures, the lack of compatibility has become a major concern and is receiving considerable industry attention.

With standardization of computer bus structures, direct communication between different types of computers is feasible, making local area networks possible. When a computer requires additional memory, communication IC chips, analog to digital convertors, arithmetic circuits and similar support chips, the bus structure must be compatible with these additional components. In fact, **bus compatibility** is a key requirement in the expansion of computer systems.

At present, little or no standardization in bus structures has been established by the industry. The wide variety of computers in existence are generally not compatible. Computer manufacturers are supporting their own bus system in the attempt to have their particular technique provide more features for specific applications, ease in expandability, at less cost, and/or with superior performance. Although adopting a standard to achieve compatibility would be of great value to the industry and to the end-users, choosing a standardized bus system has not yet been accomplished.

The non-standardized bus system problem is not unique since other aspects of existing computer systems exhibit the same lack of uniformity. These areas of incompatibility include: communications methods (serial or parallel) with differences in interface techniques and connecting hardware, disk drive sizes and format structures, internal operating systems, and the variety of data-entry techniques that must be learned for the many available application programs. Attempts on the part of the computer industry to standardize have not proven completely successful, however, efforts in this direction are still continuing and eventually, may come to fruition.

Despite the many adversities and the concomitant frustrating lack of immediate resolution, it can be safely predicted that with the rapid evolution of computer technology, so startlingly evident during the 1980s, even faster and more dramatic computer technology changes will be occurring during the last decade of the 20th Century and will be continuing into the next century and beyond.

ANSWERS TO REINFORCEMENT EXERCISES — PART II

CHAPTER SEVEN
  THE COMPUTER ALPHABET

CHAPTER EIGHT
  DIGITAL LOGIC

CHAPTER NINE
  COMPUTER MEMORIES

CHAPTER TEN
  THE BASIC COMPUTER SYSTEM

CHAPTER SEVEN
THE COMPUTER ALPHABET

1. True

2. False - The value of the least significant digit (units) in binary is "1", an odd number. The value of all the other significant digits in binary are even numbers (twos, fours, etc.). If the least significant binary digit is 1, the decimal number is always an odd number. If the least significant binary digit is 0, the decimal number is even.

3. True.

4. True - Since there is no "thousand" nor "eleven" in the binary system, binary number "1011" would properly be read as "one, zero, one, one", the *only* available digits in the binary system.

5. False - The exponential values (N x 2^e) of the decimal digits in each column must be *totalled* to produce the decimal number equivalent of a binary number.

6. True - Reading from left to right, the sequence of equivalent of binary "11011", is: $16 + 8 + 0 + 2 + 1 = 27$.

7. True

8. True - Listing a 5-bit binary sequence from left to right results in: 16, 8, 4, 2, 1. If a binary "1" is placed under each appropriate decimal digit so that these decimal digits total to 27 wherever a binary "1" exists, the sum will equal to 27 if the binary number is 11011. It would appear as:
    Decimal digits: 16   8   4   1
    Binary digit equivalent: 1 + 1 + 0 + 1 +1 = 27
    Decimal number 27 = Binary number 11011

9. False - The total number of characters that have to be converted (encoded) into pure binary is: $26 + 15 + 10 = 51$. A 5-bit system using a 5-bit word width would make possible only 32 (25) different combinations of binary digits, with each binary word representing a different character. A 6-bit system would provide 64 (26) different possible combinations which is more than enough for the desired 51 characters.

10. False - Although no industry standard on word widths have been established, the generally accepted designations are: an 8-bit binary word is a "byte", a 16-bit binary word is a "double-byte", and a 4-bit binary word is a "half-byte.

11. False - Doubling the width of a binary word does not increase the number of possible combinations by a factor of two but by considerably more. If a 4-bit pure binary word is capable of 16 (24) different pure binary word combinations, an 8-bit pure binary word width is capable of 256 (28) different pure binary word combinations. Doubling an 8-bit binary word will result in a 16-bit binary word that is capable of 65,536 (216) different possible combinations. The increase is not proportional, but exponential.

12. True

13. True

14. False - Extended ASCII is the most commonly used standard conversion code for encoding keystrokes from a computer keyboard into machine language for most computers using the English language. ASCII also includes standard punctuation marks, symbols, and special control codes.

15. True

CHAPTER EIGHT — DIGITAL LOGIC

1. True

2. False - Each gate interacts with the system by influencing the action of other gates and associated circuitry in the entire system.

3. False - The theorems of Boolean algebra apply to a logic that is based on the assumption that only two possibilities exist as far as any statement is concerned: the statement can either be "true" or "false", but never partly true and partly false. If a given statement is true, it is designated "True" by the symbol "1"; if it is false, it is designated "False" by the symbol "0".

4. True

5. True

6. False - An AND gate can have two *or more* input terminals and only *one* output terminal. When *all* input terminals are at logic "1", then, and only then, will the output be at "1".

7. False - A NAND gate is the complement or opposite of an AND gate. With a NAND gate, when *all* the inputs are at "0", the output will be at "1".

8. True - By studying their truth tables, it can be noted that the logic state at the output of a NAND gate is exactly the opposite (complement) of an AND gate, when both have the same logic states at their inputs.

9. True - The purpose of the inverter or NOT gate is to change the logic state at the output of any gate to its opposite or complementary condition by connecting the output of the gate to be changed to the inverter input and using the inverter output for the desired logic state.

10. False - A non-inverting driver is used as a power amplifier to increase the fan-out capability of a logic gate without changing the logic state of the gate, however, a driver cannot improve the fan-in capability of a logic gate.

11. False - The output of an INHIBIT gate is always at "0" when a logic "1" pulse is applied to its inhibit terminal, thereby setting the condition to inhibit the passage of logic "1" signals at any other normal input terminal of the INHIBIT gate.

12. True - A flip-flop, being a bistable element, will only change the output logic condition of both complementary outputs from an existing state to its other state when a proper signal is applied to the appropriate input.

13. False - Although the use of semiconductors, particularly monolithic IC chips provide higher speed, lower power, less use of PC board space, and at lower cost, digital computers have been designed with electromechanical relays, vacuum tubes and mechanical switches for the logic gate circuits.

14. True

15. True

16. False - A clock pulse (logic "1") at the CLOCK input of a D flip-flop acts to enable the flip-flop and allows the logic state at the DATA input to set or reset the circuit until the next clock pulse arrives. The logic that is present at the DATA input ("0" or "1") when the clock pulse arrives is sent to the output at Q with its complement sent to the output at Q-bar.

17. True - In addition to being able to serve as a means of converting one form of data transmission to another, a shift register affords the possibility of being used as a means of either multiplying by two or dividing by two, depending on the register's configuration.

18. True

CHAPTER NINE
COMPUTER MEMORIES

1. True

2. False - The act of accessing data includes both finding a desired address in the memory structure and then reading out the information that has been written at that address.

3. True

4. True

5. False - A semiconductor RAM is a volatile memory because its information is irretrievably lost when electrical power to the memory is removed, either deliberately or inadvertently. This type of memory requires that its data be transferred to a non-volatile storage medium to retain its data. By using a power back-up system, such as a battery, the loss of power to the circuit is avoided.

6. False - The use of the term "non-volatile" does not imply that information stored in this memory cannot be changed. A memory medium that is non-volatile is classified in this manner to indicate that regardless of loss of power, its information will not be lost.

7. True

8. False - Magnetic tape is a serial access memory. Its main use in modern computer systems is as a bulk storage archival memory to back-up needed information that might otherwise be lost through an inadvertent failure of a computer's memory.

9. False - Although data on a magnetic disk is non-volatile, the information on its surface can be easily and quickly overwritten, when desired, by having the computer operator enter the proper command for this procedure.

10. True

11. False - A floppy drive motor speed is about one-tenth that of a hard drive motor, therefore, its access time is about ten times longer - about 200 to 400 milliseconds.

12. False - The 5.25 inch diameter flexible, plastic disk is protected by a *non-removable*, flexible, plastic jacket. The 3.25 inch diameter plastic is protected by a hard plastic *non-removable* shell. Either floppy disk, in its protective sleeve, is inserted by the computer operator into an appropriate floppy disk drive compartment at the front or side panel of a computer.

13. False - A semiconductor RAM is an erasable read/write memory. Using the acronym "RAM" merely signifies that this particular memory is a random access memory. Although all semiconductor memories are random access memories, different, more descriptive names are used for the other semiconductor memories.

14. True

15. False - A PROM is a blank (unprogrammed) monolithic IC read-only memory intended for end-user custom programming. With the use of a proper programming machine, the end-user can access the PROM structure and convert the original blank memory into a programmed ROM. Once the programmed patterns are "burned-into" the memory, the PROM becomes a non-volatile ROM; the data becomes a permanent part of the memory and cannot be changed.

16. False - A UV-EPROM chip is enclosed in a package that has a transparent, fused silica lid positioned above a *MOSFET* chip. The chip has no connection made to its gate and is often referred to as a "floating gate" or "isolated gate" EPROM. The transparent window above a programmed UV-EPROM chip inside the package causes it to be erased when exposed to high-intensity, ultraviolet light radiation.

17. True

18. True

19. False - Unlike UV-EPROMs that are guaranteed to be programmed and erased at normal room temperature only, EEPROMs are specified to function over a wider operating temperature range, particularly those EEPROMs that are intended for installation in military or aerospace equipment.

CHAPTER TEN
THE BASIC COMPUTER SYSTEM

1. True

2. False - Essential to the functioning of a computer are both hardware and software.

3. False - When a software program is written into a hardware structure, the combination is referred to as firmware. For example, a ROM (read-only memory) is firmware. It is a hardware component containing a program or instructions (software) stored in its cells for use by the computer. Although initially a hardware component when in a blank state, a PROM (programmable read-only memory) becomes firmware after it is programmed.

4. True

5. True

6. False - Although also influenced by other factors, a computer's clock frequency and word width contribute to increasing a computer's throughput. For example, a 16-bit computer has a higher throughput than an 8-bit computer if both are operated at the same clock frequency; when operated at a higher clock frequency, the throughput will increase.

7. True

8. False - A computer is called a "powerful" tool because of the accuracy and speed with which it performs its assigned operations. A "more powerful" computer means greater speed, greater ability to store more information, and a greater facility to accommodate additional, peripheral (external) equipment.

9. False - The Central Processing Unit (CPU) consists of the ALU and the Control Unit, the sections in a computer structure where processing is done.

10. True

11. True

12. False - A computer can have an 8-bit Data Bus and a 16-bit Address Bus. If a CPU is processing 16-bits at a time, and its Data Bus is only 8 bits wide, two successive transfers are required, thereby slowing down the system. Since information being processed by a computer is moved on the Data Bus, a true 16-bit system would be structured so that both the Address and Data Bus are 16-bits wide.

13. False - Although a basic computer can be enhanced with "bus-compatible" support hardware, a careful analysis is needed to determine the technical and economic advisability of replacing an existing system. With the availability of newer, improved-performance computers, it may be more advisable to replace, rather than add to a system to achieve higher performance operation.

14. True

15. False - A synchronous system requires the transmission of clock pulses along with the data word to be transmitted from an I/O parallel port to establish synchronization (coordination), referred to as "handshaking", between a computer and a clocked peripheral. This technique is suitable for applications requiring high-speed data transfer and requires a parallel I/O port for both the computer and the peripheral device.

16. True

17. False - Although electronics technology deals primarily with the physical elements (the hardware) contained within a computer system, the software that is used to direct, coordinate, and supervise the operation of the hardware is an equally essential part of the system. A computer system without one or the other is *not* a computer system.

 GLOSSARIES

PART TWO

COMPUTERS AND
RELATED SYSTEMS

POPULAR TERMS

POPULAR SYMBOLS

GLOSSARY OF TERMS —
COMPUTERS AND RELATED SYSTEMS

ACCESS TIME - The length of time required for a WORD in the memory section of a computer to be read by the CENTRAL PROCESSING UNIT (CPU), or the time to read data from a peripheral data storage area.

ACCUMULATOR - An interface REGISTER that stores interim arithmetic information for future processing within the ARITHMETIC LOGIC UNIT (ALU) the section of a computer that contains the logic circuitry to perform its basic arithmetic functions.

ADDER - The digital logic circuits in the ALU section of a computer which generate the adding process (sum and carry) of two or more binary numbers.

ADDRESS - The location of digital information in the MEMORY UNIT of a computer, or a digital code that designates this location.

ALGORITHM - The sequence of operations which defines a solution to a logical problem.

ALPHANUMERICS - The term used to define the combined letters of the alphabet (A to Z) and the ten numerals (0 to 9). The term is sometimes used loosely to mean any text data.

AMERICAN STANDARD CODE FOR INFORMATION INTER-CHANGE (ASCII) - A 7-bit binary code, providing 128 different binary combinations for use with standard American keyboards. ASCII is used to encode all 26 letters of the alphabet (upper and lower case), all ten decimal digits (0 to 9), punctuation marks, standard graphics, and special control codes into machine language. Although ASCII has 128 different codes and only 7 bits are needed for each different code, ASCII characters are generally stored inside 8-bit bytes, providing room for the 128 ASCII codes plus another 128 codes, totalling 256 characters. This 8-bit code is referred to as EXTENDED ASCII and may be used for special commands or graphic characters that can vary from computer to computer.

ANALOG COMPUTER - A non-digital system that manipulates linear, or continuously changing data.

AND GATE - See LOGIC GATES

ARITHMETIC LOGIC UNIT (ALU) - The section of a computer that performs the four basic arithmetic functions (addition, subtraction, multiplication, and division). Larger units contain circuitry that is used for higher mathematical functions, such as: quadratic equations, etc.

ASCII DATA (ASCII FILE) - Data, or the file containing the data, that is constructed by using letters of the alphabet, numerals, punctuation marks, and the standard ASCII formatting commands, such as: "carriage return" or "line feed". These terms are used to refer to text information.

ASSEMBLER - A software program that converts (translates) each symbolic instruction written in ASSEMBLY LANGUAGE into the MACHINE LANGUAGE (binary code) of a computer.

ASSEMBLY LANGUAGE - A programming language that consists of a group of letters or labels, called mnemonics. Each mnemonic represents a *single* instruction that must be translated into the binary code of MACHINE LANGUAGE. Mnemonics are easier to use than machine language instructions. For example, the mnemonic "MUL" is used to tell the computer to "MULtiply".

ASYNCHRONOUS - A term used to describe a non-clocked, or free-running, digital signal that may be used to trigger successive computer instructions; the completion of one instruction triggers the next. The speed of operation depends only on the speed of the signal generated through the circuit or network and is contrasted with SYNCHRONOUS operation, where the computer clock controls the speed of the signals in the system.

BACKPLANE - A part of a computer into which the system's PC boards are plugged to provide a common voltage supply, reference, and SYSTEM BUS for all computer sections. A backplane is often called a MOTHERBOARD.

BASIC - The acronym for Beginner's All-purpose Symbolic Instruction Code, that is an easy to learn, easy to use programming language, originally intended for educational purposes. BASIC is available for most personal computers in varying degrees of complexity.

BAUD RATE - A measure of speed of transferring information between two or more sections of a computer system, or between two or more computers.

BAUDOT CODE - A 5-bit digital code having 32 possible combinations of binary "0" and "1"; used in Teletype (Telex) communications systems.

BENCHMARK - The specifications used to measure the characteristics of a computer system, or parts of the system, under clearly-defined conditions.

BINARY CODED DECIMAL (BCD) - A coding system in which each decimal system numeral (0 to 9) is represented by a 4-digit (4-bit) binary code.

BINARY SYSTEM (BASE 2) - A numbering system consisting of only two digits (0 and 1), as contrasted with a DECIMAL SYSTEM that uses ten digits (0 to 9). In electronics, "binary"and "two-state" are synonymous.

BINARY DIGIT (BIT) - The term "BIT" is the contraction of **BI**nary Dig**IT** and is a part of a digital "word" that consists of combinations of "0s" and/or "1s". These are the only two numerals in binary arithmetic (base 2) that is the basis for binary code (MACHINE LANGUAGE). A "bit" has the same significance in binary arithmetic that a decimal digit has in the more familiar decimal arithmetic (base 10).

BISTABLE CIRCUIT - A digital circuit having two stable electrical states. An output signal of this circuit will remain in either state indefinitely until an external input signal causes the circuit to switch its other output state. A BISTABLE MULTIVIBRATOR, generally called a FLIP-FLOP, is an example of this circuit.

BLACK BOX - A term used to refer to an electronic circuit or system within an enclosure where the concern is with its external characteristics and requirements without necessarily knowing details of its internal elements. This concept is often used to provide a useful approach in the design of a system or to properly interconnect two circuits or systems.

BOOLEAN ALGEBRA - Named after George Boole, a 19th Century English mathematician who first formulated theorems that included a mathematical analysis of the laws of human logic. It uses algebraic-like notation to describe the interaction of variables having only two states - "true" and "false". In electronics, the states are often referred to as "1" and "0" or, "high" and "low". The terms "high" and "low" refer to the voltage levels of the input and output signals of a logic gate. Boolean algebra is used in the design of logic circuits in computers and similar digital systems. The logic gates called AND, OR and NOT are the three basic logic gates in Boolean algebra. NAND, NOR, XOR and others are combinations of the three basic logic gate operations.

BOOTSTRAP (BOOT) - A software program used for initiating the operation of a computer. The function of the program is to set up the input and output (I/O) devices and load the OPERATING SYSTEM from a disk, cassette or built-in READ ONLY MEMORY (ROM).

BREAKPOINT - Location of a point in a program where program execution can be stopped to permit a visual test, printing or other performance analyses.

BUBBLE MEMORY - A high-density memory medium upon which a magnetic film is grown on a gadolinium-gallium garnet substrate. A small permanent magnet is mounted inside its package, perpendicular to the surface of the substrate. When an external magnetic field is energized with the use of an external coil, magnetic "bubble" domains are formed on the internal magnetic film which represent patterns of "ones". The absence of magnetic bubbles will represent patterns of "zeros".

BUFFER - 1. A digital logic circuit inserted between other digital circuits to reduce circuit interaction and/or to provide amplification of a digital signal. 2. An intermediate storage circuit used to compensate for a difference in baud rate or, to compensate for different times of occurrence of different events or instructions. 3. A circuit used to convert input or output voltage levels for signal level compatibility when

transmitting data from one device to another.

BUS CONTROLLER - A circuit that generates commands and control signals for sequencing and timing of the data transmitted on a bus.

BYTE - A set (group) of consecutive binary digits (bits) that forms a unit (word) or sub-unit of digital information in a computer. Depending on the size of the computer, a digital word may contain one or more bytes. Through common usage, a byte is generally accepted as containing eight bits.

CACHE - A high-speed buffer memory that is similar to a SCRATCH PAD MEMORY, but has a larger capacity. It is located between the CENTRAL PROCESSING UNIT and MAIN MEMORY and is filled from the main memory at low speed with instructions and programs and is operated at a higher speed. A CACHE can also be used as a storage section between the CPU and a hard disk to speed up access of data on the hard disk.

CD-ROM (COMPACT DISK READ-ONLY MEMORY) - An aluminized disk, 4.72" in diameter that provides an optical storage system for digital data. A laser beam is used to permanently burn data into its surface which cannot be over-written, altered, or erased, providing read-only memory capability. Larger size disks are generally called "laser disks".

CENTRAL PROCESSING UNIT (CPU) - The section(s) in which all the processing circuits of a computer are located. It incorporates a CONTROL UNIT, an ALU and related facilities.

CHARACTER GENERATOR - A circuit that accepts digital and forms the corresponding letters and numerals for a monitor or printer.

CLOCK - A digital pulse generator that controls the timing of a computer and, to a great extent, determines the speed (number of instructions per second) capability of the computer. Generally, it is located in the CPU.

CMOS LOGIC - A CMOS technology monolithic IC "logic family" characterized by low power dissipation per gate, high chip density, and relatively high propagation delay per gate compared with bipolar IC logic families.

COMPILER - A software program that converts (translates) a complete software program written in high-level language (such as BASIC or FORTRAN) into machine language, before the program is started.

COMPLEMENT - Reversal of bit values: ones become zeros; zeros become ones.

CONCURRENCY - The independent execution of two or more sequences of events that are either occurring, or appearing to occur, simultaneously.

CONSOLE - The term referring to a combination of both DISPLAY and KEYBOARD.

CONTROL BUS - A set of transmission lines whose function is to carry synchronization signals and control data as part of the SYSTEM BUS.

CONTROL UNIT (CU) - Part of the CPU containing the CLOCK, PROGRAM COUNTER and INSTRUCTION REGISTER. The CONTROL UNIT also generates control signals and manages the control bus.

COUNTER - A circuit whose output(s) change state in a specified sequence on receiving appropriate input signals. The circuit can provide a required output pulse after receiving a specified number of input pulses.

CRASH - The term used to describe a situation when part of, or the complete computer, stops working because of a hardware and/or software malfunction. A head-crash in a disk system refers to the accidental impact of the read/write head on the surface of the disk.

DAISY-WHEEL PRINTER - An impact printer that uses a print element called a "daisy-wheel" (shaped like a flat disk or large thimble) to form the alphanumerics and punctuation marks that are part of its print element. Unlike dot-matrix, ink-jet and laser printers, daisy-wheel printers can not print graphics. See LETTER-QUALITY PRINTER.

DATA BASE - A collection of structured information that can be used to create a specific format out of some, or all, of the collected data.

DATA-BASE MANAGEMENT SYSTEM (DBMS) - A software program capable of controlling and supervising the updating, editing and executing of items from multiple files in a data base environment.

DEBUG - The process of detecting, locating and correcting a problem in a software program or hardware.

DECREMENT - Reduction of the numerical contents of a counter. A decrement of 1 is usually assumed, unless otherwise specified. The complementary operation of INCREMENT.

DEVICE - When used in a computer system, this term refers to a unit of processing equipment external to the CPU and is generally synonymous with the term PERIPHERAL.

DIODE-TRANSISTOR LOGIC (DTL) - One of the first bipolar monolithic IC families of logic gates. A diode in an IC logic gate performs the required logic with a transistor amplifying and inverting the output. The DTL family has been made obsolete by the Transistor-Transistor Logic (TTL) family.

DIRECT ADDRESS - A memory accessing mode in which the contents of the accessed location is called the OPERAND.

DIRECT MEMORY ACCESS (DMA) - A method of transferring blocks of data directly between an external device and the computer system memory without the need for intervention by the CPU. This method significantly speeds up the data transfer rate, improving system efficiency.

DISKETTE - A thin, flexible, plastic circular memory medium, coated on one or both sides with a metal oxide and sealed in a protective jacket. Data is stored magnetically in binary digital form on its surface(s).

DISK DRIVE - The mechanical/electronic section that can accept and operate a compatible floppy or hard disk. It may include several motors (for disk rotation and reading/writing head positioning), position sensors and control circuits.

DISK EMULATOR - See RAM Disk.

DISPLAY - A peripheral device serving as a computer readout, such as a cathode-ray tube (CRT), flat-panel (generally used in portable computers) or other readout device. The screen can be monochrome (an amber, green or white display) or a multi-color display. Also referred to as a MONITOR.

DISK OPERATING SYSTEM (DOS) - A software program, on a compatible disk, which coordinates the operation, transfer of data, supervision and control of a computer. This software program must first be booted into the working memory of the computer from the disk before it can operate.

DISK STORAGE - A method of storing software programs and data on a rotating circular disk (either a floppy or hard disk) coated with magnetic material, such as iron oxide. Data is written (stored) and read (retrieved) by movable read/write heads positioned over data tracks on the surface of the disk. Addressable portions of the disk can be selected for read or write operations.

DOCUMENTATION - Information that explains how to use computer hardware or software. It is usually provided as a manual or stored on a disk.

DOT-MATRIX PRINTER - An impact printer that uses a computer-driven, multi-pin print element (print-head) to create images on a paper by imprinting a series of tiny dots on the paper to print a wide variety of character styles and/or finely detailed graphics. Generally, these printers are extremely fast and are used for draft-quality documents and precise graphics.

DOTS PER INCH (DPI) - The measurement of density on dot-matrix printers or other dot-matrix devices. As the DPI increases, image clarity increases.

DOWNLOAD - The transfer of files or data from a source of data in a remote computer. See UPLOAD.

DOWN TIME - A period of time during which a computer is inoperable because of temporary or permanent failure of hardware or software, or for routine hardware or software procedures.

DYNAMIC RANDOM ACCESS MEMORY (DRAM) - A type of semiconductor memory in which the presence or absence of a capacitive charge in each element of the memory represents the state of the bit (0 or 1). This charge must be periodically recharged (refreshed) to maintain the desired binary state of the element. See RANDOM ACCESS MEMORY.

EDITOR - A program used to prepare and/or modify a SOURCE PROGRAM or other file by addition, deletion or change.

EMITTER-COUPLED LOGIC (ECL) - A bipolar monolithic IC logic gate family characterized by very high speed operation and relatively high power dissipation compared with other monolithic IC logic families.

EMULATION - The process of imitation (simulation) of one computer system by another. The imitating program, or device (emulator), accepts the same data, executes the same programs and achieves the same results.

EPROM - Acronym for Erasable Programmable Read-Only Memory. An EPROM is a general term for a semiconductor memory that can be programmed, erased and reprogrammed many times over, without damage to the device. More specific types of EPROMs include: EAPROM (Electrically Alterable PROM), EEPROM (Electrically Erasable PROM) and UV-EPROM (Ultraviolet Erasable PROM). Either memory can be used for prototype and computer development work or to change the memory data when new conditions dictate the change.

EVENT - An occurrence during the execution of a task, such as the completion of an input/output operation.

EXECUTE - To run a specified instruction or software program.

EXTENDED BINARY CODED DECIMAL INTERCHANGE CODE (EBCDIC) - An 8-bit code developed by IBM for their mainframe computers, providing 256 bit-pattern equivalents of standard keyboard symbols.

FAN-IN - The maximum number of output terminals of other logic gates that can be connected to an input terminal of a specified logic gate.

FAN-OUT - The maximum number of input terminals that can be connected to the output terminal of a specified logic gate.

FETCH - The action of obtaining an instruction from a stored program.

FILE - A collection of related data treated as a single unit. In a computer, a file can exist on a disk, magnetic tape or as an accumulation of information in memory.

FIRMWARE - A combination of a software program in hardware, such as a READ-ONLY MEMORY (ROM), or a disk that has files or software programs written on its surface.

FIRST IN, FIRST OUT (FIFO) - The term refers to the sequence of entering and then retrieving data from a data storage section of a computer. With FIFO, the first data entered is the first data first retrieved.

FLAG - An indicator of a specific condition that informs a section of a program that this condition has already occurred. This condition is identified by the presence or absence of the flag. A flag can be implemented in software and/or hardware.

FLIP-FLOP CIRCUIT - A logic circuit having two stable output states. It has the ability to change from one state to the other when an input pulse is applied in a specified manner. It is also called a BISTABLE MULTIVIBRATOR.

FLOATING-POINT ARITHMETIC - A method in which the decimal point location of a number in an arithmetic operation is determined by the number's exponent value in base 10. All exponents are equalized prior to the operation to set a decimal point in its proper location in the final computation. Floating-point arithmetic extends a computer's mathematical capability beyond the limit imposed by a fixed word length and contributes to easier programming.

FLOPPY DISK (DISKETTE) - A relatively inexpensive, flexible, plastic disk used to store digital data on one or both sides of its magnetic surface.he amount of data depends on the diameter of the disk and the technology used to record the data. See DISK STORAGE.

FLOW CHART - A symbolic representation of the processing steps performed by a software program or a graphic sequence of logic operations implemented in hardware. A flow chart helps in visualizing the procedure(s) necessary to design a software program or a final hardware system.

FONT - A style of printing typeface that has a specific form and size.

FORMAT - An orderly, structured arrangement of data elements (bits, bytes, and/or fields) that is necessary to produce a larger entity, such as: a list, record, table, file or dictionary. Also, it is the term used to prepare a magnetic disk to allow it to accept digital data.

FORTRAN - A science-oriented high-level software language, derived from the contraction of the terms **FO**rmula **TRAN**slator.

FREQUENCY SHIFT KEYING (FSK) - A technique of digitally keying (modulating) an audio tone (carrier wave) so that a commercial telephone line can efficiently carry digital data. See MODEM.

FULL DUPLEX - A data transmission mode that provides simultaneous and independent transmission and reception. A conventional telephone communication is an example of this technique. See HALF DUPLEX.

GATE - See LOGIC GATE

GATE ARRAY - A group of standard logic gates that may be used to be interconnected into a complete circuit or system. Also called LOGIC ARRAY.

GENERAL PURPOSE INTERFACE BUS (GPIB) - A BUS standard (IEEE 488-1975) for controlling peripheral devices.

GIGO - An acronym used to describe the output of a computer whose operation or accuracy is suspect. (Garbage IN, Garbage Out.)

GRAPHICS - Pictures, line drawings and/or diagrams generated by using data that is entered into a computer through a keyboard or from an existing data file. Data required to perform this function are graphic representations of a model (i.e. the X and Y coordinates of a square's corner).

HALF DUPLEX - A communications mode that allows transmission and reception of digital data between computers, but not simultaneously.

HANDSHAKING - The term used for a communications synchronizing techniquehat is carried out before and after any transfer of digital data. It consists of a sequence of signals for non-clocked (asynchronous) systems in which a reply is needed to complete a data transfer operation.

HARD COPY - A printed copy of a file, message or graphic presentation, as opposed to the visual display on a screen of a computer monitor.

HARD-DISK DRIVE - A term used for a sealed unit containing high-density, high-speed, rigid metal disks and recording heads to store digital data. It reads and writes data faster than floppy disks.

HARDWARE - The *physical* equipment of a computer system, consisting of mechanical and electrical/electronic components or devices.

HEXADECIMAL - The base 16 number system using 16 symbols (0 to 9 and A to F) to represent 16 decimal numerals (0 to 15).

HIGH-LEVEL LANGUAGE (HLL) - A programming language consisting of a unique group of symbols and command statements representing a *series* of machine operations. A COMPILER or INTERPRETER is used to translate (convert) HLL into MACHINE LANGUAGE. BASIC, FORTRAN, PASCAL, ALGOL and ADA are some examples of high-level languages.

IEEE 488-1975 - See GENERAL PURPOSE INTERFACE BUS

IMPACT PRINTER - A computer-driven mechanical imprinting device where the characters are formed by striking a ribbon onto the paper.

INCREMENT - The increase in the numerical contents of a counter. An increment of one is usually assumed, unless otherwise specified. See DECREMENT.

INK-JET PRINTER - A printer which forms characters by electrostatically aiming a tiny drop of ink onto the paper to be printed.

INPUT/OUTPUT (I/O) SECTION - The section that interfaces between the computer's SYSTEM BUS and the peripherals feeding data into and taking data out of the computer. Depending on the number of peripherals in a system, the I/O sections can have a single PORT or multiple ports.

INSTRUCTION - A software statement that specifies a machine operation. Sometimes it is called a COMMAND.

INSTRUCTION SET (INSTRUCTION REPERTOIRE) - A description of the total operational capabilities of a computer, provided by the computer manufacturer, or the CPU (or MPU) manufacturer, as a listing of binary words used for each executable command. It is sometimes called the computer's "microcode".

INTERPRETER - A high-level language translator that converts individual high-level language program instructions into multiple machine instructions. It translates and executes each statement as it is encountered, during the running of the program.

INTERRUPT - The suspension of normal program execution to perform a higher priority service routine, as requested by a peripheral device. After completion of the service routine operation, the interrupted program routine is resumed at the point where it was interrupted.

JUMP - An instruction which causes the computer to fetch the next instruction to be executed from a location other than the next sequential location in memory.

KEYBOARD - A peripheral device consisting of alphanumeric, punctuation mark and other special function keys that are mechanically arranged to allow the entry of data, control commands and other information into the system.

LAN - See LOCAL-AREA NETWORK.

LANDSCAPE - A printer feature, generally controlled by software, which rotates the output image by 90° to print across the length of the paper, rather than the width of the paper.

LASER - Acronym for Light Amplification by Stimulated Emission of Radiation. It is used for generating high-intensity, highly-focused light for many purposes, including printers and high-density memory media.

LASER DISK - See CD-ROM

LASER PRINTER - Essentially a computer-driven photocopier that creates an original image of the text or graphics from the output of the computer. A computer-controlled laser beam "paints" the desired image inside the photocopier and then prints the image onto a paper.

LAST-IN, FIRST-OUT (LIFO) - A method of storing and retrieving data in a stack, table or list.

LIGHT PEN - A light-sensitive stylus used for forming graphics by touching coordinates on a display screen, thereby seeming to draw directly on the screen.

LIBRARY - A collection of standard software instructions, programs, routines and subroutines internal to a computer.

LINKAGE - Instructions that connect one program with another, providing continuity of executions between the programs.

LOCAL AREA NETWORK (LAN) - A combined hardware/software technique for interconnecting company related multiple computers or computer terminals through a high-speed networking system.

LOGIC GATE - A digital circuit resulting in an output whose state (0 or 1) depends on the specific combination of the states of input signals. Definitions of the more commonly used logic gates are listed below:
AND - All inputs must be in a "1" state to produce a "1" state output.
NAND (NOT AND) - All inputs must be in a "1" state to produce a "0" state output.
NOR (NOT OR) - Any one input, or more, in a "1" state will produce a "0" state output.

NOT (INVERTER) - A logic gate having only one input and one output. If the input is in a "1" state, the output is in a "0" state and vice versa.
OR - Any one input, or more, in a "1" state will produce a "1" state output
XOR (EXCLUSIVE OR) - If any of the inputs are in a "1" state, but **not** if two or more inputs are "1", the output is in a "1" state.

LOOK AHEAD - 1. A feature of a CPU which allows the masking of an interrupt request until the current sequential instruction has been completed. 2. A feature of an adder circuit in the ALU section which allows the circuit to look ahead to see that all the generated arithmetic carrys are available for addition.

LOOPING - The repetition of program instructions until a conditional exit situation is encountered.

MACHINE LANGUAGE - Sets of numeric instructions in binary code used by a computer to execute its operations. All other programming languages (SOURCE PROGRAMS) must be translated into machine language (OBJECT PROGRAM) before entering the CPU.

MACRO - A combination of commands, instructions or keystrokes, which may be stored in a computer's memory, to be executed as a single command by a single keystroke or a simultaneous combination of keystrokes.

MACROASSEMBLER - An assembly language translator that converts macro expressions into several machine language instructions. Although the use of macros simplifies program coding and speeds up executions of a program, a code for each macro must also be generated.

MAINFRAME COMPUTER - The largest of the computer family, in capability and, generally, in size, having a WORD-WIDTH of 32 bits and higher.

MEMORY - A general term for a data storage structure in a computer that accepts binary information for storage in electrical, mechanical or magnetic form, retains the information for as long as needed and then, when required, writes out, moves, displays, copies or erases selected information. The variety of memory media includes: paper memory, magnetic memory, bubble memory and semiconductor memory, each having different methods of operation and specific criteria for being selected. See STORAGE.

MICROCOMPUTER - A microprocessor-based computer, generally consisting of an MPU, internal semiconductor memory, input and output sections and a system bus, all on one, or several monolithic IC chips inserted into one, or several PC boards. The addition of a power supply and connecting cables, appropriate peripherals (keyboard, monitor, printer, disk drives, etc.), an operating system and other software programs can provide a complete microcomputer system. The microcomputer is generally the smallest and least capable of the computer family, however, the improvement in performance capability of newer microcomputer systems has closed this capability gap.

MICROPROCESSOR UNIT (MPU) - The Central Processor Unit (CPU) implemented in monolithic IC technology, usually, but not necessarily, on one VLSI chip. In many cases, the SYSTEM BUS is also included on the MPU chip.

MINICOMPUTER - Considered to be more capable than a microcomputer but less powerful than a mainframe. Generally, the WORD-WIDTH of the minicomputer is between 12 to 32 bits.

MNEMONIC - A symbolic label or code used to assist the user to remember a specific operation or command. See ASSEMBLY LANGUAGE.

MODEL - A representation of a process or system that can be controlled to demonstrate the effects various actions will have on the process or system.

MODEM - An acronym for **MO**dulator/**DEM**odulator that refers to specific equipment that provides a means of communication between two computer systems, over conventional telephone lines. Each remote computer requires its own MODEM and a compatible communications software program for proper interfacing. See FREQUENCY SHIFT KEYING.

MONITOR - The visual readout device of a computer system. See DISPLAY.

MOUSE - An input device used to move or enter positional information and other data or commands by accessing (pointing to) images on a monitor.

MAGNETIC MEMORY - One of the available memory media used in a computer system for mass density storage, including: hard and floppy disks and tape in both reel-to-reel and cassette form.

MULTITASKING - A technique of providing concurrent execution of more than one task in a computer system or on several terminals in a network. Multitasking separates a program or programs into two or more interrelated tasks that share memories, codes, buffers, and files while running.

MULTIUSER - The term that describes a capability of a computer system to be operated by more than one terminal at a time.

NEGATIVE LOGIC - This term refers to logic in which the less positive voltage represents the "1" state and the more positive voltage represents the "0" state. See POSITIVE LOGIC.

NESTING - Embedding commands or data in levels of other data so that specific routines or instructions can be executed or accessed continuously in loops, without returning to the main program.

NIBBLE - A sequence of four adjacent bits, or a half-byte. A hexadecimal or BCD coded digit can be represented by a nibble.

NODE - The endpoint of a network branch or the junction of two or more branches.

NONVOLATILE MEMORY - A memory whose stored data remains undisturbed by removal of electrical power.

OBJECT CODE - Machine language code produced by a translator program, such as an assembler, interpreter or compiler. Instructions in object code can be executed by a central processing unit. See SOURCE CODE.

OPERATING SYSTEM (OS) - A structured software program (set of programmed routines) used to manage, control, coordinate and sequence the hardware and software resources of a computer system. See BOOTSTRAP. The operating system is sometimes called SYSTEMS SOFTWARE.

OPERATION CODE (OP-CODE) - Part of a computer instruction word which designates the function performed by a specific instruction. For example, op-codes for arithmetic instructions include: "ADD", "SUB", "MUL" and "DIV".

OVERFLOW - An error condition occurring in a computer when a mathematical operation produces a result having a magnitude that exceeds the capacity of the computer's arithmetic register.

PASCAL - A high-level programming language that is structured to encourage good programming habits and is therefore used extensively in educational institutions and engineering circles.

PARALLEL OPERATION - A method of data transmission wherein all bits of a digital word are handled simultaneously with each bit on a separate line. Although faster and simpler to install and operate than SERIAL OPERATION, this method requires more transmission lines.

PARITY - A method of verifying the accuracy of binary data after it has been transferred to or from a storage area.

PARTITIONING - The logical grouping of electronic functions within a given set of hardware components.

PERIPHERAL - A term designating the various kinds of machines and devices that work in conjunction with a computer but are not part of the computer itself. Typically, peripherals refer to: printers, keyboards, monitors, and plotters. A MODEM is considered to be a peripheral device even when it is physically located inside a computer.

PLUG-COMPATIBLE - A term used to indicate when peripherals may be interchanged without modification.

POLLING - A process in which a number of peripheral devices, remote stations, or nodes in a computer network are interrogated one at a time to determine if service is required.

POP - The instruction used to remove a word from the top of a stack.

PORT - An input/output channel (either parallel or serial), terminated at a connector on the computer. It is used to interconnect the computer's input and/or output terminals to an appropriate source and/or destination.

PORTRAIT - A term used to designate conventional printing across the width of a page.

POSITIVE LOGIC - This logic representation (the reverse of NEGATIVE LOGIC) is the more commonly used form of logic. A more positive voltage represents a "1" state and a more negative (or zero) voltage represents a "0" state.

PRINT SPOOLER - A device for temporarily storing data to be printed when the printer is in use. It provides uninterrupted data entry and editing while the printer is in use and while other data awaits transmission to the printer.

PROGRAM - A complete sequence of computer software instructions necessary to solve a specific problem, perform an action, or respond to external stimuli in a prescribed manner. As a verb, it means to develop a program.

PROGRAM COUNTER (PC) - A special-purpose register in the CPU which contains the address of the next instruction to be fetched and executed.

PROGRAMMABLE LOGIC ARRAY (PLA) - An unprogrammed, general-purpose logic structure in monolithic IC form consisting of an array of similar, and/or compatible logic gates. Also called PROGRAMMABLE ARRAY LOGIC (PAL).

PROGRAMMABLE READ-ONLY MEMORY (PROM) - A blank read-only memory (ROM) which can be programmed after manufacture with external programming equipment. Once programmed, it is not re-programmable and is considered to be a ROM.

PROPAGATION DELAY - A measure of the time required for the output of a logic gate to respond to a combination of its input pulses.

PUSH - The instruction used to deposit a word on top of a stack.

PUSH-DOWN STACK - A dedicated temporary storage register in a computer, sometimes part of a system memory, structured so that data (words) in the stack are retrieved in reverse order of entry. See LIFO.

RAM DISK (DISK EMULATOR) - A portion of RAM configured to look like (emulate) a floppy disk with RAM characteristics. It is used to access information quickly, but its data must be stored in a nonvolatile memory for future use. Otherwise, desired information is lost when power is removed.

RANDOM ACCESS - A technique of accessing (reading) a word of data from a memory structure for use by the CPU. Since a word in the memory can be accessed directly, the time required is independent of its location (address) in the memory structure. It is sometimes called a "direct access" method.

RANDOM ACCESS MEMORY (RAM) - A volatile, semiconductor storage structure used to store temporary data by using a random or direct accessing method. It is more accurately referred to as "erasable read/write" memory. Data in this memory can be read for use by the CPU, edited, altered, erased, or new information written over existing data by computer commands, as desired. Its data must be saved for future use by writing it into a non-volatile memory. See NON-VOLATILE MEMORY and VOLATILE MEMORY.

READ-ONLY MEMORY (ROM) - A semiconductor memory whose data cannot be erased, or overwritten; it can only be accessed (read) for use by the CPU. The data in a ROM is of a permanent nature and is programmed by the ROM manufacturer. In many cases, its programmed information identifies the dedicated function of a computer. A ROM can be in the physical form of a module that is plugged into a computer to change its operation from one program to another.

REAL TIME DATA - Time-dependent data processed by a computer whose output data may be used to control other time-related events, such as traffic control. Real time is the actual time it takes for an event to occur.

REGISTER A temporary storage unit that is used for quick, direct accessibility of a small amount of data for processing. Most computers include a set of internal registers that can be accessed more quickly than the system's main memory.

RESIDENT SOFTWARE - The program(s) residing in the main memory of a computer system. For convenience of operation, several software programs can reside in RAM after the computer is turned on and booted, and can be accessed quickly from within another program.

RS-232-C - The term identifying an interconnection standard used in serial operation. It specifies the configuration and type of connectors used for the computer's serial I/O port(s) and the peripheral serial port(s).

SCRATCH PAD MEMORY - A group of internal registers used for the temporary storage of data being collected and sorted for immediate processing. It is analogous to a pad of paper used to quickly jot down notes.

SECTOR - A section of a recording track on a magnetic disk.

SEMICONDUCTOR MEMORY - Storage devices formed with semiconductor components (generally monolithic ICs), as compared to paper and magnetic memories.

SERIAL OPERATION - A method of data transmission wherein the data is hand-led in sequence, one bit at a time. See PARALLEL OPERATION.

SERVICE ROUTINE - A set of instructions used to perform a programmed operation, typically, in response to an interrupt command.

SHIFT - A computer operation consisting of moving a group of contiguous data bits either to the left or to the right by a prescribed number of positions. The move is done in a SHIFT REGISTER and is used for a carry-over operation.

SIMPLEX - A data transmission mode that provides transmission in one direction only. See FULL DUPLEX and HALF DUPLEX.

SIMULATION - The imitation of a logical operation of one computer by another to measure and evaluate the operation of the computer being designed. Simulation is primarily used to provide an analysis of program logic, independent of hardware environment, and is extremely useful for debugging a new software program prior to committing it to ROM.

SOFTWARE - Programs, languages, procedures and documentation for a computer system. Software includes: operating systems (system software), language translators (assemblers, interpreters and compilers), subroutine libraries, application programs, and the information in instruction manuals.

SOURCE CODE (SOURCE PROGRAM) - A set of computer instructions in hard-copy or stored form. When written in a language other than machine language, it requires translation by an assembler (or macro-assembler), interpreter, or compiler into object code. See OBJECT CODE.

STACK - A dynamic, sequential data list, usually contained in the computer system's main memory. It may have special provisions to allow data to be accessed from either end. Generally, storage and retrieval of data from the stack is performed automatically by the CPU.

STATIC MEMORY - A type of semiconductor read/write memory (RAM) which does not require periodic refresh cycles. As long as electrical power is ON, the data in a static memory is maintained.

STORAGE - This term is used interchangeably with the term MEMORY.

SUBROUTINE - A short program segment that performs a specific function and is available for general use by other programs and routines.

SUPERCOMPUTER - The largest mainframe computer featuring exceptionally high speed operation.

SUPPORT CHIPS - Computer-related circuits other than the CPU, main memory, I/O section, and system bus which are used for additional system operation.

STATE - The logic input or output condition of a binary digital circuit - the state is either a "0" or "1".

STORAGE CAPACITY - The amount of data that can be retained in a memory unit, expressed either by a number of bits or bytes (8-bit words).

STREAMER/STREAMING TAPES - A small tape recorder, usually in cassette form, is used to store data from a hard disk for the purpose of backing up this data, in case of loss.

SYNCHRONOUS COMMUNICATION - A method of transferring binary data in serial form between computers or between a computer and its peripherals. Transmission of data is at a rate set by the computer's clock with synchronization bits located at the beginning of each message or block of data.

SYNTAX - A set of grammatical rules defining valid use of specific commands or instructions in a computer language.

SYSTEMS SOFTWARE - A general term used for supervisory and coordination programs. Systems software may include programs, such as: operating systems, assemblers, interpreters, compilers, software debugging programs, text editors, utilities and peripheral drivers.

TEXT EDITOR - See Editor.

THIRD-PARTY SOFTWARE - Software developed by a software company rather than by a computer manufacturer or user.

THROUGHPUT - The number of instructions executed per second, generally measured in millions of instructions per seconds (MIPS).

TOGGLE - To switch back and forth between two states or conditions of operation, as in a toggle switch.

TOP-DOWN HIERARCHAL DESIGN - A hardware and/or software design approach that starts at the most general level of either a machine or software program and proceeds step-by-step to lower levels, adding detail as the design progresses.

TRACK - A ring on the surface of a magnetic disk.

TRACTOR-FEED - A pin-fed device for advancing continuous form paper through a computer printer.

TRANSISTOR-TRANSISTOR LOGIC (T²L) - A higher-speed, higher-power family of logic gates that obsoleted the DTL logic family. The first transistor in the circuit performs the required logic. Another transistor amplifies and inverts the output. Improved pin-compatible versions of this logic family are called TTL-Schottky (T²L-S) and Low Power TTL-S (LPT²L-S).

TRANSLATOR - See ASSEMBLER, MACROASSEMBLER, INTERPRETER, and COMPILER.

TRI-STATE LOGIC - The term used to designate the possible conditions of a specific logic gate output: "0" "1", or "undefined".

TRUNCATE - The dropping of digits or characters from one end of a data item, causing loss of accuracy or information.

TRUTH TABLE - A tabulation of all possible combination of states at the inputs of a logic gate which will result in a specific logic state at the output of the gate.

TURNKEY SYSTEM - A complete computer system ready to operate without any hardware or software modification or addition.

UNFORMATTED (UNINITIALIZED) DISK - A blank magnetic disk that has no track/sector identification recorded on it. This type of disk allows users to implement their own track/sector indications.

UNIVERSAL ASYNCHRONOUS/ SYNCHRONOUS RECEIVER TRANSMITTER (USART) - A circuit that converts serial-to-parallel or parallel-to-serial operation for communication between two computer or between a computer and its peripherals.

USER FRIENDLY PROGRAM - A software program that has been designed to easily direct the user through the operation or application of a program. A menu-driven program is considered to be "user friendly".

UTILITY - A software program designed to perform a computer system's routine housekeeping functions, like copying, deleting files and/or providing techniques to simplify the execution of a program.

VOCABULARY - A list of operating codes or instructions available to the software programmer for writing a program in a specific language.

VOLATILE MEMORY - A memory whose contents are irretrievably lost when operation power is removed. If data in RAM must be saved after power shut-down, back-up with non-volatile memory (magnetic disk or tape) is required.

WAIT STATE - An internal condition of delay in procession time executed by the CPU when a synchronizing control signal is not present. Wait states are used to synchronize the timing of a CPU with the relatively slower access time of the computer's main memory.

WINCHESTER DRIVE - See HARD-DISK DRIVE

WINDOWING - The ability of a program to divide a display screen into smaller sub-units that permit portions of different sections of a program, or different programs, to be displayed, edited and copied independently.

WORD PROCESSING (WP) - The term refers to a systerm, or program, that allows creating, editing, formatting, displaying, printing, and storage of text with great flexibility and ease. Different WP programs provide different, and sometimes, more desirable capabilities than others.

WORD - The set of binary bits handled by a computer as a primary unit of data. The width (number of bits) of a computer word depends on the hardware design. Wider words imply higher levels of precision, higher speed, and more intricate instructions. Typically, each location in memory contains one word.

WORM (WRITE-ONCE, READ-MANY) - A high-density optical disk memory available in a variety of formats from 5.25" to 14". The WORM can be programmed once, permanently saving a user's data and then becomes an optical disk read-only memory having essentially the same features as the CD-ROM.

WORKSTATION - The work area and/or equipment used for computer operations, including computer-aided design (CAD). The equipment generally consists of a monitor, keyboard, printer and/or plotter, and other output devices necessary for a specific application.

WRITE - The process of storing data in a memory.

X-Y PLOTTER - A computer-driven printing mechanism that draws coordinate points in graph form.

ZERO-WAIT STATE - A condition that results when no wait states are inserted into the system software to deliberately delay operation of the CPU. This can be done with the use of high-speed memory and proper design of computer architecture. Zero-wait state is desirable for high-speed operation of a computer.

ZOOM - To proportionately enlarge or reduce an image displayed on a computer monitor.

GLOSSARY OF SYMBOLS - COMPUTERS AND RELATED SYSTEMS

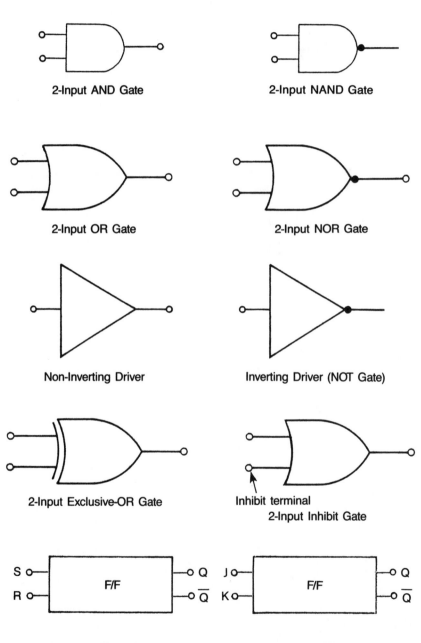

2-Input AND Gate

2-Input NAND Gate

2-Input OR Gate

2-Input NOR Gate

Non-Inverting Driver

Inverting Driver (NOT Gate)

2-Input Exclusive-OR Gate

Inhibit terminal
2-Input Inhibit Gate

R-S Flip-Flop

J-K Flip Flop

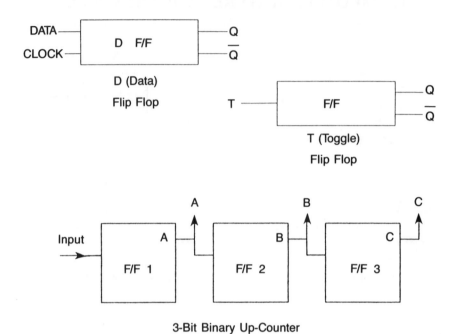

D (Data)

Flip Flop

T (Toggle)

Flip Flop

3-Bit Binary Up-Counter

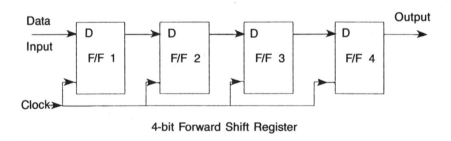

4-bit Forward Shift Register

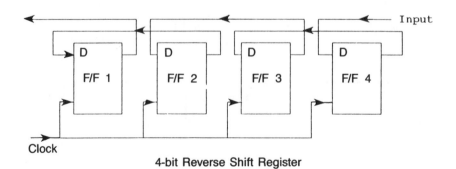

4-bit Reverse Shift Register

REFERENCES

MODERN DICTIONARY OF ELECTRONICS - Rudolf Graf
- Howard W. Sams, Inc. - 1972

ASIMOV'S BIOGRAPHICAL ENCYCLOPEDIA OF SCIENCE
AND TECHNOLOGY - Isaac Azimov
- Doubleday & Company, Inc.

ELECTRONIC ENGINEERING TIMES
- CMP Publications, Inc.

ELECTRONIC ENGINEERS MASTER (EEM)
- Hearst Business Communications, Inc.

THE RELIABILTY HANDBOOK
- National Semiconductor Corp.

HACKERS, HEROS OF THE COMPUTER REVOLUTION
- Steven Levy - Anchor Press/Doubleday - 1984

THE HISTORY OF COMPUTING - Marguerite Zientara
- Computerworld - CW Communications, Inc. - 1981

FROM CHIPS TO SYSTEMS, AN INTRODUCTION
TO MICROPROCESSORS - Rodnay Zaks
- Sybex, Inc. - 1981

DOS: THE COMPLETE REFERENCE - Kris Jamsa
- Osborne McGraw-Hill - 1987

DOS: POWER USERS' GUIDE - Kris Jasma
- Osborne McGraw-Hill - 1988

INDEX

A

abacus, 149
accumulator, 234
ADA, 259
Aiken, Howard, 155
ALGOL, 259
algorithm, 253
ALTAIR, 161
aluminum, 40
analog circuit - definition, 76
analog switch, 91
answers to reinforcement exercises
  Part One, 121
  Part Two, 275
APL, 259
Apple Computer Co., 161
APPLE II, 161
Aristotle, 179
assembler, 257
assigned, 215

B

Babbage analytical engine, 152, 156, 158
Babbage, Charles, 152-153
backplane, 240
Bardeen, John, 5
BASIC, 259
batch processing, 6, 40
Bell Laboratories, 5
BIMOS monolithic IC, 47
binary arithmetic (base 2), 165
binary code, 165
binary counter, 192
binary digit (bit), 171
binary scaler (see T flip/flop), 192
binary system (base 2), 166- 168
binary words, 171-172
  byte, 171-172,
  double-byte, 172
  half-byte (nibble), 172
binary-coded decimal code (BCD), 173
BIOS (basic I/O system), 233
bipolar monolithic IC, 47
bistable multivibrator (see flip/flop circuit), 187

N

O

P

Q